Business Ethics and Corporate Social Responsibility

About the Author

Dr. Maryan Rodriques heads the department of Communication in a post-graduate management and social work education and research institute-CSIBER at Kolhapur. He has five master's degrees and his Doctoral Research is accomplished in the area of Communicative Competence in Management. His teaching career of over three decades and active research in 'Managerial Communication' has earned him an immense popularity among students, professionals and researchers. Being a recognized University Research Guide in 'Managerial Communication' under the faculty of Management & Commerce, and in '*English*' under the Faculty of Arts, his several research students in both the areas have successfully completed their doctoral research projects.

Business Ethics and Corporate Social Responsibility

M.V. Rodriques

CONCEPT PUBLISHING COMPANY PVT. LTD.
NEW DELHI-110059

ISBN-13 : 978-93-5125-133-0 (H.B.)
ISBN-13 : 978-93-5125-134-7 (P.B.)

First Published 2015

Published and Printed by

Concept Since 1974

Concept Publishing Company Pvt. Ltd.
A/15-16, Commercial Block, Mohan Garden
New Delhi-110059 (India)
T: 25351460, 25351794, *F*: 091-11-25357109
E: publishing@conceptpub.com, W: www.conceptpub.com
Editorial Office: H-13, Bali Nagar, New Delhi-110 015, India.

Cataloging in Publication Data—*Courtesy:* D.K. Agencies (P) Ltd. <docinfo@dkagencies.com>

Rodriques, M. V. (Maryan V.), author.
Business ethics and corporate social responsibility / M.V. Rodriques.
pages cm
Includes bibliographical references (pages) and index.
ISBN 9789351251330 (HB)
ISBN 9789351251347 (PB)

1. Business ethics. 2. Social responsibility of business. I. Title.

DDC 174.4 23

Dedicated

to my beloved

mother

Archangella

Preface

The primary objective of this book is to discuss the principles and practice of business ethics and to impart to the readers knowledge and skills of using these principles in the direction of problem solving and ethical decision-making. It is intended to enhance the reader's ability to use the principles creatively, relatively, functionally and effectively in resolving the ethical problems and dilemmas in business organisations. The book should prove helpful both as a textbook for the classes and as a manual for managerial ethics.

In the development of management theory and practice, business ethics, corporate moral values, and corporate social responsibility are relatively new areas. However, in the face of globalisation, corporate wars, corporate scams, mergers and takeovers, the courses in business ethics, corporate governance, corporate codes of conduct, and corporate social responsibility are gaining central place in the management studies.

Excessive avarice and apathetic attitude of some CEOs, and their unethical business practices, especially in United States and Europe, had been the cause of global economic catastrophe during the first decade of twentyfirst century. They failed to recognise that their organisations, especially the financial organisations are the part of the society in which they operate. The failure to understand the ethical norms and corporate social responsibilities resulted in global economic uncertainty and irreparable damage to the stakeholders, especially to the small investors and millions of employees who lost their jobs in the countries across the world.

In such a context, the business schools, universities and corporate leaders are thinking seriously about 'Business Ethics' and 'Corporate Social Responsibility'. As a result, almost all the business schools, management institutions and universities have started business ethics and corporate social responsibility as a core subject in their undergraduate and post-graduate management courses. The main objective of this subject is to enable the students to understand the meaning of various concepts in business ethics, theories and the principles of business ethics, ethical problems in contemporary business, ethical programmes, policies, codes, corporate social responsibility, etc. This book deals with most of these topics with an aim to develop critical thinking and sound moral reasoning among the readers to enable them in business decision-making in the best interests of all the stakeholders and the firms.

The book is organised in a coherent manner in seventeen chapters: 'The Concept of Business Ethics', 'Theories of Business Ethics', 'Business Values', 'Code of Business Ethics', 'Ethical Aspects of Organisational Culture', 'Ethical Leadership', 'Ethical Decision-making', 'Ethical Communication', 'Ethics in Global Business', 'Ethics in Human Resource Management', 'Ethics in Marketing', 'Ethics in Accounting and Finance', 'Corporate Governance', 'Corporate Social Responsibility', 'Environmental Ethics', 'Environmental Protection', and CSR: Laws, Policies and Guidelines'.

Every chapter opens with the 'learning objectives'. These learning objectives state all the important concepts, topics and sub-topics in logical order. The learning objective capsulizes the concepts which the readers are expected to master. 'Exercises' at the end of every chapter are designed not only to test the knowledge acquired by the readers but also to apply that knowledge creatively in the real business world.

I place on record my sincere thanks to SIBER family, Concept Publishing Co. (Pvt.) Ltd., New Delhi-110059, the students, professionals, teaching community and my family who have extended their wholehearted support and cooperation. Above all, it is my duty to express my feelings of gratefulness to Almighty God who has given His helping hand in effective completion of this book.

—Dr. Maryan V. Rodriques

Contents

1
The Concept of Business Ethics

"Therefore, whatever you want men to do to you, do also to them, for this is the law and the prophets".

—Mattew 7:12

Learning Objectives

A. What is Ethics?
B. Meaning of Business Ethics
C. Significance of Business Ethics
   1. Shaping the Corporate Culture
   2. Helping to Resolve Ethical Dilemmas
   3. Shouldering Corporate Social Responsibility
   4. Protecting Environment
   5. Promoting Fair Trade and Business Practices
   6. Promoting Justice
   7. Whistle Blowing
   8. Preventing Sexual Harassment
D. Sources of Ethics
   1. Religion
   2. Law
   3. Culture
   4. Other Sources of Ethics
E. Managerial Ethics
   1. Moral Management
   2. Immoral Management
   3. Amoral Management

A. What is Ethics?

The word 'Ethics' has originated from Greek word 'Ethos' meaning character or custom. However, it is also considered to be derived from the Greek word 'Ethicos' and Latin word 'Ethicus'. According to Prof. Solomon, R.C., the etymology of the word 'Ethics' suggests two basic concerns: (i) individual character, and (ii) social rules of conduct which we call 'morality'.

However, ethics is distinguished from morality on the ground that morality is concerned with human conduct and values whereas ethics refers to the systematic study of morals and values. When ethics is applied to business, it constitutes the study of right and wrong human conduct in the context of business.

In general, ethics is referred to as some standardized form of conduct of an individual or group in a specific field. According to Oxford dictionary, ethics is related with morals and moral questions. It is also considered as the study of morals, moral standards, moral choices, rules and codes of conduct governing the individual and group behaviour. Ethics is also considered as the science of morality and branch of philosophy. According to Patrick and Quinn, ethics is the study of individual and collective moral awareness, judgment, character and conduct. Churchman C.W. defines it as 'the set of attitudes and the value systems which would be appropriate for achieving the goals of the organisation. Ethics is sometimes referred to as a code of human conduct that guides an individual behaviour in a given situation.

Accordingly, ethical conduct conforms with what a society considers to be the right conduct. The conduct has to be in conformity with the social rules. Ethics studies the assumptions and norms of good and bad conduct of a person or group. Ethics is also considered as a mass of moral principles and value systems about what our conduct ought to be. Ethics is viewed as a discipline of rules and standards of behaviours which are accepted by the society. Ethics is also viewed as a branch of philosophy which deals with the rightness or wrongness, goodness or badness of human conduct.

Ethics is a normative science. Normative sciences do not judge the facts with factual judgement. On the other hand, these sciences judge the value of the facts on the basis of 'what ought to be'. The ethical concepts are applicable to human beings only, because only the human beings enjoy the freedom of choice. Ethics is a social science which deals with a set of systematic knowledge about human moral conduct. It deals with moral judgement of voluntary human conduct.

In philosophy, ethics is the moral philosophy. The term 'moral' is derived from the Latin word 'mores' meaning conventions and practices. Accordingly, ethics can be described as a science of conventions or practices. Human conduct is the mirror of human character. This human conduct which reflects the human character is a subject matter of ethical study.

B. Meaning of Business Ethics

Investopedia defines business ethics as "the study of proper business policies and practices regarding potentially controversial issues such as corporate governance, insider trading, bribery, discrimination, corporate social responsibility and fiduciary responsibilities. Business ethics are often guided by law, while other times provide a basic framework that businesses may choose to follow in order to gain public acceptance". Accordingly, business ethics is implemented in order to ensure that a certain required level of trust exists between consumers and various forms of market participants with business.

International Federation of Accountants (IFAC) defines ethics as "A distinguishing mark of accountancy profession is its acceptance of the responsibility to act in the public interest". This definition refers only to the professional ethics in the profession of the accountants.

Stanford Encyclopaedia of Philosophy defines business ethics as 'the concept of business ethics is applied ethics discipline that addresses the moral features of commercial activity'.

According to Carter McNamara, "Business ethics is generally coming to be known as what is right or wrong in the work place and doing what is right—this is in regard to effects of products, services and in relationships with stakeholders.

According to John Donaldson, "Business ethics can be described as the systematic study of moral matters pertaining to business, industry or related activities, institutions, or practices and beliefs".

According to Churchman, C.W., "work ethics consists of the set of attitudes and the value systems which would be appropriate for achieving the goals of the organisation".

Stanwick, P.A. and Stanwick, S.D. define ethics as "the values of individual uses to interpret whether any particular action or behaviour is considered acceptable and appropriate".

According to Andrew Crane, "Business ethics is the study of business situations, activities and decisions where issues of right and wrong are addressed".

Raymond C. Baumhart defines business ethics as, "the ethics of business is the ethics of responsibility. The businessman must promise that he will not harm knowingly".

Various meanings are attributed to the concept of 'business ethics' by different people. Business ethics judges the priority of different business activities. Ethical principles which are dictated by the society are used to determine the propriety of business activities. On the other hand, business ethics refers to the ethical obligations and responsibilities of the managers and other business professionals. It is concerned with the conduct of individuals in fulfilling moral requirements of business. Business ethics requires a manager who is honest with himself, his organisation and the society.

Business ethics are viewed as moral principles that define the right and wrong behaviour in business activities. Business ethics are the norms of desirable behaviour in business interactions and commercial transactions. Business ethics is interpreted as nothing but the application of ethics in business. It is believed that business can be ethical and still it can make profit. Business ethics are the rules of business conduct by which the propriety of business activity is assessed. It also relates to the propriety of managerial activities. It provides the description of desirable conduct which is based on moral values.

In general, business ethics is considered as the application of ethical rules to the conduct of business. It is a form of applied ethics which includes not only the analysis of moral norms and values, but also the analysis of business activities, technologies used, their transactions, and other pursuits. It is concerned with moral issues in business. It examines those problems which raise the moral issues in business and makes attempts to solve them. Business ethics ensures that the goods and services which are sold to the customers, are of standard quality and are offered at reasonable prices to earn reasonable profits. Business has to promote its growth with fairness and truth, but it must take care of the interests of the customers, employees, creditors, suppliers, government, shareholders and the community.

At the level of employees, business ethics is concerned with better working conditions, welfare facilities, job security, physical safety and security, participative management and high morale. Business ethics is concerned with fair practices relating to recruitment, compensation, promotion, lay-offs, perks, etc. At customer's level, it is concerned with better quality of goods and services, reasonable prices, avoiding practice of discriminatory pricing, avoiding the practice of making false claims about product and services, avoiding the practice of customer deception etc. In regard to shareholder's interests, business ethics is concerned with disclosing all the relevant information, ensuring regular dividends, ensuring steady capital appreciation, protecting interests of minority shareholders, and protecting the interests of the shareholders at the time of mergers and takeovers.

Regarding government agencies, business ethics is concerned with complying with rules and regulations, paying taxes and other dues honestly and acting as partner in the programmes of national development. In case of banks and other financial institutions, business ethics is concerned with the safety of borrowed funds and prompt repayment of the loans.

At societal level, business ethics is concerned with contributing to better quality of life, protecting environment, preserving scarce resources for posterity, contributing to the upliftment of the poor and downtrodden, and avoiding discrimination against any social group or section.

C. Significance of Business Ethics

1. Shaping the Corporate Culture

Business ethics helps to shape the corporate culture. It clarifies the social values, morals and responsibilities of the business organisations. Every organisation can further develop their ideas regarding what is desirable organisational behaviour to suit their culture. Integrity and honesty in professional and business dealings results in important positive consequences. It promotes trust and confidence. It establishes foundations for good and long lasting business relations and positive interactions in the future. Unethical business activities usually result in serious financial loss or loss of life, or injury to the innocent people. The individuals and the organisations which are involved in unethical behaviour lose their credibility. Their image in general public and business community is tarnished, and its direct consequences can be damaging for the sales, profits and morale of the company. The distrust of the people can drive the company to bankruptcy.

On the other hand, adherence to business ethics and value systems can help to bring positive effects not only on the quality of the products and services, but it also enhances the confidence and satisfaction of all the stakeholders. Ethical behaviour of the organisational leaders is very important because it creates an ethical climate in the organisation. Ethical behaviour has an empowering effect on the parties which are involved in the business activities. An ethical manager creates the climate of trust, supportiveness and honesty. The employees feel confidence in giving positive suggestions, taking risks and responsibilities.

Temptations to satisfy the ambitions in earning higher profits can create ethical dilemmas in the functional areas of accounting, purchasing, marketing, production, quality control, etc. Education and training in business ethics can help the businessmen to survive and succeed in their future ventures. However, the ethical issues can also pose as managerial dilemmas when they raise conflict between organisation's profit earning performance and its performance in carrying out social responsibilities. Business ethics requires a manager to show integrity and honesty with his organisation and also with the society.

Ethical manager is always aware of the moral values and social responsibilities. His ethical orientation develops in him a high level of integrity and honesty. His knowledge of business ethics can help to develop ethical climate in the organisation. It can also help him to resolve the ethical dilemmas. Business ethics views the needs and aspirations of the individuals not merely as those of the individuals but as a part of those of the society.

2. Helping to Resolve Ethical Dilemmas

Business ethics helps the decision-makers to resolve the ethical dilemmas. Ethical dilemmas involve choosing between two equally acceptable and commendable options. However, the term is seldom used to refer to the situation in which one has to choose between two happy options. Often it is used to refer to those situations in which the options are equally unpleasant.

When decision-makers are required to define right and wrong conduct, the situation of ethical dilemma arises. However, the line that differentiates right from wrong is becoming increasingly blurred in recent years. Some people believe that good ethical behaviour has never been clearly defined. Moral managers write and distribute the codes of ethics to guide employees through ethical dilemmas. They try to create such an ethically healthy climate that the employees confront a minimal degree of ambiguity regarding what constitutes a morally right and wrong conduct.

Ethical dilemmas are not the sort of things that occurs only once on every blue moon. The situations in which a difficult choice has to be made between two or more equally undesirable alternatives crop up almost every day. An ethical dilemma forces the decision-makers to choose in a way that contradicts ethical values, or bulldozes them to break some ethical norms. The objective of business ethics is to guide the decision-makers to make ethical choices in such situations.

3. Shouldering Corporate Social Responsibility

Business ethics creates awareness about Corporate Social Responsibility. It is an ethical duty or obligation of business organisation towards environment, employees, government and the other stakeholders like shareholders, customers, suppliers, dealers, etc. Business organisations are expected to operate their business in ethical ways. Their socially responsible actions include promoting labour welfare, supporting social issues, protecting environment, investing in rural/urban community development, cooperating with government, and encouraging the concerned people for both ethical behaviour and social responsibility.

'Corporate Social Responsibility' has its origin in United States of America. In 1930's, the American industrialists were expected to take actions to 'protect and improve the welfare of society' as a whole along with their own interests. Later, Peter Drucker emphatically argued that industrial managements should assume social responsibility. It was further argued that managements should consider the impact of their business policies and actions upon the society, and prepare the plans and programmes to promote the public good. It has to contribute towards the social harmony and stability. Later on Sandra Holms emphasized that in addition to making profit business should help to 'solve special problems' whether or not business creates these problems.

Business organisations are under increasing pressure to conduct their business in a socially responsible manner. There is debate over the extent to which a positive image of corporate social performance is related to the corporate financial performance. Researchers have found that company's performance in social responsibility and its financial performance are positively correlated.

4. Protecting Environment

Business ethics creates awareness about environmental problems and the duties of business with respect to environment protection. Business organisations have to take precautions that their production processes do not cause pollution in the environment. Corporate managements have to abide by the various provisions of the Central Pollution Control Act to effectively control the pollution of air, water, land and sound.

For industries, causing pollution is cheaper than preventing it. It costs nothing to let the chemical effluent go into a river, stream, or a lake, but it costs to install and run an effluent treatment plant. In 1984, Union Carbide Corporation unleashed the 'Bhopal Gas Tragedy' which killed thousands of people and disabled several thousand people.

Carbon dioxide, nitrogen oxide, sulphur dioxide, etc. caused by burning of fossil fuel pose serious threats to environment. Chemical plants, paper mills, tanneries, thermal power plants discharge enormous quantities of chemical effluents, powders, particles and gases that are harmful to environment. River Ganges is severally polluted by about two hundred townships and thousands of villages on the banks of the river. The story of several other rivers and lakes in India is not different. Industrialisation has improved the standard of living. People are enabled to consume more and create more waste as a result of the increased standard of living. Consumption of disproportionately higher share of natural resources results in the depletion of the resources. Disproportionate use and high consumption of energy, metals, minerals, chemicals, fossil fuels, automobiles, etc. gives greater scope for causing pollution.

5. Promoting Fair Trade and Business Practices

For its survival and growth, every individual businessman or business organisation must earn profit, but according to business ethical standards, profit must be reasonable. Moral managements maintain the stability of prices of their products and services. But unscrupulous and immoral managements take advantage of shortages and increasing demands to raise the prices. They do not even feel morally inhibited in creating artificial shortages by hoarding.

Some business people use deceptive pricing like 'bait and switch pricing'. In it a low price offer is intended to lure customers into store, and then a sales person tries to influence them to buy high priced items. Consumers do not actually get any discount when discounts are offered on inflated prices. Sometimes unfair pricing practices are used to drive the competitors out of business.

Consumers can protect their interests when adequate information regarding product or services is provided. Adequate information is needed to make rational choices. If the required information is not properly given on product package and label, the consumers do not have any means of determining their choice.

Innumerable financial organisations have cheated the common people who trusted them. Their hard earned money is entrusted with the financial services organisations to seek better living in post-retirement period, but financial organisations have robbed people of their life savings. No stringent action is usually taken on them by the concerned authorities or by the government. It is definitely shameful on the part of those who cheat and those who do not take any action against them.

Sales people and insurance agents have developed a new vocabulary to obfuscate rather than to reveal. They avoid speaking of commissions. Commissions on mutual funds are 'front-end' or 'back-end' loads. Insurance agents whose commissions can approach 100 per cent of the first year's premium are not legally required to disclose this fact. The agents of insurance companies often address their insurance policies as 'retirement plans' and refer to the premiums as 'deposits'. Business ethics helps to prevent the unfair and deceptive practices in trade and commerce.

6. Promoting Justice

Business ethics helps to promote distributive, retributive, compensatory and procedural justice. Aristotle regards justice as a virtue. Virtue ethics presupposes a view about human nature and the purpose of life. Applying virtue ethics to business depends on a context that includes some conception of the nature and purpose of business. It means, to apply virtue ethics to business, we have to determine the aims of business activity.

The term 'justice' is used to evaluate individual actions, social actions, legal actions, political actions and economic practices. Question of justice often arises in the context of distributive justice, retributive justice and compensatory justice. Distributive justice is concerned with the distribution of burdens and benefits. Retributive justice deals with the punishment of the wrong doers. Compensatory justice deals with the matters of compensating the individuals for the wrong done to them.

A question of distributive justice often arises while evaluating distribution of burdens and benefits in our social, economic and political institutions. Compensatory and retributive justices are involved in the matters concerned with correcting wrongs. Procedural justice is concerned with impartial, equal and fair administration of the rules of procedure. The ethical question in procedural justice is concerned with the process.

7. Whistle Blowing

Business ethics supports 'whistle blowing'. This term is often used to refer to those people or government employees who give publicity to the incidents of corruption or mismanagement in government agencies. The term is also used in the private sector when an employee or ex-employee discloses the corruption or wrong doing by the authorities of the organisation. The whistle blowers have to pay heavy price for such disclosure. They face financial hardships that result from losing job and also from legal expenses. The whistle blowers are black listed, demoted and dismissed outrightly. They suffer severe emotional stress. The co-workers, friends, neighbours and even families turn against them. It is also argued that there can be more effective ways to deal with corrupt practices without making heroic personal sacrifices by the whistle blowers.

Internal whistle blowing is reporting about the wrong doing to higher authorities in the organisation. The whistle blowers can also use the suggestion box scheme to register their concerns with hidden identity. External whistle blowing is reporting about the wrong doing to the external individuals or bodies like government agencies, public interest groups and mass media. As a witness of crime, a whistle blower can notify the police or testify in the court of law. It is argued that external whistle blowing is unjustifiable because employees have a moral and contractual duty to be loyal to their employers.

8. Preventing Sexual Harassment

Ethical organisations recognise sexual harassment as a serious offence. They prevent and punish sexual harassment at the workplace. They formulate anti-sexual harassment policy which clearly states the employer's commitment to a safe work environment.

Sexual harassment is undesirable and unwelcomed sexual attention by an individual of opposite sex. It can be physical contact and advances, demand or request for sexual favours, sexually coloured remarks, display of coloured remarks, showing pornography, and any other unwelcomed physical, verbal or non-verbal conduct of sexual nature.

Sexual harassment can cost the company in the form of employee turnover, absenteeism and loss of productivity. It can have serious and devastating effects on the individual. It can result in poor public image; physical, emotional and psychological trauma; isolation, ostracism and suicide; loss of self-esteem; decreased productivity; expenses on court litigation; expensive compensation pay-outs; loss of job; strain and mistrust in interpersonal relations and unhealthy work atmosphere.

Supreme Court guidelines lay down certain responsibilities on the employers. The employers have to set up a complaint committee through which complaints of the women can be heard. An express prohibition of the sexual harassment must be notified, published and circulated. Employers must prevent and punish sexual harassment at workplace.

D. Sources of Ethics

1. Religion

Religion is one of the oldest sources of ethics. Major religions of the world have the belief that values, morals and ethics are the expressions of divine will. Christianity believes in transcending nature and realising everlasting life after death even though man is born in original sin and bound to flesh and its lusts. A Christian believes in crucifixion of an immoral man in him with the crucifixion of Jesus and receiving a new moral life through the resurrection of Christ from death. His purpose of life is to love and serve the God, and the only way of loving and serving God is to love and serve the neighbour. Christ's greatest commandment is "love others as you love yourself". The life of Jesus gives an expression to highest Christian virtue— "love".

Golden rule for Christians is "Do unto others as you would have them do unto you" (Mathew, 7:12). The Jews love and serve God through the obedience to Mosaic laws and with commitment to justice, humility, righteousness, kindness, truth and fidelity. Rules of personal and social conduct were laid down for the Hindus in Manusmriti, *Yadnya*-walkyasmṛuti, Kautilyasmruti, etc. *Hitopdesha* is another book that gives advice regarding moral code of conduct for the individuals in the society. For Hindus, the moral code of conduct depends upon the 'Yati-dharma' or the caste system. Every caste has to follow different ethical standards and behavioural patterns. It is believed that four castes are formed from four divisions of the body of God: Brahmins from the head, Kshatriya from the arms, Vaishya from the abdomen and Stri-shudra from the feet.

According to classical Jewish, Christian and Islamic teachings, God rewards the righteous and punishes the wicked. According to Bhagwadgita, every individual ultimately reaps the fruits of his own *karma* (deeds). God or Creator does not feature anywhere in the ethics of the Jains and Buddhists though they have clearly defined their respective codes of ethics.

If the moral code of conduct can exist without God in a religion, it can also exist without religion. But the religions bind the people together. A religion can give its followers a sense of belonging to a community, culture and tradition.

2. Law

Constitutional laws, statutes and regulations serve to educate people about the ethical behaviour, values and moral course in life. However, this does not mean that all the people agree to accept law as a vehicle to express all the ethical preferences of the society. It can only represent a rough approximation of society's ethical norms and standards. Legality and morality are two different concepts. Legality of an action need not always be interpreted as an appropriate moral action. An illegal action can be sometimes moral, and a legal action can be sometimes immoral. Mahatma Gandhi's 'civil disobedience movement' was against British law. In the context of freedom struggle, violating the law was morally required and even morally permissible. Morality and legality are different but correlated.

Laws are generally considered as the codification of social norms, values, customs, mores and ideals. Therefore, modifications and changes in law generally reflect the changes in the social attitude about rightness and wrongness of the conduct. However, the changes and modifications in law sometimes bring about change in people's perception of an action or individual's conduct.

Some economists and social critics like John Kenneth, Galbraith and Reich have the opinion that society should not expect business to behave morally but rather should simply use government to direct business' pursuit of profit in socially acceptable directions—by using law. All those who defend corporate social responsibility believe that business interactions and transactions should not only be socially and morally acceptable, but also legally permissible. It is also argued that law is an adequate vehicle to direct the moral behaviour of business.

There are some counter arguments which say that there are limits to what the law can be expected to achieve in this context. Sometimes laws are made when business has already done damage through its immoral behaviour. Formulating appropriate law is also a difficult procedure. Generally, government bodies have limited expertise, staffing and time. Therefore, they give opportunities to industrial experts to make significant inputs in writing the laws. However, once formulated, the laws guide the moral conduct of individuals, groups and organisations in business.

3. Culture

Culture refers to a set of morals, values, beliefs, rules, standards, traditions, ideals, arts, customs and the behavioural practices followed by the individuals and groups in a society. These cultural values, morals and beliefs form the source of ethics. The physical and social environment of living, religious practices and education contribute their share to create culture.

Individual growth, social order and development are possible by adherence to the positive cultural standards and norms. The cultural values, ideals, beliefs and morals are transferred from one generation to the other. Cultural impact makes majority of people law-abiding citizen. Respect for cultural norms and maintenance of law and order provides social security to the people. A good culture recognises the importance of nature and ecosystem, and recognises the gifts of nature as the gifts of God. Ethical value system is created by culture which guides man to behave honestly, legally and in a socially responsible manner.

Religions are the main contributions to the cultural patterns of society. Christianity has given special characteristics to the cultures in many parts of the world. Hinduism, Islam, Buddhism and other religions have founded the basis of cultures in many countries of the world, especially in Asian and African countries. Religions create cultural norms of social behaviour. Religious ethics also contributes to formulate the judgments of right and wrong. The cultural values are expressed through aesthetic sensibilities in the work of arts like literature, music, painting, sculpture and dancing. These fine arts are closely associated with religious traditions in many cultures.

Cultural values of duties and responsibilities are associated with the religious beliefs. Usually, the value crisis is understood as the cultural crisis. Cultural tradition is exhibited as the cultural identity. Contemporary cultural crisis is associated with the speedy changes in the moral standards, life styles and social relationships.

The guidelines for moral conduct and formation of value system are decided by the cultural experiences of an individual. Opportunity and reward system, social stratification, values, norms, use of time, food habits, dress and appearance, language, law, communication, media, education, arts, crafts, customs, historical background, religion and geographical factors provide a wide scope for cultural experience of an individual.

4. Other Sources of Ethics

The 'Ten Commandments' are the earliest recorded code of conduct in the world. Ten Commandments are given by God to Moses. The first three commandments are concerned about our responsibilities towards God, and the remaining seven commandments are about our responsibilities towards mankind. These commandments are given and discussed in Chapter 20 of the book "Exodus", and in Chapter 5 of the book "Deuteronomy". Laws of 'sexual sins' are given in Chapter 18 of the book "Leviticus". The laws of 'Social Order' are given in Chapter 19 of "Leviticus". These books are included in the Old Testament of Holy Bible. Exodus was written about 1445 B.C., Leviticus was written about 1405 B.C.; and Deuteronomy was written about 1400 B.C. The authorship of these books is Mosaic.

Philosophical systems like puritanism, stoicism, advaitism, altruism, epicureanism etc. are considered as some other sources of ethics. Socio-biologists have collected evidences which suggest that certain traits of human nature are inherited through genetic factors. Certain inherited characteristics and illnesses have the genetic source. Therefore, genetic screening is used to identify the individuals who are susceptible to certain genetically based illnesses, and also to single out the persons who have certain genetic traits.

Business houses develop their own operating policies, code of ethics, and corporate codes of conduct which are also considered as the sources of business ethics.

E. Managerial Ethics

Managerial ethics deals with the moral standards and moral judgments of the managers. Managerial ethics determines how socially responsive an organisation can be in long run. Ethical standards of a manager decides the kind of response an enterprise may give to the stakeholders and the society.

Archie B. Carroll states that there are three levels of ethical judgment that characterise managers and their morality:

1. Moral Management
2. Immoral Management
3. Amoral Management

1. Moral Management

The activities of moral management conforms to the ethical standards. It complies with the accepted professional standards of behaviour and right conduct. The managers of moral management firmly believe that they should not do anything that may harm their own self-esteem, or damage the reputation of their organisation. Moral management prefers to operate well above what law mandates because law is considered as a minimal ethical behaviour. Moral management desires to succeed, but its success is guided by ethical fairness and justice. It earns profit within the confines of ethical standards and law.

2. Immoral Management

Immoral managements are actively opposed to ethical codes of conduct. They have exclusive concern for gains and profits. They have strong desire to achieve success at any price. Their activities show total lack of principles and practice of ethics. They have no desire to treat others with fairness and justice.

3. Amoral Management

Amoral managements are neither moral nor immoral. They ignore the ethical considerations, and do not think about the ethical issues. They are inattentive and insensitive to the moral aspects of their decisions and actions. They believe that general-ethical standards are not appropriate to be followed in business.

EXERCISES

1. Define business ethics and discuss its relevance in business activities.
2. "Business has to promote its growth with fairness and truth". Discuss.
3. Write a detailed note on meaning and scope of business ethics.
4. Elucidate on the significance of business ethics.
5. What are the sources of business ethics?
6. Discuss the role of business ethics in promoting justice and fair trade practices.
7. Write a note on the moral, amoral and immoral managements.
8. Write short notes on the following:
   (i) Whistle Blowing
   (ii) Environment Protection
   (iii) Preventing Sexual Harassment
   (iv) Ethical Dilemmas
   (v) Shaping Corporate Culture
   (vi) Religion as a Source of Ethics
   (vii) Legal and Cultural Sources of Ethics
   (viii) Managerial Ethics

2

Theories of Business Ethics

"A theory can be proved by experiment; but no path leads from experiment to the birth of a theory".

—Albert Einstein

Learning Objectives

A. Introduction
B. Theory of Ethical Egoism
C. Theory of Ethical Utilitarianism
D. Theory of Eudemonism
E. Theory of Kantianism
F. Theory of Egalitarianism
G. Theory of Ethical Relativism
H. Theories of Teleological Ethics
I. Theories of Deontological Ethics
J. Theory of Capitalism
K. Theory of Ethical Altruism
L. Theory of Dualism
M. Theory of Existentialism
N. Theory of Contractarianism
O. Theory of Ethical Intuitionalism
P. Theories of Positive and Negative Rights
Q. Theories of Social Justice
R. Theories of Virtue Ethics
S. Theory of Ethical Feminism
T. Theories of System Development Ethics
   (a) Theory of Personal Improvement Ethics
   (b) Theory of Organisational Ethics
   (c) Theory of Extra-organisational Ethics

A. Introduction

Ethics is a traditional area of philosophical inquiry that dates back to the ancient Greeks. There are three historical periods of the development of ethics—Greek period, medieval period, and modern period. Socrates, Plato and Aristotle emphasised the need and importance of good conduct. Laws of morality were considered natural, rational, and comprehensible to human nature. Medieval ethics refers to those aspects of morality which developed into ethical theories with the spread of Christianity in Europe. Modern ethics gives emphasis on human freedom, individualism and human accomplishment.

Ethical theories are needed to resolve those controversial issues on which reasonable people disagree. Ethical questions in business arise when people have to decide how to balance competing concerns. Controversial issues cannot be settled easily by our simple moral rules and ordinary moral beliefs. When reasonable persons disagree about some really hard ethical question, they require some understanding of ethical theory. Ethical theories represent the best efforts of philosophers and thinkers over the ages that help us to understand morality and to resolve our controversial issues in business ethics.

In this chapter, we deal with several theories of ethics like egoism, utilitarianism, eudemonism, Kantianism, egalitarianism, relativism, teleological ethics, deontological ethics, capitalism, altruism, dualism, existentialism, contractarianism, intuitionalism, rights theories, theories of social justice, virtue ethics, ethical feminism, etc.

B. Theory of Ethical Egoism

Theory of ethical egoism is a teleological theory. Ethical egoism holds that an action is right if it tends to produce or produces the outcomes by which a particular person's self-interests are maximised. This maximisation of self-interests can result even at the expense of the others. Ethical egoism does not permit a person to help, assist or serve the others if that person does not get anything from doing so.

Egoism refers to the individuals whose decisions are based on their self-interests. Thomas Hobbes is credited for the development of ethical egoism. It focuses on each individual's self-interest. It is founded on the belief that every individual should act in such a way that it will promote himself or herself.

Ethical egoism allows an individual's actions for self-interests so long as it also produces the positive benefits for others. Some ethical egoist believe that all of their actions on balance generate more positive benefits than the negative ones. **Psychological egoism** is different from the ethical egoism. Theory of psychological egoism holds that people always want something out of their actions for themselves. They deny the reality of **ultimate altruism**. Ultimate altruism is the intentional sacrifice of one's own self-interests for the sake of the welfare of others.

Theory of **Enlightened Egoism** emphasises the decisions for serving the self-interests but it also allows for the altruistic concern for the welfare of the others. An enlightened egoist may support the community welfare projects, but he does so because it helps to achieve some ultimate object for himself. It tries to justify that pursuing a person's self-interests is required to generate some positive outcomes for others. An ethical egoist argues that without self-interests nobody would do any action.

C. Theory of Ethical Utilitarianism

Utilitarianism is a teleological theory. It holds that an action is right if it tends to produce or produces the greatest amount of satisfaction for the greatest number of people.

Theory of utilitarianism was originally developed by Jeremy Bentham in his 'Principles of Morals and Legislation' (1789) and by John Stuart Mill in his 'Utilitarianism' (1863). Supporters of this theory argue that the people would not do actions that help others if the action does not benefit their own self-interests.

Classical utilitarianism states that an action is right if it produces the greatest pleasure over pain for everyone. However, a problem arises in the attempts to decide exactly how much pleasure each course of action produces, because pleasure cannot be measured in quantity. John Stuart Mill's writings do not give any guidance for comparing the quantity with the quality of pleasure.

Utilitarianism puts emphasis on the consequences of action. Results of a person's actions and his intention behind the action are considered important in utilitarianism. Happiness producing consequences are considered to be important. Actions are good when they produce happiness. Actions are bad when they produce unhappiness. **Consequentialism** claims that, what makes an action right or wrong is the consequences of the action and not the internal character of action. Utilitarianism is a theory with specific emphasis on happiness producing consequences. Therefore, it is a particular version of consequentialism. But, consequentialism is considered as a particular form of utilitarianism. Utilitarians focus on the net results of the actions rather than on the means and the motives.

It is practically impossible to determine what would be the greatest good for the greatest number of people. Those who oppose utilitarianism, generally stress this difficulty. They also find inherent contradictions in this theory. By emphasising greatest good for the greatest number, utilitarianism treats the minority unfairly, because the minority does not receive the greatest good.

D. Theory of Eudemonism

Eudemonism or eudemonia is a classical Greek word which is commonly translated as 'happiness', but the meaning can be better described as 'good life' or 'well-being'. Eudemonism is a teleological theory. It holds a view that an action is right if it tends to promote or promotes the goal of human happiness. If a manager promotes the labour welfare activities, and implements the policies of employee health, safety and security standards, he ensures the natural components of human happiness.

Aristotle had argued that there is a difference between having a good time and leading a good life. Having a good life is maximising happiness. On the other hand having a good time is maximising the pleasurable activity or utility. Aristotle preferred 'maximising happiness'. According to eudemonism, an action can be right or wrong depending on the consequences of that action. These consequences vary with the varying circumstances. Every person is counted equally and no person's happiness or unhappiness is more important than that of the another. Killing one person and using his organs to save the lives of ten other persons by transplantation is not a justifiable action.

Eudemonism holds 'well-being' of an individual as an essential value. Therefore, it considers that action as a right action which leads to the 'well-being' of the individual. According to ancient Greek philosophers, 'good life' or 'eudemonia' is an outcome of a life time practicing of the virtues in one's everyday activities which are subject to the exercise of practical wisdom to resolve any conflicts or dilemmas. The dilemmas might arise during the course of the right action. As an ultimate goal, eudemonia is an objective state, not a subjective state of a person. It characterises 'well-being' and 'well lived' life, irrespective of the subjective and emotional state of the person.

Eudemonism and virtue (arête) are two central concepts in ancient Greek ethics. All ancient Greek theorists understand eudemonia as the highest human good, but they differ from one another regarding how to achieve it. According to Aristotle eudemonia results from the rational activity in accordance with the virtues over a period of complete life. To him, eudemonia is not constituted by honour, wealth or power. Epicurus, a subsequent hedonist agreed with Aristotle that happiness is the highest good. But he identified eudemonia with pleasure. He considered pleasure as the only thing that people value for its own sake. The stoics also believed that eudemonia was the highest good. But for them 'virtue' or 'well-being' consists in living according to nature. According to St. Augustine and St. Thomas Aquinas eudemonia is found ultimately in a 'direct perception of God'. It is a state of complete blessedness.

Immanuel Kant, an opponent of eudemonism, rejected the view that happiness is the highest good. According to him happiness can be an ingredient of the highest good, but only if it is deserved. Existentialists also reject eudaemonist because they consider happiness as just a bourgeois fantasy.

E. Theory of Kantianism

Kantianism is an ethical theory given by German philosopher Immanuel Kant. For Kant, an action is morally right only if it is motivated by a goodwill. Kant gives an excellent example of thoroughly non-consequentialist approach to ethics. In contrast to utilitarianism, Kant's theory states that an individual does not have to know about the possible consequences of his action.

According to Kant nothing is good in itself except a goodwill. This does not mean that health, happiness, intelligence, courage, etc. are not good, but their good depends on the will of the person who makes use of them. For example, intelligence is not good when it is used by an evil person. The concept of duty is included in the notion of goodwill. Our actions can have moral worth only when we act from duty. If one does not will the action from a sense of one's duty to be fair and honest, his action does not have any moral worth. True moral worth of actions comes from a recognition of duty and a desire to discharge that duty.

Kant believed that reason alone can produce moral law. According to him, an action is morally right if and only if we can will it to become a universal law of conduct. Kant's 'categorical imperative' gives firm rules to follow in moral decision-making. These rules do not depend on circumstances, nor do they permit any individual exceptions. Much good may come from lying or deceptive, but deliberate lying or deception is always wrong. Kant stresses the importance of motivation and of acting on principle. It is not enough just to do the right thing. An action is right only if it is done from a senses of duty. It is the desire to do the right thing for its own sake. According to Kant if action is motivated by self-interest it does not have moral worth, even though the action is a right thing. If a person does a right thing out of instinct, habit or sympathy for other person, then still the act does not have the moral worth. Only if an action is done out of a sense of duty, that action has moral value. Critics of Kant ask, if one is emotionally moved by pictures of starving children to give money to famine relief fund; has that action no moral worth? A person with strong human sympathies can be more admirable person than someone who gives to the relief fund solely out of a sense of duty.

F. Theory of Egalitarianism

Egalitarianism holds the view that all human beings are equal in some fundamental respect, therefore, each person has an equal claim to society's goods. There are no relevant differences among the people, therefore unequal treatment given to them cannot be justified. All benefits and burdens should be distributed among the people by giving exactly equal shares to each one of them. Goods should be allocated to everyone in equal portions.

Egalitarian view of equality—"All men are created equal"—is an attractive social ideal. The ideal of equality is a driving force behind emancipation of women, emancipation of slaves, and elimination of racialism, sexual harassment and other forms of social, political and economic injustice. Equality is not only a principle of justice for entire societies but also for its smaller groups, institutions and organisations. When workgroups work with solidarity and cooperation, all the workers should receive equal compensation.

Egalitarians have a positive attitude towards group decision-making. Egalitarianism is considered as political doctrine that all people should be treated as equals and should have the same political, economic, social and civil rights. It advocates the removal of economic inequalities among people. It views equality as the natural state of humanity. It also refers to equality of opportunity and a state of economic affairs in which the government promotes equal prosperity for all citizens.

John Locke believes in equality of human rights and refers to them as natural rights. Another form of egalitarianism refers to **distributive egalitarianism** in which the wealth created by workers is organised, controlled and distributed in equal manner. Karl Marx is the proponent of this form of egalitarianism.

Christian egalitarians hold the view that Bible teaches the fundamental equality of men and women of all racial and ethnic mixes, all economic classes, and all age-groups based on the teaching and example of Jesus Christ.

Egalitarianism is subjected to criticisms also. Many critics claim that there is quality that all human beings do not possess in precisely the same quantity. All human beings vary in their abilities, intelligence, needs, virtues and the other physical and mental attributes. Therefore, they say, all human beings are not equal in all respects.

G. Theory of Ethical Relativism

Theory of ethical relativism holds that ethical standards for judging an action varies with different cultures, periods, places and circumstances. What is right is determined by varying factors at different times and places. Relativism proposed that ethically right action is relative to the social, cultural and personal circumstances in which one finds oneself. It holds that every person has his own ethical standards that enables him or her to make decisions. One cannot make a moral judgment about another person's social conduct. What is morally right at one place for one person may be wrong at another place for another person.

If abortion is legally permissible in one country, it is morally right or neutral for an ethical relativist in that place; but if it is condemned in the another country, it is morally wrong there for a relativist. Therefore, the ethical relativists have no absolute ethical standard which is independent of socio-cultural context. Moral requirements are relative to socio-cultural customs, norms, traditions and laws.

Many global corporations who operate in different parts of the world, adopt different ethical standards. According to them, many criticised business practices are not considered to be unethical by the local standards of some other countries. Should those global companies be bound by prevailing moral standards of the home country? Or should they behave in Rome as Romans do? No easy answers are available for these questions. However, according to '**absolutism**' business ought to be conducted in the same way all over the world, and a single code of conduct should be followed. On the other hand, according to relativism, the only way for the conduct of business abroad is doing what is legally and morally accepted in a given country.

H. Theories of Teleological Ethics

Teleological ethics is also known as consequentialist's ethics. "consequentialism" is the class of normative ethical theories which hold that the consequences of one's conduct are ultimately basis for any judgment about the righteness of that conduct. According to consequentialist, a morally right act is one which produces a good outcome or consequences.

Teleological ethics is based on ancient Greek philosophy. Greek word 'teleos' means 'end' and 'logos' means 'science'. It is an ethical theory that holds that an action can be determined as morally good or evil by its 'end' or 'consequences'. This theory maintains that good ends or results determine the 'ethical value' of the actions. If a stakeholder obtains more benefits than costs than by any other alternative, then teleological ethics endorses the goodness of that choice. Therefore, it is a theory of ethics that derives duty or moral obligation from what is desirable as an end to be achieved.

Teleological ethics is distinguished from deontological ethics which derives the rightness or wrongness of one's actions from the 'character of the behaviour' rather than the outcomes or consequences of that behaviour. Teleological theories are often discussed in opposition to deontological theories. Deontology holds that actions themselves are inherently good or evil regardless of their consequences.

Teleological theory is also distinguished from 'virtue ethics'. Virtue ethics focuses on the character of the person rather than on the nature or consequences of the actions of that person.

Some thinkers argue that consequentialist and deontological theories are not necessarily mutually exclusive. They argue that 'human rights', which are commonly considered as a deontological concept, can only be justified with reference to the consequences of having those rights.

I. Theories of Deontological Ethics

The word deontology comes from the Greek roots 'deon' which means 'duty' and 'logos' which means 'science'. Thus deontology is a science of duty. Theories of deontological ethics hold the view that ethical value of actions is determined by fulfilling obligations, doing the right things and adhering to the moral standards of conduct. Deontological ethics maintains that 'an action is right independent of its consequences'. It is right to obey the 'Ten Commandments' without being bothered about its benefits or costs.

Deontological ethics focuses upon adherence to independent moral rules or duties. To make correct moral decisions a person has to understand what his moral duties are and what rules exist to regulate those duties. If he follows his duties, he behaves morally. If he fails to follow his duties, he behaves immorally. Duties and obligations should be determined objectively, not subjectively. Deontological systems have no room for subjective feelings. Deontologists condemn relativism and subjectivism in all their forms.

Divine command is the most common form of deontological ethical theory. According to many Christians an action is correct if it is in agreement with the rules and duties established by God. Duty theories hold that an action is morally right if it is in accordance with some list of duties and obligations. Rights theories hold that an action is morally right if it respects the rights of all humans. This is also sometimes referred to as libertarianism. '**Libertarianism**' is a political philosophy that holds the view that people should be legally free to do whatever they wish to do so long as their activities do not affect or impinge upon the rights of the others.

Deontological moral principles are completely separated from the consequences of the actions. If one has a moral duty not to lie, then lying is always wrong, even when telling truth results in harm to others.

Some critics argue that deontological ethics is, in fact, consequentialist ethics in disguise. According to them, duties and obligations which set forth in deontological systems are actually those actions which have been demonstrated to have the best consequences over a long period of time.

J. Theory of Capitalism

According to William Shaw, "capitalism can be defined ideally as an economic system in which the major portion of production and distribution is in private hands, operating under what is termed a profit or market system". Market and private ownership aspects of capitalism are in contrast with its polar opposite socialism. Socialism is characterised by public ownership of property and a planned economy. It depends on centralised planning rather than on the market system. Major economic decisions are not made by individuals, but by the government.

Capitalism allows to create companies or business organisations that exist separately from the people associated with them. It is "an artificial being, invisible, intangible and existing only in the contemplation of law". The second characteristics of capitalism is the motive of a company to make profit.

Profit earning is considered as ubiquitous motive of mankind. Profit or money is the lifeblood of capitalist system. Capitalists are motivated by their robust voracity for profit. Appetite for money and equal access to raw materials, manpower and markets sets the capitalists free to pursue their own interests. Further, capitalism allows the capitalists to have the private ownership of the major means of production and distribution. Capitalists control the basic economic assets and productive resources.

A common defence of capitalism is that people have a fundamental moral right to property. Capitalism is considered as the outcome of this fundamental, natural and moral right to property. Certain fundamental moral rights to property cannot be denied but these rights need not be unlimited. Unlimited rights to property can lead to profound economic inequality and enormous disparity in personal incomes. It can lead to exploitation and alienation of the proletariat (labourers) by the capitalists (bourgeoisie).

K. Theory of Ethical Altruism

The term 'Altruism' was originally coined in 19th century by philosopher and sociologist August Comte. In simple terms it means caring about the welfare of other people and acting to help them.

Altruism is a theory and practice of concern for the welfare of others. It is a traditional virtue in various cultures and religions. Altruism is the opposite of selfishness. It is a motivation to provide something of value to anyone who needs it. But altrûism differs from duty. Duty is concerned with the moral obligation towards a specific individual or group. Altruism consists of sacrificing something like time, money, efforts, possessions, etc. for someone other, without expecting any direct or indirect benefits or compensation. There is a great deal of debate over the possibility of 'true' altruism. It is argued that no act of sacrificing, sharing or helping can be considered as truly altruistic. An individual who is involved in such acts may receive an intrinsic reward in the form of personal gratification. However, this argument is rejected by many people for its subjectivity. For them, the intrinsic rewards do not qualify as 'benefits'.

Ethical altruism claims that every person is morally obliged to benefit the others. In this sense ethical altruism is opposed to ethical egoism. Ethical egoism supports the actions that benefit one's own self.

Altruism is demonstrated through pro-social behaviours such as community service, cooperation, comforting, helping and sharing. Altruism is evoked by the empathic desire to help someone who is suffering. Altruism is central to the teachings of Jesus. St. Thomas Aquinas states in '***Summa Theologica***' that we should love our neighbour more than ourselves. His interpretation of Pauline phrase "love seeks not its own interests", is that 'we should seek common good more than the private good'. In Sufism altruism means devotion to others through complete forgetfulness of one's own concerns. Judaism defines altruism as the desired goal of creation. Altruism towards humanity leads to altruism towards the creator or God.

L. Theory of Dualism

Henry Sidgwick propounded this theory in his book "The Methods of Ethics" published in 1874. He bridges the gap between the two competing ethical frameworks of ethical egoism and utilitarianism.

He attempted to find a common ground between the two contending theories. His theory of dualism is founded on the common ground that exists between the two theories. He argues that both the theories had the elements of using cost-benefit analysis to analyse the actions of the persons involved.

Sidgwick attempts to find out whether the actions of a person's self-benefit has an impact on that person only or on the others also. He considered utilitarianism as a foundation component of any ethical framework. He called it 'rational benevolence'. He also includes the self-interest of ethical egoism in the ethical framework which he called 'prudence'.

Rational benevolence is necessary in the actions of the people, but prudence is also necessary because happiness of the people is the common goal of the action. It is not logical for anybody to sacrifice his or her own happiness for the sake of others.

M. Theory of Existentialism

Existentialism holds that the starting point of philosophical thinking should be the experiences of an individual. Existentialists like Kierkegaard, Dostoyevsky, Nietzsche, Sartre believed that moral and scientific thinking together do not suffice to understand the human existence. Therefore, a set of categories governed by the norm "Authenticity" is needed to understand the human existence. In the context of existentialism, authenticity is 'being true to one's own personality, spirit or character'.

A central proposition of existentialism is that 'existence precedes essence'. It means the most important consideration for an individual is the fact that he is an individual. Individual is an independently acting and responsible conscious being (existence), rather than what labels, roles definitions or stereotypes the individual fits (essence). In his work, "Existentialism is a Humanism" Sartre writes "man first of all exists, encounters himself, surges up in the world—and defines himself afterwards". An individual can choose to act in a different way. Since humans can choose to be either cruel or good, they are, neither of these things essentially.

The underlying belief of existentialism is: 'the only person who can determine the right and wrong is the person who makes the decisions'. Each individual determines his own actions, therefore, he is ultimately responsible for the consequences of his actions.

Individuals are able to develop their own sense of personal virtue through authenticity of their actions. Existentialism does not accept universal principles because every individual determines the acceptance of his own actions.

N. Theory of Contractarianism

Contractarianism or social contract theory holds the view that all individuals agree to social contract to shoulder certain duties and responsibilities so that they can become the members of the society. John Locke and Rousseau were the founders of this theory. Individuals agree to follow the social rules, regulations and norms by establishing a social contract with the other social members. According to social contract theory, all the members of the society are guided by the principles which are equally fair to everyone. Everyone in the society agrees to abide by the principles, if the principles are fair. John Rawls (1971) in his book "A Theory of Justice" argues that everyone should have the equal social rights and duties.

According to Rousseau, for a stable social life, some restrictions are essential. The society willingly accepts them. With a view to ensure self-discipline, the society creates a 'political' state. Therefore, Rousseau says, that the state is not a divine creation, but it is an outcome of a sort of unwritten social contract. If the state fails to abide by the terms and conditions of the contract, the people have the moral and natural right to overthrow the state authority.

John Rawls argues that if there are social and economic inequalities, it would be acceptable to the members of the society only if these inequalities generate the benefits for all the members of society. Thus Rawls challenged the philosophy of utilitarianism by stating that it is not acceptable to focus on actions for the greatest good of greatest number of people if the minorities do not benefit from the decision. The social contract theories of Locke, Rousseau, Garret Nardin and John Rawls hold that an action is right if it conforms to the agreed terms, rules and conditions.

O. Theory of Ethical Intuitionalism

Ethical Intuitionalism or Moral Intuitionalism is recognised as a meta-ethical theory that embarrasses the following assumptions:

1.` Moral realism, the view that there are objective facts of morality.
2. Ethical non-naturalism, the view that these evaluative facts cannot be reached to natural facts.
3. The thesis that our intuitive knowledge of evaluative facts forms the foundation of our ethical knowledge.

Sometimes the term 'ethical intuitionalism' is associated with a pluralistic deontological position in normative ethics, a position defended by W.D. Ross. However, the term refers to the general position that there are basic moral beliefs. This usage encompasses both empiricist and rationalist accounts of non-inferential moral knowledge. The empiricist version of ethical intuitionalism is standardly called 'moral sense theory' (or sometimes 'sentimentalism').

The rationalist version of ethical intuitionalism is simply called 'rational ethical intuitionalism'. Rationalist ethical intuitionists characterise moral intuitions as a species of beliefs that are self-evident in that they are justified simply by virtue of one's understanding of the proposition believed. Others characterise intuitions as a distinct kind of mental state in which something seems to be the case as a result of intellectual reflection.

Ethical intuitionalism was popular in the early 20th century particularly among British Analytic Philosophers like H.A. Prichard, G.E. Moore and Michael Huemer. Michael Huemer defines intuition as 'a sort of seeming reasoning sometimes changes how things seem to us but there is also a way things seem to us prior to reasoning, otherwise reasoning could not get started. The way things seem prior to reasoning we may call an 'initial appearance'. An initial intellectual appearance is an intuition. An ethical intuition is an intuition whose content is an evaluative proposition.

According to moral sense theorists, certain moral truths are known via moral sense simply on the basis of experience, not inference. One way to understand the moral sense is to draw on analogy between it and other kinds of senses, e.g. beauty is something we see in some faces, art works and landscapes. We can also hear it in some pieces of music. We clearly do not need an independent aesthetic sense faculty to perceive beauty in the world. Our ordinary five senses are quite enough to observe it, though merely observing something beautiful is not by itself enough to appreciate its beauty. Suppose we give name to this ability as 'the aesthetic sense'—the ability to appreciate the beauty in things—this aesthetic sense does not come automatically to all people with perfect vision and hearing. Similarly we can understand the moral sense as informing us of what is good. People with a functioning moral sense get a clear impression of wrongness when they see puppies being kicked.

P. Theories of Positive and Negative Rights

Positive rights theories hold that an action is good if it provides an individual or group with whatever they need to exist. If a person has a right to adequate health care to survive, the other agents (the government) have a duty to provide it to him or her. The negative rights theories hold that an action is good if it protects an individual or group from unwarranted interruption and interference from government and/ or other people in the exercise of that right. Political conservatives are of the opinion that government's responsibility should be restricted to protecting the negative rights of the people (e.g. right not to be deprived of the property, right not to be injured or killed, etc.)

A person has a right when he is entitled to an act in a certain way. Secondly, he also has a right when he is entitled to have the others act in a certain way towards him. If that entitlement is derived from a legal system, then it is called a legal right. If such entitlements are derived from a system of moral standards, they are called as moral rights or human rights. Legal rights are limited to a particular jurisdiction where the legal system is enforced, but moral and human rights are universal, and they are not limited to a particular jurisdiction.

The main purpose of rights is to enable an individual or group to pursue certain interests and activities and to protect those chosen interests and activities. Moral rights are strongly correlated with the duties. The moral rights of one person can be defined in the terms of the moral duties of the other people toward that person. Velasquez says, "To have moral right necessarily implies that others have certain duties toward the bearer of that right. Moral rights impose correlative duties on the others. These duties can be either duties of non-interference or the duties of positive performance.

Contractual rights and duties are the special rights and duties that arise when one individual or group enters into an agreement with the another person or group. These rights and duties are attached to specific individuals and groups. But, they depend on publicly accepted system of rules.

Q. Theories of Social Justice

Social justice theory holds that an action is right if it promotes fairness in the distributive, retributive, and compensatory aspects of social benefits and burdens.

Philosophical concern with ethics goes back to the age of Socrates, Plato and Aristotle, to whom justice was a paramount virtue. Today, philosophers generally distinguish justice from morality on the ground that something 'unjust' is more specific than something 'immoral'. But, unfortunately, the terms 'just' and 'unjust' are also vague because different people use them in different ways. The term 'justice' is often used to mean 'fairness'. Fair treatment of the members of groups or the fair compensation of prior injuries and damages, is generally referred as justice.

However, 'what exactly requires fairness is difficult to explain in precise terms. If one manager is justly punished for bribery, and the another is allowed to escape the punishment for committing the equally serious and same type of crime, then the first manager is unfairly singled out and suffers injustice.

An idea which is commonly bound up with the concept of justice is that of equality. Justice requires that people should get what they deserve. Each should receive his or her due. A person is treated unjustly when his moral rights are violated. Such injustice can be in the form of treating someone worse than the others, or depriving someone of his possession, etc.

Distributive justice is the proper distribution of social benefits and burdens. As a basis of such distribution different principles are recommended—according to individual need to each person, an equal share to each person, according to personal efforts to each person, according to social contribution to each person and according to personal merits to each person. Each of these principles seems to be acceptable and credible in different circumstances. Though there are advocates of every one of these principles, there are problems with each. For example, if equality of income is guaranteed, an idle and unenterprising person will receive an equal share of income with a hardworking and industrious person.

R. Theories of Virtue Ethics

Virtue ethics descends from the classical heuristic tradition represented by Socrates, Plato and Aristotle. They view cultivation of virtuous traits of human character as the primary function of morality. Aristotle held that virtue is a disposition bred on innate capacity which is developed by proper training and exercise. According to him virtue is neither a feeling nor an innate capacity. An individual acquires virtues as he acquires the skills such as carpentry, playing a musical instrument or cooking. He becomes just by performing just, and becomes temperate by performing temperate actions. According to Aristotle virtuous character is neither natural nor unnatural, it is acquired and cultivated like language.

According to Velasquez, a normal virtue is an acquired disposition that is valued as a part of the character of a morally good human being and that is exhibited in the person's habitual behaviour. A person has a moral virtue when he is disposed to behave habitually in the way and with the reasons, feelings and desires that are characteristics of him as morally good person. A person has a virtue of honesty when he is habitually disposed to tell the truth, and he does so because he believes that telling truth is right.

Aristotle held the view that humans are distinguished from all other creatures because humans possess the ability to reason. Therefore, the distinguishing purpose of human beings is to exercise reason in all their activities. Moral virtues are the habits that enable an individual to live according to reason. Aristotle argues that moral virtue is a habit that enables a human being to act in accordance with the specific purpose.

However, virtue ethics is more than just a habitual training. A just person should not only have a disposition to act fairly but he should also have a morally motivated desire to do so. A Kantian is motivated to act in accordance with a rule of obligation. But performing obligation does not allow the person to cherish. If the desire is absent, a necessary condition of virtue also seems to be lacking. A desire to perform is a necessary condition of virtue. If a person takes jobs simply for earning wages, he may meet his obligations, but he is not engaged in a morally appropriate action. When a person does some business in which he sells a quality product with a desire to give real value for the price, he is engaged in a morally appropriate practice. An action in business is morally justified when it is conducted by the people whose character manifests the virtues like truthfulness, respectfulness, justice, etc. A morally motivated person is more likely to follow the moral ideals and to perform the right actions.

St. Thomas Aquinas also held that moral virtues enable people to follow reason in dealing with their desires, emotions and actions. To Aristotle's four cardinal virtues of courage, temperance, justice and prudence, Aquinas added the Christian virtues of faith, hope and charity.

Virtue ethics theories maintain that ethical value of a person is determined by habitual development of sound character traits. Character is the pattern of intentions, inclinations and virtues that dispose a person or organisation to act ethically. Individuals with good character have soundly cultivated intellectual, moral, emotional and social virtues to do the right things.

'Individual Character Ethics' holds that the identification and responsible development of noble human traits like courage, justice, self-discipline, moderation, sincerity, gratitude, sense of humour, etc. determine both the instrumental and intrinsic value of all human ethical interactions.

'Work Character Ethics' holds that the identification and responsible development of noble traits at work such as creativity, competence, fairness, honesty, trustworthiness, loyalty, shared work pride, tolerance, dependability, supportiveness, cooperativeness, civility, etc. determine the instrumental and intrinsic ethical quality of work life.

'Professional Character Ethics' holds that credentialed expertise, self-regulation, autonomy, altruism, impartiality, independence of judgment, loyalty, collegiality, etc. determine the instrumental and intrinsic ethical quality of individuals in associational or professional communities.

S. Theory of Ethical Feminism

Feminist ethics is an approach which is based on the assumption that traditionally ethical theories have undermined and underappreciated the moral experiences of women, and therefore, it chooses to reimagine and reformulate ethics through a holistic feministic approach. The feminist scholars are committed to reformulate the ethical theory that does not subordinate the interests of the women. However, the issues are complex and there are disagreements among the feminists regarding how to accomplish the task. Feminists have different perspectives on matters like equality, impartiality, community and the objectivity.

Contemporary feminist philosophers have widely criticised the Kantian and utilitarian theories because these theories advocate a concept of morality that leaves little room for virtues such as love, compassion, fidelity and friendship. Feminist philosophers criticise traditional ethics because it pre-eminently focussed on men's perspectives and have little regard for women's viewpoints. Caring and the moral issues of private life and family responsibilities were traditionally regarded as trivial matters. Generally, women were regarded as ethically immature and shallow in comparison to men.

Feminist approach to ethics holds the view that the subordination of women is as wrong as it is common; and, the experiences of women are worthy of respect and they should be taken rather seriously. Traditional ethics favours the masculine cultural traits like independence, autonomy, intellect, will, dominion, war, death, etc. It gives less emphasis on culturally feminine traits like interdependence, emotion, body, trust, absence of hierarchy, joy, peace and life.

T. Theories of System Development Ethics

System development ethics theories hold the view that ethical value of actions is determined by the nature of "supportive framework" for continuous improvement of ethical conduct. Ethics development systems are implemented by the managers to sustain the environment of integrity building. They implement the recognition process for exemplary moral conduct and take swift action against wrongdoers at work. They are sensitive to the needs of the assessment and development of work culture which is supportive of ethical conduct.

Managers do not exclusively rely on the character of the employees to sustain sound business practices. They do not neglect the implementation of morally supportive intra-organisational systems. Personal improvement ethics, organisational ethics, and extra-organisational ethics are the three theories of system development ethics.

(a) Theory of Personal Improvement Ethics

Personal improvement ethics holds the view that an action is right if it promotes personal responsibilities for continuous learning, holistic development, and moral excellence. Manager generates new ideas to promote the personal improvement of the employees in order to achieve the goals of the organisation. He uses the educational benefits package of the organisation to improve himself and his organisation. Families and friends who support the moral progress and personal improvement of the employees, energise the on-going programme of personal development.

(b) Theory of Organisational Ethics

Organisational ethics holds that an action is morally right if it promotes the formal and informal organisational processes, which enhance the innovation, respectful caring, systemic justice and procedural outcome in ethical work culture. Manager takes care to develop fair reward system, a system for employee feedback, etc. to support the individual and organisational moral development.

(c) Theory of Extra-organisational Ethics

Extra-organisational ethics holds that an action is morally right if it promotes or tends to promote the improvement of collaborative partnerships in the human and natural environments. Manager willingly takes the social responsibility, and respectfully considers the global and domestic political, legal, social, ecological, economic and philanthropic concerns that affect the organisation.

Theory of open system of management advocates innovative adaptability and acquisition of external resources as the criteria for managerial effectiveness. Managers who support this approach exhibit the system development ethics. This approach emphasises resourcefulness, creative change management, respectful global negotiation and collaborative networking with diverse global interests. Managers adopt organisational flexibility and concurrently manage both people and processes ethically.

EXERCISES

1. Briefly elaborate on various theories of business ethics.
2. Discuss ethical egoism as a teleological theory.

3. What is the difference between enlightened egoism and psychological egoism?
4. What is 'Utilitarianism'? What are the strengths and weaknesses of this theory?
5. Comment on the statement, "There is a difference between having a good time and leading a good life".
6. Explain the theory of Eudemonism.
7. Elucidate the concept of 'eudemonism' and 'virtue' in Greek ethics.
8. Why did Emmanuel Kant opposed eudemonism?
9. What is 'Kantianism'?
10. Explain the Egalitarian view of equality.
11. Comment on egalitarianism as a theory of political, economic, social and civil rights.
12. Discuss the views of distributive egalitarians and Christian egalitarians.
13. What is 'Ethical Relativism'?
14. Discuss the consequentialist's views in the theories of teleological ethics.
15. Explain the theories of deontological ethics.
16. How does deontologist condemn relativism and subjectivism?
17. Why does deontologist oppose consequentialism?
18. "Profit earning is an ubiquitous motive of mankind". Discuss.
19. Explain the theory of capitalism.
20. Elucidate the concept of 'Ethical Altruism'.
21. Write a note on the theory of 'Dualism'.
22. Explain the existentialists' concept of 'Authenticity'.
23. "The only person who can determine the right and wrong is the person who makes the decisions". Discuss.
24. Explain the theory of existentialism.
25. What is 'Contractarianism'?
26. Write a note on ethical intuitionalism as a meta-ethical theory.
27. What is rational ethical intuitionalism?
28. Elaborate on the theories of positive and negative rights.
29. Explain the theories of Social Justice.
30. Write a detailed note on 'Virtue Ethics'.
31. Briefly comment on ethical feminism.
32. Write short notes on:
    - (i) System Development Ethics
    - (ii) Personal Improvement Ethics
    - (iii) Extraorganisational Ethics
    - (iv) Feminism
    - (v) Virtue Ethics of St. Thomas Aquinas
    - (vi) Positive and Negative Rights
    - (vii) Ethical Intuitionalism

(viii) Contractarian Ethics
(ix) Existential Ethics
(x) Dualism
(xi) Altruism
(xii) Capitalism
(xiii) Teleological Ethics
(xiv) Ethical Relativism
(xv) Egalitarianism
(xvi) Eudemonism
(xvii) Utilitarianism
(xviii) Egoism
(xix) Kantianism
(xx) Consequentialism
(xxi) Deontology
(xxii) True Altruism
(xxiii) Rawl's Theory of Justice
(xxiv) Social Justice
(xxv) Distributive Justice
(xxvi) Professional Character Ethics

3
Business Values

"Values are determined by systems, contexts and circumstances"
—Edward de Bono

Learning Objectives

A. The Concept of 'Value'
B. Characteristics of Values
C. Determinants of Values
D. Classification of Values
 (a) Wide Spectrum of Categories
 (b) Temporal Values and Universal Values
 (c) Instrumental Values and Terminal Values
E. Personal Values
F. Organisational Values
G. Workplace Values
H. Managerial Values
I. Essentials of Developing Managerial Values

A. The Concept of 'Value'

An individual or people make their choice of alternative courses of action in different situations. This choice is based on a set of normative standards or beliefs. These normative standards or enduring beliefs are called as values. An individual's value system is an enduring set of beliefs concerning his preferable way of living or behaving. Different value systems are used to explain a wide variety of differences of behaviour.

Value is the term derived from its Latin and French origin. The Latin root word 'valerie' means strong and vigorous, whereas, the French root word 'valoir' means important, worth, merit and usefulness of a thing. It is a relative concept which determines the worth of human behaviour or conduct. However, there are some other aspects of its meaning also. For example, value can be ideas like integrity, love, etc. It can be a quality and quantity of product, or it can be the respect shown by a young man for the elders.

Individuals need values so that they can become ethical in their conduct. Values are always associated with some fundamental principles and enduring beliefs. Values do not belong only to the individuals but they are also societal and corporate. Companies show their concern for values when they facilitate the process of transparency and accountability. Non-violence, love, truthfulness, etc. can be regarded as the societal values.

According to Oxford dictionary, value means 'worth'. However, this worth is interpreted by different social sciences as 'moral obligations', 'needs', 'duties', 'interests', 'pleasures' and such other modalities of social orientation. The judgments regarding values are influenced by a thing's usefulness, quality and worth. Values are also described as those desirable and selective ends of the actions which are supported by a worthwhile principle, merit, quality or a standard. As the values have the selective or directive quality, they serve as criteria for selection of action. They also serve as criteria for judgment, choice and preference. They constitute the basis for decision-making because they influence the choice of human behaviour or action. Therefore, values are all those social, moral, religious, artistic and other standards which an individual prefers to choose and follow. However, there appears to be no other term used with more recurrence and ambiguity than the term 'value'.

Values are the desirable 'end-states' which guide the individual and social action. Values are those normative standards which influence an individual's or group's choice among the alternative courses of action. It can be said that values characterise as the selective and desirable ends of any action. Therefore, values are all those principles and standards which are considered desirable and worthwhile to be followed. Values are also used as standards by which choices and courses of actions are evaluated. Values are all those abstractions and ideas about the quality of things and behavioural standards which the people think as important in their lives. The opinions, pre-conceived notions, judgments, viewpoints, likes-dislikes, prejudices and attitudes of the people determine their views of the world and influence their behaviour.

Thus, the concept of value generally refers to the principles or standards which the people use to determine what is desirable and important in their lives. It is the quality of anything that is esteemed, desired and respected. When a system of dominant values is accepted by a person, it becomes a centre around which his thoughts, feeling and actions keep revolving. It gives meaning and purpose to his life. For example, the value of 'love and service to humanity' becomes the only purpose of the life of a missionary.

B. Characteristics of Values

- Values differ from person to person.
- Values have the content attribute which shows the importance of a mode of individual behaviour or the end-state of existence.
- Values influence individual's ideas and opinions regarding what is right or wrong. Therefore, values are said to have the judgmental attribute that contributes in making decisions and selections.
- Value system of an individual or group is formed of the values which are hierarchically organised. All the individuals and groups have such a separate hierarchy of values.
- Values are not static. They are dynamic. Individual as well as group values may change overtime.
- If values are relatively enduring and stable, it is due to the way they are learned.
- Values have the intensity attribute which indicates how significant they are in the lives of the people.
- Values are considered as a dominant force that affects human behaviour.
- Values give shape to human personality. Personal values occupy central place in an individual's personality.
- Group values are the motivating force behind group behaviour.

C. Determinants of Values

Values are determined by several factors, like culture, parents, education, friends, teachers, etc. What a child learns about right and wrong is largely influenced by family members, especially the parents. Parents demonstrate ethical values by punishing wrong behaviour and rewarding right behaviour. As the child grows, he or she develops contacts with other relatives, neighbours, schoolmates, playgroups, etc. These social agencies exert great amount of influence on the beliefs and behaviour of the child. An individual's values are also determined genetically. As a person matures, he or she goes through varying situations and experiences that shape his or her value system. Schools and higher educational institutions decide the intellectual values like quest for knowledge and truth, scientific temper, etc.

Social institutions, organisations, and associations decide and develop the social values like cooperation, mutual respect, equality, brotherhood, etc. Constitution of a country, laws of the land, customs, traditions and norms of the society are the important determinants of the values of the people. Most of the Constitutions of various nations around the world propagate the values of liberty, equality, fraternity, democracy, social justice, etc.

Religious scriptures, churches, gurudwaras, etc. decide the moral, ethical and spiritual values like righteousness, faith, purity, self-control, etc. Religion binds the people together and postulates faith in the divine power of God.

Culture formulates and develops the ideologies and fundamental values of a society. Culture generates the noble qualities of heart and intellect like love, compassion, gratitude, cultivation of knowledge and wisdom, etc. There are multiple theories and principles regarding the determination of the values. Subjective theory views that the personal notions formulate the values of an individual. On the other hand, objective theory considers that the circumstances in which a person lives determine the individual values.

Emotive theory considers that our emotions are naturally expressed. These emotions determine our values. Utility theory decides the values on the basis of utility of the things. Hedonistic theory views that anything that has the power and ability to satisfy human needs, is the determining factor of the values. Perfectionism views that anything has a value if it contributes to the perfection of human life.

D. Classification of Values

(a) Wide Spectrum of Categories

Values can be classified under several categories such as religious values, recreational values, economic values, political values, social values, moral values, spiritual values, material values, aesthetic values, associational values, academic values, socio-political values, cultural values, global values, axiological values, scientific temper values, historical values, psychological values, traditional values, functional values, etc. Some of these values are grouped under the categories of 'instrumental values and terminal values', and 'temporal values and universal values'.

(b) Temporal Values and Universal Values

Temporal values include the social, political, economic, cultural, psychological, intrinsic, extrinsic, axiological, historical and corporate values. Social values are concerned with the social relations in social institutions and organisations. Political values are concerned with the spectrum that range from conservative to liberal political structure. Economic values are related with buying, producing and selling. Cultural values are related with the manners, norms, customs and traditions of the people.

'Extrinsic values' are the instrumental values. These are considered as the means and instruments to achieve the higher ends. On the other hand, intrinsic values are desired as end states like peace, love, happiness, truth, etc. Historical values are those values which have acquired institutional form such as religious, aesthetic, moral, etc. Axiological values are the values of truth, beauty and goodness. Psychological values are concerned with interests, desires, instinctive tendencies, etc.

Universal values are the values adhered and followed by all the people around the world from generation to generation. These values are found across all the cultures, religions and philosophies of the world. These values are of three types—moral, spiritual and human. Non-violence was held high as universal moral value by Mahatma Gandhi. Moral values shape our lives. Devotion to community service, courtesy, justice, honesty and integrity are the universal moral values. The human values include equality, self-control, freedom, responsibility, etc. The spiritual values include truth, love, compassion, forgiveness, tolerance, etc.

(c) Instrumental Values and Terminal Values

There are two types of values according to M. Rokeach? (1) Instrumental values, and (2) Terminal values.

Instrumental values relate to the means of achieving the desired end-states. These are concerned with the ways to approach the desired results. On the other hand, the terminal values are those end-states that we desire, praise and prefer, for example, security, equality, love, self-respect, etc. The way we process and understand information, the way we feel about different issues and the patterns of our behaviour are mainly influenced by a wide variety of our personal values.

Instrumental values include hard work, obedience, truthfulness, honesty, courteousness, open-mindedness, education, dependability, assertiveness, helping and caring for others, etc.

The Terminal values consist of happiness, sense of accomplishment, recognition, knowledge, wisdom, peace and harmony.

E. Personal Values

Every individual has a core set of personal values which can be defined as broad preferences regarding appropriate courses of action. Personal values are the assumptions that form the basis of a person's ethical action, and reflects his sense of what 'ought' to be. Personal values influence one's own attitudes and behaviour. These values range from the common place values like hardwork, punctuality, etc. to more psychological values like self-reliance, high morale, etc.

According to Morris Massey values are formed during three significant periods:

1. Imprint period from birth to seven years;
2. Modelling period from eight to thirteen years;
3. Socialisation period from thirteen to twentyone years.

Personal values provide an insight into what a person considers to be desirable, beneficial, useful, beautiful and constructive. Personal values give answers to the questions of why people do what they do, and in what order they do them. Personal values guide and motivate the people in achieving success and accomplishments. A person can energise and motivate himself by making the full efforts to implement his personal values. Once he identifies the values which are meaningful to him, he can develop the strategies to implement them. It can result in material, psychological and spiritual benefits. What really motivate a person in his life are the things he truly values. Values help to solve common human problems. If personal values get public expression over a period of time, and people recognise the importance of those values in their day to day lives, those personal values can lay the foundation of laws and customs.

Personal values exist in relation to the cultural values. Personal values can be in agreement with or divergent from the cultural values. A culture is a social system in which people share a set of common values. Social expectations and collective understanding of what is good, beneficial, beautiful, important, etc. influence the formulation of personal values. The virtue of individual values can be measured against the collective understanding of cultural values and norms. An individual's identification with a culture depends upon how he relates his personal values with the values of his culture.

Personal values relate to what one prefers and in what order he desires and prefers them. These values are obtained and imbibed in many ways. The main source of obtaining and building personal values is a person's family. Family teaches children what is right and wrong long before the other agencies of socialisation do it. School, playgroup, neighbours, friends and religion play their role in socialising the child and teaching him what is right and wrong.

Values influence the thoughts, feelings and actions of a person. If the values are positive and gracious, the thoughts, feelings and actions of a person will also be positive. It leads to creating happiness, joy and satisfaction.

Values influence the perceptions and motivation of the people. Values also influence their attitudes and opinions. Values have directional attributes which results in providing guidelines for decision-making and conflict resolution. Generally, values place limits on human behaviour by determining correct course of action.

F. Organisational Values

There is an unprecedented growth of population, industrialisation, urbanisation, environmental pollution, materialism, crime, corruption and social evils in today's world. However, there is a no similar growth in ethicality, goodness, righteousness, honesty and other virtues of human character. Real social growth and human excellence is possible when human hands work with value oriented head and heart.

Value orientation of managers is essential to understand various dimensions of human behaviour as well as managerial behaviour in organisation. Values are the determining factors in the selection of goals, missions and objectives of business organisations. Managerial functions like organising, communicating, planning, controlling, etc. have to be consistent with the value system of the management.

Not only the attitudes of the management and employees but also their morale and motivation are based on the value system of the organisation. A particular style of leadership of a manger and his leadership effectiveness are founded on his value orientation. When manager evaluates his subordinates and their performance, it clearly reflects the personal value system of manager. Most of the managerial decisions are subjective in nature. The effectiveness of these decisions are critically dependent upon his value system.

In organisational context, values serve various purposes. Values serve as the influencing factors on employee motivation because they are used to decide the rewards which are sought by the employees. Values also influence the employee's attitudes, perceptions, performance and job satisfaction. Values provide guidelines to the managers for decision-making. Above all, the values serve as the standards of organisational ethical behaviour and also the standards of desirable organisational course of action and performance.

Organisational values foster the spirit of organisational trust, confidence and commitment. Values also help in the organisational cohesion, unity and loyalty. Organisational and managerial effectiveness is determined by the values. Values help in building adaptability to the changes in the organisation.

G. Workplace Values

A distinctive factor of the successful organisations, is their ability to trust in the competence and loyalty of their employees. Some organisations give high value for personal growth, development, accomplishments and self-actualisation whereas others have high expectations for employee performance. Some managements value organisational and group processes over the personal achievement. They value collectivism rather than the personal accomplishments.

Work values are beliefs which influence the occupational choices of the workers. These values indicate an individual's beliefs regarding what he considers to be of importance in his assigned duties and responsibilities. Work values are based upon the perception and evaluation of the work needs. When these work needs and requirements are met, the employees and the management are satisfied. Its result is job satisfaction. Therefore, the work values can be only those beliefs which are carefully chosen from the alternatives that lead to satisfaction of work needs.

Some of the major work related values of the work places are: Entrepreneurship or desire to be self-employed; leadership in order to meet the organisational goals; fair supervision by a person who is considerate, just and even-handed; friendship with the colleagues to develop social interactions and personal relationships; helpfulness in helping the co-workers directly or indirectly; recognition for the achievements and quality of work; respecting and noticing the contribution of work; aesthetics in appreciating beauty of the ideas, things and performances; loyalty in strict fulfilment of the promises, duties and responsibilities entrusted by the authorities; honesty to be truthful and sincere towards the co-workers, superiors and subordinates; reliability, to show consistency, dependability and trustworthiness to the others at the workplace; privacy, to respect the private and personal matters of the colleagues and others; integrity in the behaviour that indicates virtuousness, righteousness, honesty, goodness and honour towards others; creativity, to think and act differently, to innovate, invent and discover new ideas, things and programmes; excellence in being the best in performance by putting all the necessary abilities, skills and efforts.

The workplace values can be classified in four categories — Empowerment values; compliance values; individualism values; and collectivism values. The empowerment values are those which give organisational freedom to the individuals for the growth and development of the individuals and the organisation. Compliance values require adherence to rules, norms, morals, traditions, disciplines, beliefs and guidelines of the organisation. Values of individualism give priority to personal goals, objectives, ambitions, aspirations and accomplishments. The values of collectivism give priority to the objectives and achievements of the group rather than those of an individual.

H. Managerial Values

Managerial values guide the manager as a leader of the company. He is expected to achieve the common goals of human welfare at the individual and organisational levels. These values give not only the positive guidance and direction to the manager's behaviour but also bring out the best in him. Values exert influence on his vision and performance in a strong way. Several studies have proved that the managerial values and managerial effectiveness are positively interlinked and correlated. In fact, the efficiency and effectiveness of the managers and employees is the functional outcome of the values.

If the managers are not aware of the managerial values and their functional significance in management, they cannot perform their roles effectively. These values can help the managers to resist the temptations and to avoid the mistakes. Managers' behaviour patterns and their managerial strategies are determined and shaped by their particular value orientations. When the varying values between the managers and employees are adjusted, the organisational conflicts can also be resolved.

Values in management serve as the accepted standards of behaviour for both the managers as well as the employees. When these values are adhered, right and ethical decisions are made and correct course of action is decided and followed. Managerial values also serve as the motivating factors to enhance the productivity. Positive managerial values consequently result in organisational excellence, and better performance.

There are some managerial values which emerge as the most preferred or favoured values in the business organisations. The executives from different functional areas of the organisation are expected to be truthful, trustworthy, honest, reliable, capable, competent, qualified, skilful, effective, efficient, objective, unbiased, fair-minded, just, open-minded, flexible, broad-minded, dependable, conscientious, comforting, supporting, helpful and visionary.

I. Essentials of Developing Managerial Values

1. Managerial values must be adhered to facilitate ease in the communicative interactions between the internal and external stakeholders.
2. Management should be fair-minded in adjusting and fulfilling expectations of conflicting stakeholder groups.
3. Reward system of the organisation should be based on the principle of integrity.
4. Management should be objective and just in its approach.
5. Self-interest and the interests of others should be treated equally.

6. Responsibilities should be counted individually rather than collectively.
7. Individuals should accept personal responsibility for their actions.
8. Economic and pragmatic values of the management should direct the organisation towards effective planning, ensuring quality, enhancing performance standards and organisational discipline.
9. Management should view and interpret all the organisational activities in terms of ethical purpose and moral responsibility.
10. Management should actively support the social values like honesty, loyalty, respect and integrity.
11. The emotional and development values like creativity, self-confidence, adaptability, flexibility, freedom, happiness, etc. should be directed towards creating new opportunities for organisational action.
12. Managerial values should be used as a major force for rebuilding of sustainable and competitive culture in the organisation.
13. Managerial values should be used to shape the behaviours of individuals and groups in the organisation.
14. Managerial values should be used to form self-control teams, and to create personal self-control environment.
15. Manager's behaviour and his decisions should be directed towards uplifting moral climate.
16. As a leader manager must develop his moral character before he makes attempt for the moral development of his subordinates.
17. Managers should create and develop moral environment by influence strategy.
18. Managers should prioritise the managerial values.
19. Core managerial values should be identified and defined in terms of how people have to behave actually.
20. Managerial values should be communicated and made evident to all the stakeholders.
21. Managers should try to identify the gaps between values and behaviour.
22. Managers should objectively assess how well these values are practiced by the employees.

EXERCISES

1. Write a note on the nature and characteristic of 'Business Values'.
2. "Values are the desirable 'end-states' which guide the individual and social action". Explain.
3. What are the determinants of business values?
4. Discuss different types of business values.
5. What are the basis on which business values can be classified?
6. Write a note on the nature and formation of personal values.
7. Explain the nature and significance of organisational values.
8. "Work values are beliefs which influence the occupational choices of the workers". Elucidate.
9. How do the managerial values guide the manager as a leader of the company?
10. What are the essentials of developing managerial values?
11. Write short notes on the following:
    - (i) Determinants of Values
    - (ii) Workplace Values
    - (iii) Personal Values
    - (iv) Wide Spectrum of Values
    - (v) Temporal Values
    - (vi) Universal Values
    - (vii) Intrinsic Values
    - (viii) Universal Values
    - (ix) Instrumental Values
    - (x) Terminal Values

4
Code of Business Ethics

"I cannot give you a code; go and watch the best and wisest that you can find and imitate them". —Aristotle

Learning Objectives

A. Meaning of 'Code of Ethics'
B. Significance of Code of Ethics
   1. A Way to Institutionalising Ethics
   2. An Effective Mechanism to Enforce—Ethical Behaviour
   3. Improving Self-Image and Self-Regulation
   4. Enhancing Ethical Communication
   5. Providing Philosophical Basis and Moral Status
C. Developing Code of Ethics
   1. Precedence of the Groups
   2. Priorities of the Values
   3. Impact of Individual Code of Conduct
   4. Constituting Ethics Committee
   5. Articulation and Communication of Code
D. Some Do's for Developing Effective Code of Ethics
E. Essentials of Effective Code of Ethics
F. Common Features in Codes of Ethics
G. Implementation of Code of Ethics

A. Meaning of 'Code of Ethics'

A code of ethics is a written document which clearly and openly states what is right and what is wrong, or what is acceptable and what is unacceptable for all the employees of the organisation. It is a detailed statement of an organisation's ethical policies. It identifies and interprets what a firm considers to be ethically correct and acceptable behaviour in all its interactions and transactions.

Code of ethics makes the employees aware of their moral duties and obligations towards their organisation. Code of ethics constitutes the beliefs and norms of an organisation in the form of statements. These statements define the purpose of the organisation and clarify its moral values and principles.

In establishing its ethical standards, an organisation is influenced by personal factors, organisational factors, and social factors. The values and moral standards of the decision-makers, government laws, firm's own voluntary business guidelines, the social values and ethical standards together contribute to the formulation and establishment of a code of ethics.

Code of ethics shows company's commitment to do the right things in the right manner for the benefits of its stakeholders. It represents a statement of the values and morals of the organisation. It gives guidelines to the employees regarding how to face the grey areas while working for their company. It helps the employees in keeping themselves away from ethical misconduct. It's net outcome is the formation of a strong ethical climate in the organisation.

The code of ethics helps a company to communicate its ethical vision to the stakeholders. The ethical needs of various stakeholders can be addressed with the company's code of ethics. Values like justice, integrity, utility and competence are necessary to be considered while developing the code of ethics. The value of justice is indicated by the company's commitment to unbiased and fair interactions with the stakeholders. Company's integrity is an ideal that highlight its attributes like transparency, honesty and sincerity. The value of utility highlights the company's actions that result in doing greatest good to the greatest number. The value of competence is shown by capabilities of the company to execute its ethical vision.

When a code of ethics is written, it helps the employees and the external stakeholders to know which behaviours are acceptable, and which behaviours are unacceptable and undesirable. The employees have to understand the consequences of violating the code of ethics. If the sanctions section in the code of ethics is selectively used or overlooked, a code of ethics becomes meaningless.

A code of ethics is meaningful and valuable only if the employees believe in the code and their behaviour is influenced by it. It should improve the human factor in the business. It is expected to result in giving as nearly as possible the complete satisfaction to the stakeholders. Firm's policies, methods and actions should be guided by the code of ethics.

B. Significance of Code of Ethics

1. A Way to Institutionalising Ethics

Business community faces a variety of ethical issues every day. If they develop a code of ethics in their firm, and if that code is implemented effectively, manifold benefits can be reaped of it. The different advantages can be: improved industrial relations, enhanced self-confidence of the managers and the employees, enhanced customer satisfaction, enhanced loyalty of the employees, improved competitive position of the firm, and decreased undesirable behaviour. Code of ethics breaks down the communication barriers among the employees.

Establishing a code of ethics is the most common way of institutionalising ethics and creating healthy organisational environment. In every corporation the ethical rules, values and principles develop gradually overtime and require time to change. The existence of code of ethics in organisation indicates that earnest efforts have been made to ensure moral conduct in the organisation.

2. An Effective Mechanism to Enforce—Ethical Behaviour

Apart from legal obligations and socio-cultural compulsions, introduction of code of ethics improves organisational standards of behaviour. It is an effective mechanism to enforce ethical behaviour in the organisation. Their behaviour is guided by the respect for core human values and beliefs that help in deciding what is right and what is wrong. The code also leaves room for the individuals to use their individual judgment in sensitive situations.

3. Improving Self-Image and Self-Regulation

A code of ethics helps to improve self-image of an individual employee, a company, a professional and a profession. Their ethical concern is shown by the way they reconcile their business priorities with the considerations of public interest. A code of ethics fulfils their need of self-regulation. Most of the business organisations, especially the advertising agencies, insurance companies, tobacco and liquor industry, the print media, audio-visual media, stock market, etc. have a strong need for self-regulation.

4. Enhancing Ethical Communication

Corporate ethical codes help the employees to interpret their individual and organisational goals and activities in ethical terms. Business corporations have to clearly state and communicate equitable ethical standards to all the employees so that they can be expected to behave morally in an environment where code of ethics is institutionalised and enforced. To institutionalise ethics in a company the top management should articulate the firm's values and goals, and set up a high ranking ethics committee to develop, oversee and enforce a code of ethics which is applicable to all the members of the company.

5. Providing Philosophical Basis and Moral Status

A code of ethics provides philosophical basis and moral status to business organisation. Scholars believe that philosophical basis of ethics is essential for constructing a view of ethical organisation. Holistic, teleological and deontological philosophies provide various approaches to ethics in business management. Holistic philosophy consists eternal ethics and empirical ethics, teleological philosophy consists ethical egoism and utilitarianism and deontological school deals with the rights principle and justice principle. Various schools of thoughts look into various dimensions of ethics. Philosophical basis of an organisation formulates its ethical approach to managing the means to achieve the ends in an appropriate manner. Philosophy of holistic school states that there are two approaches to ethics—the eternal and the empirical—Eternal ethics believes in the code divinity of individuals and considers man as divine in all his behaviours and actions. All the worldly things come under his empirical self, whereas the timeless, space less dimension comes under the eternal self.

Ethical egoism holds that an action is good if it produces or tends to produce results that maximise a particular person's self-interest. Utilitarianism focuses on the ends. If the end is good, then the action is good. Rights principle holds that humans have the moral rights on the basis of their being humane. Justice principle states that morally correct action is one that produces a fair distribution of benefits and costs. Philosophical foundation and ethical approaches of a code plays a role in including and promoting particular ethical standards and values of the organisation.

C. Developing Code of Ethics

1. Precedence of the Groups

Code of ethics is an instrument that helps to strengthen the ethical working of an organisation. It is not something that is imposed on the employees. It is developed with a view to protect the organisation legally and to guard the interests of the stakeholders carefully. Management needs to be sensitive enough about stakeholder's expectations regarding ethical conduct of the organisation. But, stating the norms and beliefs of the organisation relative to various constituents like stockholders, employees, customers, suppliers, distributors, etc. with their level of precedence is not possible without at least one of them is being hurt. Therefore, code of ethics needs to be written in general terms without stating the level of precedence of the groups.

2. Priorities of the Values

Difficulties in decision-making can arise when the code of ethics does not include the priorities of the values of the firm. For example, the code of ethics may include both 'respect for employees' and 'expectation of fair profits'. But, when a division of company shows declining profits a controversial situation arises regarding which one of the codes is to be given a priority.

3. Impact of Individual Code of Conduct

The corporate activities and cultures are substantially and significantly influenced by the ethical values, moral principles and activities of the individuals. Individuals with different kinds of qualities, competencies and ethical priorities can bring about the changes and developments in the ethical culture of the organisation. Their individual code of conduct can greatly influence the corporate code of conduct, especially when such individuals are in the leadership position. Leader's vision, patience, good relationships, his ability to love, listen and motivate the employees, his self-control, knowledge, wisdom, morality, integrity, skills, values, etc. can create and develop an ethical environment in the organisation. His character and action contributes to shaping of company's code of ethics.

4. Constituting Ethics Committee

A high ranking ethics committee contributes to developing and enforcing a code of ethics in the firm. Ethics committee incorporate ethics training to the employees. The ethics committees should have the authority and responsibility to address the ethical issues, and to communicate the code and the decisions which are based on the code to all the employees. The ethics committee should interpret the code whenever required, and investigate into the violations of the code. It has to discipline the violators and reward the compliance. It investigates into grievances regarding the code, and reviews, upgrades and revises the code.

5. Articulation and Communication of Code

Corporate mission and code of ethics is an important form of company's value articulation and communication. Value structure of the organisation gives guidance regarding ethical dilemmas to the decision-makers. Some companies appoint the ombudsman to interpret, update and communicate the general areas of business conduct and to investigate the complaints and grievances. Though many firms have corporate codes of ethics, they neither communicate their codes to the stakeholders, nor adhere to it in practice.

D. Some Do's for Developing Effective Code of Ethics

1. Code of ethics begins with mission statement.
2. Mission statement explains why the company exists and what it stands for.
3. Mission statement identifies all the stakeholders.
4. Mission statement follows with the company's values, vision and guiding principles.
5. Mission statement clearly shows the company's commitment.
6. The representatives from all the levels of organisational

hierarchy come together to form a task force to write the code.

7. An ethical decision-making framework is prepared to help the employees in making the choices. A code guides the employees in making an ethical decision about a desirable course of action.
8. A listing is made of available resources for obtaining guidance on ethical issues.
9. The employees are informed about how to report the ethical issues anonymously, if required, and whom to report about it.
10. The employees are informed about how to contact the Ethics and Compliance Officer whenever required. They are also informed about the reporting chain of command.
11. The employees are informed about the Ethics and Compliance Websites for obtaining further details, if needed.
12. For accountability of ethical-unethical behaviour some relevant and generic examples are given.
13. The ethical enforcement and implementation mechanism ensures the integrity of records and safeguards the confidential information.
14. Internal ethical auditors monitor the corporate code of conduct. The ethical auditor's examiners and legal advisers periodically update the ethical policies. The code excludes the things that no longer make any sense.
15. Care is taken to make the code ethically and legally valid.
16. Foresight is shown in developing the code of ethics which is globally acceptable.
17. The code covers newly developing risks.
18. The code is also approved and certified by the employees.
19. The code specifically and clearly explains the values of the organisation.
20. The code covers all the employees of the organisation.
21. The employees who review and revise the code are provided the periodic training on the ethical issues.

E. Essentials of Effective Code of Ethics

1. Having a good code of ethics does not ensure that the employees will comply with it. Actions speak louder than

the words of the statements. The ethical code is useless, if no one follows it. The code is not merely for posting on the notice board without any action.

2. The board of director should be committed to the code of ethics.
3. The code of ethics should be distributed to everyone in the organisation.
4. The senior staff and the higher authorities should set the correct examples of good conduct.
5. It should not be difficult for all the employees to have a continuous access to the code and the periodic changes in the code.
6. The code should be made available in all the languages used by the organisation to conduct the business.
7. When there is a breach of the code of conduct, the management should not fail to follow-up.
8. It is advisable to establish an ethics committee within the board of directors.
9. The code of ethics should feature in the programmes of training and development.
10. When needed the code should be reviewed, and necessary revisions and adjustments should be made by keeping in view the core ethical values of the firm.
11. Ethical commitments should be made a part of the contract for employment.
12. The code should be distributed to the business partners, suppliers, distributors, agents, etc.
13. A report regarding use and enforcement of the code should be included in the firm's annual report.
14. A system for prompt reporting of ethical breaches should be established.
15. A code should not be considered as an internal and confidential document.
16. There should not be exceptions to the code's use and application for selective circumstances.
17. The ethical committees should seek the feedback of the employees regarding their ethical concern.
18. A special care should be taken by the top management that they do not fail to set an ethical example.
19. The responsibility for the effective implementation of code

of ethics should not be considered as an assignment of one unit within the organisation.

20. Reaching, understanding and adhering to the code should be responsibility of all the employees of the organisation.
21. Ethical training programmes should be organised.

F. Common Features in Codes of Ethics

Codes of ethics help the business organisation to improve their performance, efficiency and goodwill. Such codes give guidelines, rules and norms as follows:

(i) Customers must get the goods and services that conform to the promised commitment.

(ii) Customers must be treated with respect and fairness.

(iii) Customers must be given the best services.

(iv) Highest standards of behaviour must be maintained.

(v) The needs, concerns and welfare of the society must be respected.

(vi) The capital, technology, knowledge, skills, expertise and experience should be used for public good and for upgradation of quality of life.

(vii) The decisions and actions of a firm should result in the benefit of the organisation, investors, employees, customers and society.

(viii) An organisation should give highest priority to the management of environmental issues. Management should assess the environmental effects of its activities. They should follow the positive environmental policies and best international practices to protect the environment.

(ix) An organisation should not deal with illicit activities and projects. It should not manufacture, store, purchase or sell the adulterated goods. It should not deal with the smuggled products.

(x) Free distribution of goods should be supported and the creation of artificial shortage should be averted.

(xi) Misleading advertisements should not be released or published.

(xii) Accuracy in weights and measurements of goods should be maintained.

(xiii) The quality of articles manufactured, processed or sold should be ensured. The information regarding the contents of the products, date of manufacture and expiry, etc. should be provided.

(xiv) For consumer durables, effective after-sale-services should be provided.

(xv) Professional managers should consider themselves as the trustees of the stakeholders.

(xvi) Company should consider society as an important stakeholder.

(xvii) The employees should not engage in any activity, relationship or business which might conflict with the interest of the organisation. They should avoid the situations in which their personal interests can conflict with the interests of the organisation.

(xviii) The legal and regulatory compliance is the responsibility of the employees, especially chief executives and the divisional executives are responsible for the organisational compliance of all the applicable laws and regulations both in letter and spirit.

(xix) The actions and transactions in the conduct of the business should be transparent except those where the needs of business security dictates otherwise.

(xx) The facilities in the organisation should not be misused. Employers should take care that the costs are reasonable and there is no wastage. Employees should avoid ostentation in the organisational expenditure.

(xxi) The senior managers should act professionally. They should visibly exhibit high professional and ethical standards. They should become role models for the others.

(xxii) All the employees should be committed to make the organisation a gender friendly workplace. There should be equal opportunities for men and women. Management must be responsive to the employee complaints of sexual harassment.

(xxiii) Employees should not disclose any confidential information about the organisation to the press or other mass media unless specifically authorised to do so.

(xxiv) All the employees, including the full time directors and managing director should be professional and honest. They should follow high ethical standards.

(xxv) Management should strive to provide safe and healthy working environment. It should prevent wasteful use of natural resources.

(xxvi) Equal opportunities should be given to all the employees and all the qualified applicants for employment without regard to their caste, religion, race, colour, marital status, sex, age, nationality, veteran status and disability. All employees should be treated with dignity.

(xxvii) An organisation and its employees should neither receive or offer, directly or indirectly, any illegal gifts, payments, donations, remuneration, etc. to obtain business or favours.

(xxviii) An organisation should provide physical safety, healthy environment, good physical working conditions, high standards of hygiene and housekeeping.

(xxix) An organisation should be committed in all its activities to help the economic development of the country in which it operates.

(xxx) An organisation should actively assist the improvement of the quality of life of the people in the society in which it operates. It should initiate and support the activities in the field of family welfare, community health, water management, education, social forestry, etc.

(xxxi) An organisation should be committed to enhance shareholder value. It should comply with all the laws and regulations that govern the rights of the shareholders.

(xxxii) An organisation should be committed and supportive to the functioning democratic Constitution. But it should not support directly or indirectly, any political party or candidate for political office.

G. Implementation of Code of Ethics

The following factors are crucial in implementing the corporate code of ethics:

1. Pivotal Elements

Statements of the ethical mission of the organisation, a broad philosophy of the firm, appointment of the firm's ethical committee, meetings and discussions with the external stakeholders, constant consciousness of the norms and values, periodic auditing for assuring compliance, fair and well-defined enforcement procedures, organising staff training programmes, etc. are the important measures of implementing the code of ethics.

2. Ethical Climate and Valid Motivation

A strong ethical climate is required for effective implementation of code of ethics in the firm. A valid motivation can be introduced with insistence on the significant benefits which can be obtained by adopting and adhering the code of ethics.

3. A System of Sanctions

An absence of some system of sanctions can definitely make the code of ethics ineffective and meaningless. Therefore, some system of sanctions must exist so that compliance with the code of ethics can be enforced. The system has to monitor and enforce the ethical behaviour which is described in the code of ethics. It should provide incentives for ethical behaviour rather than disincentive for it.

4. Effective Communication and Continuous Feedback

Living up to a code of ethics does not mean that every employee should blindly comply with it. In diversities of situations and conditions a number of difficulties can occur. Therefore, a continuous feedback from the employees is needed to make the necessary changes, adjustments and revisions. Orientation programmes, newsletters, in-house communications, etc. can be used to communicate the rules, norms, standards and morals to the employees. Advisory system can be used to answer the employees' questions about whether or not a course of action is ethical.

5. Clearly Written Code of Ethics

The written statement of code of ethics should have clarity in describing organisation's mission, purpose, beliefs, values, standards, rules, norms, objectives, obligations, vision of future, tradition and procedures. It should describe the main constituencies or stakeholders of the organisation to whom the organisation is obligated. The kind of sanctions which can be imposed on the transgressors of the code of ethics should be clearly described.

6. Priorities of the Norms and Values

The priorities of the norms, beliefs and the true values of the firm must be decided and understood by the employees in the practical context.

7. Commitment to the Code of Ethics

Company's commitment to ethics is its valuable asset. Top executives have to play a major role in securing organisation's commitment to ethics. They must support ethical behaviour throughout the organisation. They should integrate ethics in all the aspects of organisational activities. Ethical policies should be implemented in human resource management, decision-making, industrial relations, customer interactions, TQM, production and marketing, etc. An atmosphere should be created where the customers can trust the products and services of the company.

8. Moral Standards of the Seniors

Moral standards of the senior executives must be made known to the employees, so that it can be followed throughout the organisation. They should treat the employees as the internal customers of the company. Ethical approaches should be followed in the areas of employee data, equal opportunities, continuous development, employee involvement and participation, redundancy, harassment, compensation and counselling. Every employee should get what is just and fair.

9. Employee Training

Training and development is an effective way to foster the ethical programme of the business organisations. It focuses on creating ethical culture in the organisation. The content of ethical training programme emphasises the moral values which are cherished by the organisation, and highlights its expectations. For ensuring high level of ethical culture throughout the organisation, management can conduct workshops periodically that provide ethical training, which ultimately helps the management in implementing ethical programme.

10. Creating Broad Acceptance

In order to create broad acceptance of the code of ethics, it is necessary that the representatives from all the departments of a company should come together in the process of identifying, elaborating, discussing, analysing, redefining and implementing the code of ethics.

11. Deciding New Guidelines

If some rules in the code of ethics prove to be inadequate and inconsistent, new guidelines can be decided through verifications and discussions. Feedback from the concerned people can be useful to disclose the inconsistencies between the rules and the practice.

EXERCISES

1. What is the meaning of 'Code of ethics' in business?
2. Explain the significance of ethical code in business.
3. How does code of ethics help to strengthen the ethical working of an organisation?
4. How should a firm develop its code of ethics?
5. What are the essentials of developing a code of ethics for a business organisation.
6. Enumerate some important DO's for developing a code of ethics.
7. What are the essentials of effective code of ethics?
8. What are the common features in codes of business ethics?
9. Which factors are crucial in implementing the corporate code of ethics?
10. Write short notes on the following:
    (i) Institutionalizing Ethics
    (ii) Mechanism for Enforcing Ethics
    (iii) Enhancing Ethical Communication
    (iv) Ethics for self-regulation
    (v) Priorities of values
    (vi) Ethics committee
    (vii) Developing code of Ethics
    (viii) Ethical Climate
    (ix) Clarity in code of Ethics
    (x) Commitment to code of Ethics
    (xi) Moral Standards of the Seniors.

5

Ethical Aspects of Organisation Culture

"Culture may even be described simply as that which makes life worth living". —T.S. Eliot

Learning Objectives

A. Culture: Meaning and Definition
B. Characteristics of Culture
  - ➢ Culture is Learned
  - ➢ Culture is Shared
  - ➢ Culture is Cumulative
  - ➢ Culture Changes
  - ➢ Culture is Ideational
  - ➢ Culture is Diverse
  - ➢ Culture is Symbolic
  - ➢ Culture Provides Norms

C. Organisational Culture: Meaning and Definition
D. Characteristics of Organisational Culture
E. Types of Organisational Culture
  1. Normative Culture
  2. Pragmatic Culture
  3. Academic Culture
  4. Collaborative Work Culture
  5. Baseball Team Culture
  6. Club Culture
  7. Fortress Culture
  8. Tough Guy Culture
  9. Bet Your Company Culture
  10. Process Culture

Introduction

Organisational ethics is the ethics which is concerned with how an organisation ethically responds to an internal and external stimulus. Organisational ethics is interdependent with the organisational culture. Organisational ethics expresses the values, beliefs and moral standards which are associated with the culture of organisation.

A. Culture: Meaning and Definition

Culture is a socially transmitted behavioural pattern and life style of the people that brings a particular class or community together with shared values, beliefs, ideologies, attitudes, assumptions, expectations, customs, arts, laws, education, language, religion, technology, economy, social organisations, institutions, norm and social structure which is expressed in a given period. Culture is expressed through various verbal and non-verbal means of communication. Language gives an identity to culture. It is a most powerful medium of cultural expression. Behavioural patterns, a particular type of dress material, food habits, time consciousness, punctuality, system of rewards and recognition, opportunity structure, values, customs, norms, traditions, books, literature, scriptures, music, painting, dancing, sculpture, architecture, artefacts, crafts, designs, signs and symbols are some other means of expressing culture. Communication technology and mass media like print media, audio-visual media, cinema, radio, websites, etc. are used to convey cultural messages.

B. Characteristics of Culture

Culture is Learned

Culture is learned by any individual especially if he grows as a member of a particular social group, organisation or community that share a particular culture. He can learn behavioural patterns, language and many other attributes of that culture.

Culture is Shared

Members of groups and organisations share a common culture. A thought or action can be considered as a culture if it is shared, believed and practised by a group of individuals, and then, it can be recognised as their culture.

Culture is Cumulative

Culture is passed from one generation to another generation in a cumulative process. More and more knowledge is added in a particular culture as time passes by.

Culture Changes

Knowledge, thoughts, customs, traditions, norms, etc. are changed, modified and lost as the new cultural traits are added. Culture is 'dynamic'. It changes constantly as new ideas and new techniques change or modify the old ways. Culture is 'adaptive' because it depends on human capacity to adapt changes and innovation.

Culture is Ideational

Culture forms ideal behavioural pattern which are expected to be followed by the individual members of a group or community. These behavioural patterns serve as guidelines that are expected to be followed by the members to gain social acceptance.

Culture is Diverse

It is believed that culture is formed by bringing together the traits of many separate cultures. It is a system of several mutually interdependent parts that form the culture as a whole.

Culture is Symbolic

Culture is symbolic because it depends on the human capacity to symbolise, and to use one thing to represent the another. Language is a common and arbitrary symbol system used by individual members to communicate with each other in a particular linguistic community.

Culture Provides Norms

Culture gives norms and appropriate behavioural patterns. It provides a range of permissible behavioural patterns regarding how an individual should act in different social relationships and occasions.

C. Organisational Culture: Meaning and Definition

Organisation culture is a common perception regarding the ways in which people think, feel, interact and work in the organisation. It comprises of different components like organisational mission, goals, objectives, work forms, and financial resources. It is based on power and authority structure, leadership and various other aspects of work and social relationships in organisation. It is expressed through formal work behaviour and informal non-work behaviour of the employees. It is a product of values, beliefs and morals of the organisation.

D. Characteristics of Organisational Culture

Organisational culture is a system of shared meaning. It is a common perception held by the members of the organisation. It is a pattern of beliefs, values and learned ways of coping with the persons and situations within an organisation. It is visible in the structures and processes of the organisation, and it is perceived from the ways its employees behave. It conveys the ways in which the people of the organisation think and work. Some of the characteristics of organisational culture are given below:

Identity. It is the extent to which the members of the organisation identify themselves with the organisation as a whole rather than with their particular work group or field of professional expertise.

Innovation and Risk Taking. It is the extent to which the members of the organisation are encouraged to take the immediate steps and calculated risks.

Structure: It is an extent to which the rules and regulations of the organisation are used to supervise and control the behaviour of the members of organisation.

Reward system. It is an extent to which 'reward and recognition' in the organisation are based on the performance of its members.

Customer orientation. It is the extent to which the organisation is responsive and honest to its customers.

Pride and Excitement. It is an extent to which its members have perceptibly good feelings like pride, loyalty, excitement, etc. about the organisation and activities.

Commitment. It is an extent to which the members of the organisation are willingly and efficiently working towards the achievement of its goals and objectives.

Direction. It is an extent to which the organisation creates and communicates its objectives and performance expectations with clarity and precision.

Standards and Values. It is expressed by the performance levels, values practiced and behavioural standards followed by the organisation.

Management support. It is an extent to which an assistance, support and warmth is provided by the management to the subordinates.

Integration. It is an extent to which all the units in the organisation are encouraged to operate in a well-coordinated manner.

Stability vs. growth. It is an extent to which organisation activities emphasise on stability in contrast to growth.

Aggressiveness. It is an extent to which the members of organisation are aggressive and competitive rather than unconcerned, easy going and relaxed.

Attentiveness. It is an extent to which the members of the organisation are expected to pay attention to details.

Team orientation. It is an extent to which the work activities are organised around the teams rather than individuals.

People orientation. It is an extent to which management is attentive to the effects of their decisions on the people working in the organisation and on the shareholders.

Result orientation. It is an extent to which management focuses on results rather than on the means, techniques and processes to achieve those results.

Individual autonomy. It is an extent of responsibility, freedom, independence, and opportunities that the individuals have in the organisation to exercise their initiative.

Attitude towards change. It is an extent of response given to new ways, methods and values by the people in the organisation.

Communication pattern. It is an extent to which the organisational communication is restricted to the formal channels of communication.

Conflict tolerance. It is an extent to which conflict is present in relationships between the peers and work groups, and secondly, the extent to which they are motivated to be open and tolerant about the differences.

E. Types of Organisational Culture

1. Normative Culture

In normative organisation culture, the norms and rules of organisational procedures are clearly pre-defined. The norms, rules and regulations are strictly implemented. The employees follow the organisational procedures in correct manner. They strictly adhere to the organisational policies and try to behave in an ideal way. They do not dare to break the rules. This culture is perceived to indicate a high standard of business ethics.

2. Pragmatic Culture

In contrast to the normative cultures pragmatic culture places more emphasis on satisfying the needs and wishes of their clients. Customer satisfaction is the main motive of the employees. The clients are virtually deified. Every employee strives hard to satisfy the customers. Their prime concern is to cater to the needs of the customers and to obtain and retain the maximum business by attending and serving them.

3. Academic Culture

The organisations which follow the academic culture, hire the highly skilled and qualified individuals. Organisation provides them an environment for further development and honing of the skills. The roles and responsibilities are delegated according to the knowledge, skills, experience, educational qualification and efficiency of the employee. Such organisations are very particular about conducting training programmes for their employees. They make sincere efforts to improve the competence and upgrade the knowledge of their employees. Employees tend to stay and grow with their organisation.

4. Collaborative Work Culture

This culture is often called as "clan culture" that offers a congenial and amiable work environment. Such an organisation is a friendly workplace where leaders act like father figures. While working in such organisations workers derive a feeling of comfort and strong motivation. The superiors provide more of guidance and less of governance. The organisation cares for employee welfare, developing team work and rewarding performance handsomely.

5. Baseball Team Culture

Organisations following the baseball team culture consider the employees as the most treasured possession of the organisation. The employees have a major role in the successful functioning of the organisation. Therefore, they are considered as the true assets of the organisation.

6. Club Culture

The employees stay with the organisations for a long time in the club culture. Organisations following this culture are particular about the specialisations, educational qualifications and interests of the employees they recruit. The employees with high potential, skills, knowledge and expertise are promoted suitably to higher positions.

Only those employees are hand-picked who possess specific skills required by the organisation.

7. Fortress Culture

Organisations following this culture are often found undergoing the massive changes. The employees in such cultures are not very sure about their career. They are terminated if the organisation is not performing well. Stock broking firms, large car companies, etc. are the examples of such organisations in which the employees suffer the most when the organisation is at loss.

8. Tough Guy Culture

The employees working in tough guy culture or macho culture are expected to possess a strong mentality for survival in the organisation. In such organisations, feedback is essential. The work of the employees is thoroughly monitored, and their performance is reviewed from time to time. They are under constant watch of the superior authorities. This kind of culture is associated with organisations which are involved in quick financial activities like brokerage, currency trading, or in the activities related with sports team, police team, etc.

9. Bet Your Company Culture

The organisations following this culture are involved in huge amount of risks. The consequences of their risks are also unforeseen. They make big decisions over high stake endeavours. An organisation which designs experimental military weapons, or an organisation involved in experimental research projects, are the examples of the organisations which follow this kind of culture.

10. Process Culture

In process culture organisations take low risk. The feedback and reward is slow. Comfort, security, low stress and plodding work are the results of this culture. Stress may result from the internal organisational politics and stupidity of the system. They focus on security of the past and of the future. The employee in such a culture, mainly adhere to the processes and procedures of the organisation.

11. Work Hard, Play Hard Culture

In this culture, employees experience stress coming from quantity of work, rather than from uncertainty. In it, high speed action leads to high speed recreation. Examples: software companies, restaurants, etc. They give steadfast customer help service.

F. Characteristics of Ethical Organisation

1. Comprehensive and Well-organised Code of Conduct

A good code of conduct is comprehensive, well-organised and equally applicable to all the employees of the organisation. It is usually a booklet which includes the background of the organisational policies on ethical conduct. It gives details about how to apply the policies in different departments. It also includes the questions and answers that help to interpret the code.

2. Value Statement as 'Value in Action'

Value statement of an organisation is not just words but values in action. These statements are expected to grow out of the experiences of the organisation. Value statements go wrong when they are not related to the decisions and functions of the organisation. There should be no difference between the current organisational practices and the value statements.

3. Honour and Special Attention to Strong Performers

Organisation gives special attention and honour to the strong performers and achievers. Morally upright and industrious people are the fundamental part of the ethical organisation. They exemplify the spirit of the organisation. Organisation gives recognition to their performance and achievements, and shows gratitude for their exemplary behaviour, hard work, dedication and sacrifices. Their contributions are acknowledged privately as well as publicly.

4. Executives as Embodiment of Values

Senior executives of the organisation oversee the good governance of ethics and values. They are the dedicated ethics officers, and active members of the audit or ethic committee which periodically reports to the board. The CEO and the management team are a walking embodiment of values in public as well as in private. CEO puts the values to work, and shares his experience with the subordinates about the ethical problems and how to resolve those problems. His private and personal behaviour is always consistent with the values of the organisation.

5. Doing Best to Build Mutual Respect

The employees of the organisation have the self-respect, and they surround themselves with the people whom they can respect. The mutual trust and respect enable them to avoid the micro-management of people. They do their best to rebuild mutual respect when existing relationships weaken. They usually do not hire or do business with the people whom they do not respect or who do not respect them.

6. Evaluation Systems Embody Ethical Values

An organisation needs to have a performance evaluation system that has an explicit reference to the ethical values of the organisation. Their values are integrated in the operating systems. Their important decisions are examined in the light of the values of the organisation. They do not allow the financial criteria or the performance pressure to trump the values and ethical norms.

7. Always Standing by Their Word

They make their word their bond, and always stand by their word. It is known that they never lie, steal or cheat. They treat others as they'd want to be treated. They do not retain or hire people who do not have integrity.

8. Mechanisms to Vet Ethical Cases

An ethical organisation needs to have the mechanisms to vet the difficult cases. Mechanisms such as a corporate committee is a committee dedicated to the rights and well-being of the concerned parties. For example, ethics and environmental assurance committee may monitor the non-financial aspects of management activity such as ethical conduct, health, safety and environmental matters, etc. in the organisational context.

9. Re-inventing, Innovating and Risk-taking

Organisations grow by taking risks, by innovating and by re-inventing themselves. The ethical organisations need not be timid and mousy. They should not stick to the safe path. They can take risks and try new things. As long as the organisation sticks to its code of ethics, risk-taking does not pose any threat to their moral conduct. Management can encourage, support and reward their employees for taking calculated risks.

10. Ethical Enforcement and Auditing

Ethical organisations enforce the code of ethics, audit the conduct of business, investigate the ethical cases thoroughly and respectfully, and maintain the discipline appropriately and justly. Audits generally deal with quantitative, easily measurable data. Ethical issues are often qualitative or subjective in nature. Considering multiple perspectives of an organisation's commitment to ethics is the key to an ethical audit.

11. Focussing on Responsibilities to Customers

A business organisation is nothing if it does not have customers. Serving all the customers is a part of organisation's ethical responsibilities. Ethical organisations provide service to the customers before, during and after the purchase. This service consists of a series of activities designed to enhance the customer satisfaction. This satisfaction is the feeling that a product or service has met the customer expectation.

12. Passion, Enthusiasm and Excitement for Work

Great ethical organisations are comprised of employees who have a passion and enthusiasm for what they are doing. They work for organisation, for thrill and challenge, and not only for the salary. They believe that their work and efforts can make a difference. They are excited, driven and motivated to achieve the organisational goals and objectives.

13. Achieving Results within Ethical Values

Ethical organisations do not aim for results at any cost. They focus on ethics factor into the results. They work for achieving the results within their organisation's ethical values. An ethical company's results are attained in satisfying customers, by producing and delivering what they want at a fair price.

14. Constant Communication and Regular Training

Best practices of ethical organisation include constant communication about ethical norms and values. This communication is on a regular basis for all the employees, and it includes the ethical training also. Obviously, the trainers and the executives do not pay only the lip service to the ethical values.

15. Creating Ethical Culture: An Ongoing Process

Creating ethical culture is an ongoing process in any ethical organisation. Building the sense of ethical backbone, ethical courage, accountability, responsibility, etc. is an ongoing process in the ethical organisations.

16. Periodic Renewal and Revision of Standards

In ethical organisations values and ethical standards are revised periodically and the freshness of message is retained. The recent incidents are neither ignored nor overemphasised. A renewal becomes successful when message remains fresh and efforts are made to seek input from the people.

EXERCISES

1. What are the characteristics of ethical culture in business organisation?
2. Write a note on meaning and characteristics of culture.
3. What are the components and characteristics of organisational culture?

4. "Organisational culture is a product of values, beliefs and morals of the organisation". Elucidate.
5. What are the types of organisational culture?
6. "Organisational ethics and organisational culture are the two sides of the same coin". Discuss.
7. What are the characteristics of ethical organisation?
8. Write short notes on the following:
   (i) Ethics and Culture
   (ii) Normative Culture
   (iii) Collaborative Culture
   (iv) Work Hard, Play Hard Culture
   (v) Value Statement as 'Value in Action'.
   (vi) Achieving Results within Ethical Values
   (vii) Creating Ethical Culture
   (viii) Mutual Respect and Trust

6
Ethical Leadership

"Civilisation is always in danger when those who have never learned to obey are given the right to command".

—Bishop Fulton Sheen

Learning Objectives

A. Meaning and Definition of Leadership
B. Significance of Leadership in Management
C. Ethical Use of Leadership Powers
   (i) Legitimate Power
   (ii) Reward Power
   (iii) Expert Power
   (iv) Referent Power
   (v) Coercive Power
   (vi) Information Power
   (vii) Rational Persuasive Power
D. Leadership Styles
   (i) Democratic Leadership
   (ii) Paternalistic Leadership
   (iii) Autocratic Leadership
   (iv) Laissez-faire Leadership
   (v) Coaching Leadership
   (vi) Pacesetting Leadership
E. Theories and Approaches of Leadership
   (i) Trait Approach
   - Limitations of Traits Approach
   (ii) Behavioural Approach
   - Michigan Studies
   - Ohio Studies

(iii) Situational Theory of Leadership
- Fiedler's Contingency Model
- Hersey and Blanchard Situational Model
- House's Path Goal Theory
- Vroom-Vetton and Jago's Contingency Model
- Likert's System of Management Leadership

(iv) Charismatic Leadership Theory

(v) Transformational Leadership Theory

(vi) Transactional Leadership Theory

F. Ethical Qualities of Managerial Leadership
- Ability to Motivate and Inspire
- Patience and Fortitude
- Dedication
- Combines Values with Competencies
- Builds and Maintains Relationships
- Impartial
- Mutual Respect
- Visionary
- Empowering the Employees
- Open-minded and a Good Listener
- Building Character and Integrity
- Cooperation and Teamwork
- High Energy, Initiative and Tenacity
- A Desire to Lead
- Seeking Power as Means
- Developing Networks and Coalitions
- Self-Confidence
- Cognitive Abilities and Strategic Thinking
- Adequate Knowledge
- Creativity
- Honesty, Integrity and Trustworthiness
- Moral Courage
- Identifying and Cultivating Talents
- Judgment and Decision-Making Power
- A Winner's Mindset
- Enthusiasm for Achievement
- Calm yet Strong
- Learning Aptitude
- Dynamism and Optimism for Change and Progress

- Perseverance and Determination
- Cultural Sensitivity and Flexibility
- Democratic Approach
- Humility and Modesty
- Reliability

A. Meaning and Definition of Leadership

Leadership is a personal quality which exists only if there are followers. There is no leadership without followers. A person becomes leader when people have willingness to follow him. He influences the attitudes, beliefs and behaviour of his followers. The purpose of the existence of leadership is only for the realisation of common goals. Leadership indicates readiness to accept complete responsibility in all situations. A leader has a function to motivate the followers to attain organisational objectives. The styles of leadership change under varying circumstances. Different situations demand different leadership styles. To be an effective leader, an individual must possess the ethical qualities like personal integrity, social responsibility, vision, empathy, initiative and self-confidence. He must have an ability to integrate, to build self-confidence and zeal among his people, and to stimulate the best in his people.

Real leader is a person who actually exercises the influences over the group and runs the things, rather than the one who has the formal title and apparent authority. Leadership has been defined in various ways by different authors and experts.

> *"Leadership is not making friends and influencing people i.e. salesmanship. It is the lifting of man's visions to higher sights, the raising of man's personality beyond its normal limitations".* —Peter Drucker
>
> *"Leadership is the ability of a manager to induce subordinates to work with confidence and zeal".* —Koontz and O'Donnell
>
> *"Leadership is the process whereby one individual influences other group members toward the attainment of defined group or organisational goals".* —Yuki, G.
>
> *"Leadership is the exercise of authority and making of decision".* —Dubin, R.

"Leadership is the activity of influencing people to strive willingly for group objectives". —George R. Terry

"A leader is best when people barely know that he exists, not so good when people obey and acclaim him, worst when they despise him. 'Fail to honour people, they fail to honour you'. But of a good leader, who talks little, when his work is done, his aim fulfilled, they will all say, 'we did this ourselves'." —Lao Tzu, Chinese Founder of Taoism

"A leader shapes and shares a vision which gives point to the work of others". —Charles Handy

"As we look ahead into the next century, leaders will be those who empower others". —Bill Gates

"Leadership is an attempt at influencing the activities of followers through the communication process and toward the attainment of some goals".

—Donnelly, J.H., Ivaneevich, J. and Gibson, J.L.

"Leadership is influence—nothing more, nothing less".

—John Maxwell.

"Leadership is that process in which one person sets the purpose or direction for one or more other persons and gets them to move along together with him or her, and with each other in that direction with competence and full commitment". —Jaques, E.F. Clement, S.D.

"Leadership is the art of influencing others to their maximum performance to accomplish any task, objective or project".

—Cohen W.A.

"Leadership is the art of mobilising others to want to struggle for shared aspirations". — Kouzes, J.M. and Posner, B.Z.

"Leadership is the capacity to translate vision into reality

—Warren G. Bennis

"Leadership is the influential increment over and above mechanical compliance with the routine directives of the organisation". —Katz & Kahn

B. Significance of Leadership in Management

Leadership in management helps the organised group of people to set goals, to initiate action, to direct their efforts, to coordinate their activities, to keep them motivated, to build up confidence and zeal, to cooperate with each other, to resolves the conflicts, to solve the problems and ultimately, to realise the common objectives and goals. Therefore, the significance of leadership in management is emphasised by the management experts.

A dynamic manager generates energy and enthusiasm in the organisation. He motivates the employees to do their best in order to achieve the goals. He raises the morale of the employees. He creates and shapes the organisation, and assigns the appropriate roles, responsibilities and duties to the employees. He facilitates various components of the organisation to operate sensitively towards achieving organisational goals.

It is not always possible to bring the desired results by using formal position of authority. Leadership acts as an aid to formal authority because leadership influences, inspires and initiates actions. Leader takes initiative in all the matters of group's interests. He has creative ideas and his decisions reflect original thinking. A leader reconciles the interests of individual employees with those of the organisation. He ensures voluntary cooperation and coordination in the organisational activities at all the levels of management.

C. Ethical Use of Leadership Powers

Leaders use power to influence the behaviour of others. Some do it ethically and effectively, but inept and ineffective leaders use it unethically, unproductively and in vain. Legitimate power, reward power, expert power, referent power, coercive power, information power and rational persuasive power are the seven main sources of leadership power which are used to influence the followers:

(i) Legitimate Power
(ii) Reward Power
(iii) Expert Power
(iv) Referent Power
(v) Coercive Power
(vi) Information Power
(vii) Rational Persuasive Power

(i) Legitimate Power

An individual acquires this power to influence the people on the basis of his formal position in the organisation. Managers have the legitimate power and right to assign tasks and to give orders to their subordinates.

(ii) Reward Power

An individual acquires this power to influence the behaviour of others by providing the desired and valued rewards like promotions, appreciations, monetary benefits, etc. Manager influences the behaviour of the employees because they desire to be rewarded for their compliance. Managers who realise the consequentiality of rewarding and recognising employees when they achieve the organisational goals, become the mentors and motivators of those employees.

(iii) Expert Power

An individual acquires this power to influence the behaviour of others on the basis of his talents, competencies, knowledge and skills. Managers who demonstrate their expertise in specialised field of knowledge, acquire this power. Their problem solving ability indicates this power. The lack of expert power often causes problems in organisational functioning for managers as well as employees.

(iv) Referent Power

An individual acquires referent power on the basis of his admired personality, charisma and reputation. Subordinate's identification with a leader and his desire to be like that leader creates referent power. In this way, a young manager tries to follow and imitate the leadership style of his older, admired and experienced leader. Manager's referent power can motivate the employees to achieve the goals of an organisation.

(v) Coercive Power

Coercive power of an individual depends on his ability to influence the behaviour of others by punishing them. The subordinate employees comply because they are afraid of the punishment for their failure to respond favourably to their leader's orders and instructions. However, the punishments can bring the undesirable side effects also.

Coercive power can reduce or stop undesirable behaviours of the employees, but it does not encourage the desired behaviour. Punishments for the undesirable behaviour can be in the form of undesirable work assignments, reprimands, strict enforcement of rules, close supervision, suspension without pay, etc.

Thus, coercive power results from the leader's capacity to control punishments. Most managers do not like to use the threats of punishments, but many people rely on their coercive power, and many employees are too familiar with it. They know that if they fail to comply, the request can turn into an order and there can be severe consequences for disobeying.

(vi) Information Power

An individual acquires information power on the basis of the data and other knowledge he has at his disposal. Usually, the individuals at the top positions in the organisations have the unique sources of information which are not available to the others. This information makes them powerful. Now-a-days information technology has made more information available to more people than ever before. Due to increasing use of information technology, information power is losing its significance as potent source of influence in many business organisations. Information may no longer be the unique property of few people at top positions, but by virtue of their positions, the managers have an access to the closely guarded information about their employees and the processes. They are also expected to maintain confidentiality regarding the information about their employees. Therefore, it seems that information remains an important source of power even today.

(vii) Rational Persuasive Power

An individual can exert influence by using his rational persuasive power. Effective and repetitive use of rational persuasion tactic can result in acquiring this personal power. The strength of logical arguments and the effective style of presenting those arguments can easily influence the others and help the leader to acquire power over them.

D. Leadership Styles

"Leadership style" refers to the consistent behavioural pattern of a leader. It results from his philosophy, personality traits and past experience.

(i) Democratic Leadership

In this leadership style, leader encourages the subordinates to take initiative and to give suggestions. He is participative in his approach. He acts according to mutual consent, and makes decisions after consulting the subordinates. He motivates the employees by ensuring their participation in decision-making process. It results in job satisfaction, high morale, self-confidence and mutual trust. This leadership may cause delay in decision-making, but it reduces employee's grievances, industrial unrest and strikes.

(ii) Paternalistic Leadership

Paternalistic leader treats his subordinates like his children. He is loving and compassionate like a father to his subordinates. Therefore, this leadership style is based upon the sentiments and emotions of the concerned people. The subordinates become dependent upon the teacher who helps, guides and protects them all.

(iii) Autocratic Leadership

An autocratic leader is one who wants to control virtually everyone and everything, makes all the decisions, tells his subordinates precisely what to do, and literally runs the whole show. He expects complete obedience from his subordinates and never entertains suggestions and initiatives from subordinates. In fact, autocratic leader is not a leader but merely a formal head of the organisation who is generally disliked by his subordinates.

(iv) Laissez-faire Leadership

A leader with 'Laissez-faire' style gives maximum freedom to his subordinates. The subordinates are allowed to decide their own policies, procedures and methods. He provides help only when it is required by the subordinates, otherwise he does not meddle in their work. This leadership style builds self-confidence in the employees and gives them the opportunity to develop their skills, competencies and talents. Such a style is suitable to the organisations where the employees are self-disciplined, competent and committed to organisation's goals and objectives.

(v) Coaching Leadership

The leadership has an objective of developing his people for the future. This style can be summed up in a phrase, 'Try this'. This style gives best results when the leader wants to help the group to build lasting personal strengths.

(vi) Pacesetting Leadership

Pacesetting leader expects excellence and self-direction. This style can be summed up in a phrase "do as I do, now". This style works effectively when the team is already motivated, skilled and ready to give the quick results which are expected by the leader. However, if this style is extensively and intensively used, it can overwhelm team members and discourage innovation.

E. Theories and Approaches of Leadership

The traits and the behavioural theories are probably the earliest, basic and most popular of the leadership theories. Many recent complex theories often draw on these two theories of leadership.

(i) Trait Approach

An individual becomes a leader because he is different from others in some special ways. Some people are born to lead. Great leaders of past as well as the contemporary leaders seem to differ from ordinary people in many respects. They possess high level of ambition and clear vision of their future. They possess an aura that sets them apart from the others. This approach to the study of leadership is known as 'The Great Person Theory'. This theory contends that great leaders possess key traits that set them apart from most other human beings, and these traits remain stable over time and across different countries.

The advocates of this theory hold an opinion that the leaders are physically, psychologically and socially better adjusted to display better judgment. They believe that the traits of leadership are inherited or innate, and these cannot be acquired by learning. They generally have higher intellectual powers than their average followers. They are emotionally stable, confident and consistent in action. Their height, weight, physique, appearance and health contribute to their success in leadership. They generally have very strong inner urge and motivational drive to accomplish something. They have vision and foresight to look into future and devise plans and policies. Their empathetic attitude enables them to observe the things and situations from the point of view of others. They develop social understanding, interpersonal relationships and possess knowledge about how human being react in different situations.

They have social skills and abilities to win loyalty and confidence of the people. They display fairness and objectivity in dealing with people. They have flexibility and open-mindedness to accommodate others point of view. They are extrovert, persuasive and confident enough to communicate effectively. They display technical as well as soft skills like organising, planning, decision-making, analysing, delegating, controlling, supervision and wining cooperation. They have will power, initiative, persistence, alertness, originality, creativity, enthusiasm, cheerfulness, politeness, expressiveness, sociability, self-esteem, integrity, self-assurance and decisiveness.

Limitations of Traits Approach

However, no uniformity was found in the list of leadership traits given in various research studies. There are no consistent patterns between sets of traits and leadership effectiveness. There are numerous traits of successful leadership positions. There are disagreements over which traits should be considered as most essential for an effective leadership. Several decades of study could not produce a set of qualities or one personality trait that can be used to differentiate leaders from non-leaders. This theory also fails to show comparative significance level of different traits.

There are many outstanding business leaders who are found to be authoritarian and narrow minded. People have various traits with different degrees, therefore, it is difficult to decide the degrees of the various traits required for effective leadership. Traits model often attempts to relate physical traits like appearance, height, physique, etc. with effective leadership. In business, such traits are not required for leadership positions. Traits approach is fatalistic in suggesting that, by traits some people are more prone to be leaders than the others. There are no definite, reliable and valid tests for the accurate measurement of these traits.

(ii) Behavioural Approach

Behavioural approach focus attention on the actual behaviour and actions of leaders as against the emphasis on personal qualities in traits approach. Behavioural model investigates into what leaders actually do and how they do it. Leadership involves interpersonal relationship between a leader and his subordinates. According to behavioural approach, in interpersonal relationship, a leader's behaviour towards his subordinates constitute the most critical element.

Effective leaders help the subordinates or teams to achieve their goals. They build task-centred relations with employees that focus on the quality and quantity of work. They are also considerate and supportive of the employees' attempts to achieve the goals. They build up self-confidence, raise the morale, and spirit of the team members. They work hard to settle the disputes, keep the subordinates happy, provide positive reinforcement and support them to achieve personal goals like promotion, recognition and work satisfaction.

Michigan Studies

The empirical studies conducted by Institute of Social Research at the University of Michigan on leadership identified leadership styles that results in higher performance and group satisfaction. These are two distinct leadership styles:

1. Production Centered Leadership
2. Employee Centered Leadership

Production centered leadership is known as task oriented leadership. It stresses on certain points like close supervision of the subordinates; rigid rules, regulations, procedures, and work standards; consideration of employees as tools to accomplish the organisational goals; and the various technical aspects of the job.

The employee centered leadership style is 'relation oriented' leadership which emphasises the importance of human relations. This style gives priority to treat the employees as human beings. It shows concern for employee needs, welfare, career advancement, etc. It encourages employee participation in managerial decision-making. It allows high degree of freedom to the subordinates.

However, the boss centered leadership and employee conferred leadership are two extreme types of leaderships which are rarely found in practice. These studies ignore the personal characteristics of individuals and groups, and other situational variables. A leader is supposed to follow either of the two extreme styles rigidly. However, in practice these two extremes cannot be followed rigidly. Leaders adopt both the styles in varying degrees to suit the requirements of a particular situation. They cannot restrict themselves to particular style.

Ohio Studies

The main objective of Ohio State University Leadership studies was to identify the major aspects of leadership and to find out the effects of leader's behaviour on the employees. It describes the leader's behaviour in two dimensions:

(i) Initiating Structure
(ii) Consideration

Initiating structure refers to leader's behaviour in defining and organising relationship between himself and the subordinates. The purpose of this structure is to establish patterns of organisation, to develop channels of communication, to develop methods or procedures, and to supervise the activities of the employees. On the other hand consideration refers to the behaviour which is characterised by friendliness, openness, supportiveness, respect, mutual trust and concern for the welfare of the employees.

This theory states that leadership behaviour is based on two axes rather than on a single continuum. A leader can be (i) High on both the dimensions, (ii) Low on both the dimensions, (iii) High on one and low on the other, (iv) Low on one and high on the other. There is positive relationship between consideration and regularity of employees and low grievances. There is positive relationship between initiating structure and employee performance, but initiating structure

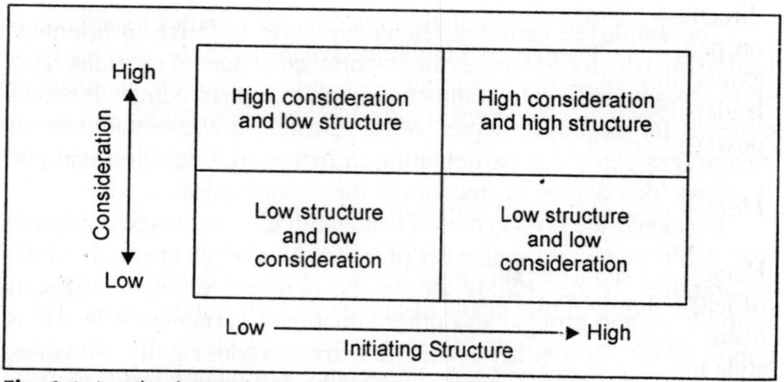

Fig. 6.1: Leadership Behaviour: Two Dimensions

is also associated with grievances and absenteeism. When both these dimensions are high, performance and job satisfaction tends to be high, but in some cases high productivity was accompanied by grievances and absenteeism.

Ohio studies found two characteristics which could be high or low and were independent of one another. The research was based on questionnaires to the leaders and subordinates. Consideration is the degree to which a leader acts in a friendly and supportive manner. On the other hand initiating structure is the degree to which a leader defines or structures his role and the role of the subordinates towards achieving goals of the organisation. Consideration is the people orientation and initiating structure is the task orientation. Both Ohio studies and Michigan studies focused on 'task' and 'people'.

(iii) Situational Theory of Leadership

Situational theories of leadership hold the view that leadership is largely affected by a situation. These theories do not emphasise on the personal traits of a leader. An effective leader is one who moulds himself and modifies his behaviour to suit the requirements of a given situation.

Fiedler's Contingency Model

Fiedler's theory assumes that leaders are either task oriented or relationship oriented. Task oriented leaders focus on task assignments, directives and deadlines whereas relationship oriented leaders focus on people. A situation is favourable when it enables the leader to extend influence over the group. The most favourable situation for leaders is one in which they are liked by the subordinates and have a powerful position.

Hersey and Blanchard Situational Model

Hersey and Blanchard believed that leaders have to match their style of leadership with the needs of maturity of the subordinates. These needs move in stages and have a cycle with which the leadership style has to adjust. Therefore, this model is also called as 'life cycle theory of leadership'. It is based on an interaction among three variables—task behaviour, relationship behaviour, and maturity level. According to this theory, as the level of subordinate's maturity increases to accomplish a given task, a leader should reduce task behaviour and increase the relationship behaviour. This theory was not based on any empirical studies.

House's Path Goal Theory

Fielder's theory and House's Path goal theory are both contingency theories. Robert House's situational leadership theory is based on the Ohio state leadership studies and Vroom's expectancy model. Path goal theory considers leader's role as one that affects a subordinate's motivation to reach the desired goals. Leader's role is to create a work environment that helps subordinates to reach organisational goals. Leaders have to create a goal orientation and they have to improve the path towards the goal. Its major concern is how the leader influences the subordinate's perceptions of their work goals, personal goals and paths to goal's attainment.

Vroom-Vetton and Jago's Contingency Model

Victor Vroom, Philip Vetton and Arther Jago developed a contingency model which emphasises the role played by leaders in making decisions. It focuses on the degree to which the employees may be allowed to participate in decision-making. Decision quality, decision acceptance and decision timing are three factors which are considered important in this context. The quality of a decision is highest when the best alternative is chosen. Decision acceptance is important whenever decision is concerned with subordinate's work motivation and when a decision is to be implemented by the subordinates. Decision timing is important whenever timing can have certain constraints on decisions.

Likert's System of Management Leadership

Rensis Likert was the Director of Michigan Institute of Social Research who conducted extensive research in the field of leadership. According to him organisation is a complete system which is founded on the principle of supporting relationship. In this system leadership, communication, motivation, decision-making and control move together. He holds the view that these variables are measurable and they can be correlated to profit and production overtime.

Likert considered traditional job oriented supervision as a cause of low morale and low productivity. He also considered organisation as a complex system of interrelated work groups. He was supportive of participatory management in the area of decision-making.

According to him, there are four types of leadership styles—

(i) Exploitative Autocratic
(ii) Benevolent Autocratic
(iii) Participative
(iv) Democratic

In 'Exploitative Autocratic' style of leadership there is no participation of workers in decision-making because these leaders have no trust and confidence in the subordinates. In 'Benevolent Autocratic' leadership style the relationship is that of a master and a servant because these leaders have no proper confidence in the subordinates. In "participative' leadership style, leaders do not have full confidence in the subordinates, but the subordinates are given freedom to discuss about the decisions regarding their job and their lives. In 'Democratic' style of leadership leaders have full confidence and trust in the subordinates. They meaningfully participate in decision-making. Leaders always ask the subordinates for their ideas and opinions.

(iv) Charismatic Leadership Theory

Charismatic leaders direct and motivate the subordinates primarily by creating a set of shared values and a strong emotional commitment to a shared vision in them. Charisma is a form of interpersonal attraction of a leader that inspires acceptance and support of the followers.

Charismatic leaders create a shared vision of a highly desirable future and their values. They link these values to the goals and mission of the organisation and expected behaviours of the subordinates. These leaders possess extraordinary gifts and qualities that attract the followers emotionally and personally. They promote shared identity regarding 'who they are' and 'what they stand for'. They create common bonds among the followers. They display the impression of self-confidence, determination, innovation, optimism and social and physical courage. They focus on success rather than the potential for failure.

(v) Transformational Leadership Theory

Transformational leadership includes charisma, inspirational motivation, individualised consideration, intellectual stimulation and idealised influence. Transformational leader anticipates future trends, inspires followers to understand and embrace a new vision of possibilities, develops others to be leaders or better leaders, and builds the organisation as a community of rewarded leaders. Transformational leaders can be described as visionary, inspiring, daring and ethical. Their vision does not blind the followers but empower them.

Transformational leaders encourage the followers to be innovative and creative, to explore new ideas and methods, to revaluate their own perspectives and assumptions, and to find productive and positive solutions. They demonstrate the behavioural patterns which their followers strive to follow. They provide special attention to individual follower's needs for growth and achievement. They use all the sources of power like expert power, legitimate power, reward power, referent power and coercive power to move individuals and teams towards a vision and goals. They may willingly sacrifice their personal gains for the gains of followers. Their individualised consideration compels them to play the roles of counsellors, teachers, mentors, confidants and facilitators.

(vi) Transactional Leadership Theory

Both transactional and transformational models were developed by J.M. Burns. Transactional relationship between leader and follower involves exchange relationship. Fiedler's model and Path-goal model are transactional in nature. Transactional leadership involves motivating and directing the subordinates through appealing to their self-interests. Transactional leader sets performance expectations and goals, and provides feedback to the subordinates. Leadership power of a transactional leader originates from his formal authority and responsibilities in the organisation.

Transactional leaders focus on the managerial functions of planning, organising and controlling. They identify paths that link the achievement of goals to the rewards. They set and clarify the goals, clarify expectations, exchange resources for support, exchange assistance for efforts, provide commendations for successful performance and ultimately obtain short-term measurable results. They actively monitor the employee performance. They may wait to take action until the mistakes of the subordinates are brought to their notice. Punitive methods and corrective measures are used for unacceptable behaviours.

F. Ethical Qualities of Managerial Leadership

If both the employers and employees uphold the ethical code, it contributes to long-term organisational success. The role of top management in setting up behavioural standards is crucial. Often, the general perception is that senior managers follow the double standards when they have one rule for themselves and another for the rest of the corporation. Managers have to set an example of ethical behaviour in their own actions.

A code of ethics is adhered in the organisation when manager emphasises ethics, talks about it, encourages the employees to raise the ethical issues, and keeps their attention focused on ethical standards. As a leader, manager has to develop realistic goals which can be achieved by the employees. If the employees cannot achieve the goals, they are inclined to forfeit ethics in order to achieve the goals. Manager can avoid ethical problems by discussing various sorts of temptations which might arise before the employees. He has to identify the areas which are vulnerable to unethical practices. He has to encourage the employees for reporting unethical activities in the organisation. If the employees see that the unethical behaviours are practiced and tolerated, they will not pay attention to the code of ethics and statement of mission. Values cannot be just preached, they must be lived. Manager has to integrate ethics in his personal life as well as business life. Ethics and morality has to become an internalised part of his personality.

Leadership competencies of a manager includes his integrity, vision, initiative, customer orientation, innovation, creativity, flexibility, technology adoption and its management, general awareness (internal and external), speed in decision-making, ability and willingness to learn, team building and teamwork, interpersonal skills, communication skills and ability to take risks.

An ethical manager never looks at ethics as an inconvenience. He never stretches the law for his personal or organisational gains. In dealing with the people he never behaves unethically. He deals fairly with the customers. His staff is motivated to understand and follow his ethical guidelines. He is known in the organisation for honesty and fairness. He never exploits the loopholes in laws for his personal or organisational benefits.

An ethical manager creates a clear statement of values for the employees. He knows and follows the applicable business laws, never bends the truth, and vigorously argues for fair dealing. He is known for being honest and scrupulous in all activities. He always opts to do what is right without getting disturbed by its consequences. He is praised for speedy and generous remedies for the defects in products and services. He gains and retains new customers due to his honesty. Some of the ethical qualities of managerial leadership are given below:

Ability to Motivate and Inspire

Manager as a leader should be able to inspire and motivate the employees for a righteous cause. He should be able to mobilise and channelize their energies, strengths, skills and competencies for that cause.

Patience and Fortitude

He consistently holds on to the goals of an organisation. He shows extreme patience and fortitude.

Dedication

He rises above his own individual importance for the sake of organisation and the stakeholders.

Combines Values with Competencies

He combines his values with competencies and skills for progress and development.

Builds and Maintains Relationships

He builds and maintains good relationships with the people. To him, these relationships are more valuable than monetary and material gains.

Impartial

He selects and appoints right persons for right jobs to achieve organisational success.

Mutual Respect

He respects the rights, authority and freedom of others.

Visionary

He has complete vision of the organisation, its objectives, its place in the country and the world, and its future status.

Empowering the Employees

He loves his employees. He makes every employee feel great. He does not become great by making other people small. He empowers his people to fulfil their duties and obligations. He is warm, kind and friendly.

Open-minded and a Good Listener

He is open-minded and a good listener. He has ability to adapt to the needs of the people.

Building Character and Integrity

He focuses on building character and developing morality and integrity of his employees.

Cooperation and Teamwork

He gives importance to cooperation, collaboration and teamwork.

High Energy, Initiative and Tenacity

He has a strong drive or desire for achievement. He has high energy and initiative. He is ambitious and tenacious.

A Desire to Lead

He has leadership motivation, a desire to influence others, and a desire to lead.

Seeking Power as Means

His leadership motivation can cause him to seek power as a means to achieve desired or shared goals.

Developing Networks and Coalitions

His socialised power of motivation urges him to cooperate with others, and to develop networks and coalitions.

Self-Confidence

He displays self-confidence and trusts in his own abilities, competence and performance. He must be self-confident to inspire confidence in others.

Cognitive Abilities and Strategic Thinking

He has strong cognitive ability or intelligence, emotional intelligence and cultural intelligence. He has conceptual skills for abstract and strategic thinking.

Adequate Knowledge

He has adequate knowledge of industry, relevant processes, procedures, technology, business transactions, market and environment.

Creativity

He has creativity and originality. He has ability to invent and develop original ideas.

Honesty, Integrity and Trustworthiness

Above all, he is known for his honesty, integrity, reliability and trustworthiness.

Moral Courage

He displays physical, mental and moral courage. If required, he is prepared to take risk. He can be severe, but can never be cruel.

Identifying and Cultivating Talents

He has an ability to identify and cultivate talents in the individual employees.

Judgment and Decision-Making Power

He displays good judgment. He has an ability to make sensible guesses about a situation or sensible decisions about what to do. He has an ability to make difficult decisions in short time frame.

A Winner's Mindset

He has winner's mindset. He knows how to survive in the present business environment which is global, competitive, and sometimes unethical and frustrating.

Enthusiasm for Achievement

He is enthusiastic. Great achievements are impossible without enthusiasm.

Calm yet Strong

When others are perturbed, he is calm, composed, undisturbed and confident of handling the crisis.

Learning Aptitude

He has strong learning aptitude for new knowledge and skills that equip him to face dramatic changes and chaos in business environment.

Dynamism and Optimism for Change and Progress

He is dynamic, active and energetic. He is prepared for constant change and progress. When he gives orders, he also gives out strength, good cheer and optimism to the employees.

Perseverance and Determination

He has a quality of perseverance. He takes on his tasks and continues steadfastly and determinately even though it is difficult.

Cultural Sensitivity and Flexibility

He recognises and celebrates the value of diversity in organisation. He is flexible enough to accommodate global cultural diversity.

Democratic Approach

He is a democratic leader who favours social equality and justice. He uses group decision method.

Humility and Modesty

He has self-confidence and self-esteem, but has total lack of arrogance. He displays humility in his willingness to admit his mistakes and errors. He does not pass the buck.

Reliability

He is reliable. His actions suit the words, and his words suit the actions. He gets the things done without creating any confusion, distrust and enmity.

EXERCISES

1. "To be an effective leader, an individual must possess the ethical qualities". Elucidate.
2. Define leadership and explain the concept of ethical leadership.
3. Elaborate on the significance of ethical leadership in management.
4. How can a leader make ethical use of his/her leadership powers?
5. What are the types of leadership powers? How can these powers be used ethically?
6. Comment on the ethical dimensions of leadership styles.
7. Which leadership styles are ethically appropriate according to you?
8. Discuss various theories and approaches of leadership.
9. What are the ethical qualities of managerial leadership.
10. Write short notes on the following:
    - (i) Laissez-fair Leadership
    - (ii) Democratic Leadership
    - (iii) Persuasive Power of Leader
    - (iv) Paternalistic Leader
    - (v) Autocratic Leader
    - (vi) Trait Approach of Leadership
    - (vii) Transactional Leadership Theory
    - (viii) Charismatic Leadership
    - (ix) Behavioural Approach of Leadership
    - (x) Legitimate and Coercive Powers of Leader
    - (xi) Situational Model of Leadership
    - (xii) Contingency Model of Leadership
11. Explain the situational theory of leadership.
12. Comment on the contingency models of leadership.

13. Compare the 'Trait approach' and 'Behavioural approach' of leadership.
14. Compare the 'Transactional' and 'Transformational' leadership theories.
15. Write a detailed note on various ethical qualities of Managerial Leadership.

7

Ethical Decision-making

"The best decision is only an approximation and a risk".

—Peter Drucker

Learning Objectives

A. Meaning and Definition
B. The Process of Ethical Decision-making
   1. Introduction
   2. Potential Decision Need
   3. Identification and Definition of Problem
   4. Setting Specific and Measurable Objectives
   5. Collecting Information
   6. Developing Alternatives
   7. Selecting the Best Alternatives
   8. Implementation Phase
C. Techniques to Improve Decision-making
   1. Group Decisions
   2. Individual Decisions
   3. Brainstorming
   4. Delphi Techniques
   5. Nominal Group Technique
   6. Electronic Meeting
   7. Fish Bowling Technique
   8. Didactic Interaction Technique
   9. Stepladder Technique
   10. Synthetic Technique
   11. Morphological Analysis Technique
D. Guiding Principles for Ethical Decision-making
E. Ralph Potter's Model of Making Ethical Decisions

A. Meaning and Definition

Decision-making is forming a conclusion in which a best course of action or behaviour is rationally chosen from a number of possible alternatives in a given situation. The term 'decision' is taken from its Latin origin 'decidere' meaning to 'cut off'. It is regarded as a mental process which results in selection of a course of action among many alternatives. The output can be an action or an opinion of choice. Individual decisions are examined in the context of a set of needs, preferences and values of an individual.

Decision-making is also regarded as a cognitive continuous process which is integrated in the interaction with the environment. From a normative perspective, the analysis of individual decision is concerned with the logic and rationality of decision-making. Decision-making is also regarded as a problem solving activity which comes to an end when a satisfactory solution is reached. It is a reasoning or emotional process which can be rational or irrational, moral or immoral. It can be based on explicit assumptions or tacit assumptions. According to rational choice theory decision-making encompasses the notion that we seek to maximise benefits and minimise the costs. Given below are some definitions of decision-making.

According to Oxford Advanced Learner's dictionary, decision-making is "the process of deciding about something important, especially in a group of people or in an organisation".

> *"Whatever a manager does, he does through decision-making".* —Peter Druckor.
>
> *"A course of action chosen by the manager as the most effective means at his disposal for achieving goals and solving problems".* —Haimann, T.
>
> *"A decision is an act of choice wherein an executive forms a conclusion about what must be done in a given situation. A decision represents a course of behaviour chosen from a number of possible alternatives".* —McFarland, D.
>
> *"Decision-making is the selection based on some criteria from two or more alternatives".* —G.R. Terry
>
> *"A decision in its simplest form, is a selection of alternatives".* —R.A. Killian
>
> *"Decision-making is a blend of thinking, deciding and acting".* —F.G. Moore

"Decision-making is the selection of a course of action from among alternatives, it is at the core of planning".

—Harold Koontz and H. Weihrich

B. The Process of Ethical Decision-making

1. Introduction

Ethical managers are those who make ethically acceptable decisions. Decisions are not only influenced by moral code of conduct, but they are also influenced by the present conditions, past experience and the future expectations. A good decision maker tries to fully comprehend the objectives, background, alternative courses of actions and their possible consequences on stakeholders and also on the other people in the various sections of the society. Once a decision is taken, it becomes difficult to reverse the course of action. Therefore, the choice of an alternative course of action should be consistent with the ethical standards and the objectives of the decision.

2. Potential Decision Need

The process of decision-making starts with the awareness of potential decision need which is founded on some hard evidence, or it could be based on the intuition and general feeling of the decision maker. After observing and noticing the existence of decision opportunity in the organisation, an individual manager is convinced that the need for a decision is real. He accumulates the evidence and gives formal recognition to it. Consequently, he feels the need to diagnose the true nature and perspective of the problem. Faulty diagnosis can lead to formulating a wrong problem which can result in a bad decision that is made in a careless and irrational manner.

3. Identification and Definition of Problem

It is believed that a problem well defined is a problem half-solved. A problem must be understood in clear and specific terms in order to find out the best or optimal solution. Manager has to critically examine the present situation, past background and experiences and the future expectations. The problem can be identified and understood correctly in the context. A problem may be associated with some other related problems. Manager has to clarify the details of the problem. He has to turn the agreed interpretation of the problem into its operational form. A problem can be formalised by making a written statement and drawing the boundaries of the decision.

4. Setting Specific and Measurable Objectives

It is necessary to set a specific and measurable objective of problem-solving and decision-making. The decision must be made to achieve the desired goals of the organisation.

5. Collecting Information

Decision-makers have to rely on the facts and available information which is related to the problem. The situational information, information regarding human factor, time factor, place and causative factors must be gathered in order to find the answers to 'what', 'who', 'where', 'when' and 'why' regarding the problem.

6. Developing Alternatives

Generating maximum and better alternatives is needed for better analysis of a problem from different perspectives. Possible alternatives can be developed by brainstorming and taking suggestions from the concerned people. Different perspectives like product, planning, potential and people can be considered to generate alternative ideas. Different ideas can be combined into a comprehensive alternative.

The feasibility, risks and other implications involved with the alternatives is necessary to be evaluated carefully.

7. Selecting the Best Alternatives

When the consequences of each alternative option are spelt out and evaluated, the next step is to select the best and comprehensive option that meets the decision objective satisfactorily. In selecting the most appropriate alternative, the decision-maker gives preference to the alternative that carries more weightage over the others. Decision Tree Analysis can also be used to select the best option. It involves placing all the available alternative options in a tree—like diagram and selecting the best.

8. Implementation Phase

Before implementing the selected option, a proper review of the selected alternative is required. It is required for detecting the loopholes and avoiding the errors. Then, the decision is to be conveyed to those who are involved in the implementation and to those who are affected by it. The reasons behind selecting particular alternative may be explained to them. Implementation depends on the implementability of the option and also on the skill and ability of the manager who is charged with that task.

It is necessary to monitor and see how effective the option is in solving the problem. If the decision has effectively solved the problem, the phase of implementation and monitoring comes to an end.

C. Techniques to Improve Decision-making

1. Group Decisions

Techniques for improving effectiveness of decisions are gained by bringing together the best features of 'individual' and 'group' decision-making, and by minimising their disadvantages. A situation in which an important decision has to be made about a complex problem like 'whether one organisation should merge with another', anyone individual would not be able to make a good decision. Highly complex decision tasks can overwhelm even the experts. A group can do a better job in such situations. For groups to outperform individuals, groups should be composed of heterogeneous group members with complementary skills. Diversity of opinions, knowledge, expertise, skills and experience offered by the group members is a major advantage of group decision-making.

However, it is not simply enough to have diversity of this kind. Group should be able to communicate their ideas with each other in an effective, free, open and amicable manner. Individuals in a group should not intimidate or obstruct other members from contributing their views, opinions and expertise. Having an expertise is different from making concrete contribution by using that expertise. When such contributions are made, it helps the group to achieve success. Group decisions can be superior to individual decisions if the groups are composed of heterogeneous experts with complementary skills who communicate openly to contribute to the groups' decision.

Whether groups perform better than individuals in simple decision tasks depends on the nature of the task and the expertise of the people involved. An individual expert working alone may do better than a group.

2. Individual Decisions

Groups may perform better than average or even exceptional individual under certain conditions. But, under certain conditions expert individuals prove superior to groups. If anyone in the group has a correct answer and the group members accept it, group performs as well as the best individual. But, if the other group members reject the correct answer, the group performs worse than the best individual.

Organisations require a lot of creative thinking to face most of their problems. Research has shown that individuals perform better than the groups in creative tasks. A commonly used approach by groups to solve the creative problems is brainstorming. This tool is a technique developed by advertising executive Alex Osborn to generate new, creative ideas. The members of brainstorming group are encouraged to present their ideas freely and openly. The members share even the far-fetched suggestions. They avoid criticising the ideas and opinions of others. They can use the ideas of others to create their own. They offer as many ideas as possible.

Researchers have compared the effectiveness of individuals and brainstorming groups who worked on the creative problems. The results showed that individuals were more productive than the groups. When they work on creative tasks, groups perform worse than individuals. The basic problem is that some individuals feel inhibited by the presence of the others in a brainstorming group.

3. Brainstorming

Many creative professionals strongly believe in the power of brainstorming. The members of brainstorming groups are encouraged to express their views and ideas freely and in uncritical way. But if the members wish to avoid feeling foolish for expressing even far-out suggestions and silly things, their creativity is inhibited in group communication. Brainstorming efforts are made to find a solution for a specific problem by gathering a list of ideas which are spontaneously contributed by the group members. Brainstorming is considered more effective than individuals working alone to generate new ideas.

For effective brainstorming, it is necessary to reduce social inhibitions among group members. Idea generation should be stimulated. Overall creativity of the group can be increased by focusing on quantity. It means enhancing divergent production of ideas with an aim to facilitate problem solving. It is assumed that the greater the number of ideas generated, the greater the chance of producing a radical and effective solution.

In brainstorming, criticism of ideas generated should be put 'on hold'. Criticism should be reserved for a later 'critical session' of the process. Unusual ideas should be welcomed. Such ideas can be generated by looking from new perspectives. It is assumed that new ways of thinking can be useful in providing better solutions.

Ideas generated in brainstorming may be combined and improved in order to form a single better idea. Ideas can be built by a process of association. Memory operates in a chain of associations of concepts, words and ideas.

4. Delphi Techniques

Delphi technique was developed by the Rand Corporation. It is a systematic way of collecting and organising the opinions of several experts into a single decision. This process begins by enlisting cooperation of experts and presenting the problem to them. Then each expert proposes what he believes to be the best solution. Experts record those solutions and recommendations. The group leader compiles all these individual responses and reproduces them for sharing with all the other experts. Each expert comments on the ideas of the other experts and proposes another solution. These individual solutions are again compiled by the group leader who looks for a consensus of solutions and opinions. The decision is finalised when a consensus is reached. If consensus is not reached, the process of sharing the reactions is repeated till the consensus is reached.

Communication of the experts with the group leader is through letter or e-mail. It helps to avoid the pitfalls of face-to-face group communication. It allows to collect the expert judgments without bringing them together in a face-to-face meeting. However, this process can be time consuming. Sending letters or e-mails to the experts, waiting for their response, sending their responses to all the others for sharing, and again waiting for their comments on each other's solutions till the consensus is reached, can consume a lot of time. Minimum time required to use this technique can be 45 days, if postal mail is used. Use of e-mail reduces the time consumed in this process. Delphi technique is not considered to be appropriate in crisis situations.

5. Nominal Group Technique

In nominal group technique (NGT) a small number of individuals, usually about 7 to 11, are brought together to systematically offer their individual solutions to a given problem. Then, they share their personal reactions to other's solutions. The technique is called as 'nominal group' because participants do not attempt to agree as a group on any solution. They form a group in name only. They vote on all the proposed solutions by the group members. The process begins by gathering the members together. They identify the problem at hand. Each of them writes down a solution. Then each member presents his solution before the group. Then each solution is discussed and evaluated. Each member is given a chance to express his reactions to the gathered solutions. After evaluating all the solutions, each member privately ranks the preferred solutions. The solution which gets highest rank is taken as the group's decision.

This technique can be used to arrive at group decision in a few hours. The technique discourages any pressure to conform to the wishes of a high status group members. The solutions are evaluated and preferences are conveyed in private balloting. This technique requires trained group leader. It requires one well-defined problem to be considered at a time. In case of a complex problem, NGT can be used only if that problem can be broken into smaller parts.

6. Electronic Meeting

In a recent approach to group decision-making, the NGT blends with the sophisticated computer technology which is called 'Electronic Meeting. The group members sit around in a horse shoe shaped computer terminals. When the issues are presented to the members, they type their responses on their computer. Individual comments as well as aggregate votes are displayed on the projection screen. Speed, anonymity and honesty are the major advantages of this technique.

The group members can anonymously type their comments and it flashes on the screen for all to see. It allows the participants to be honest without any penalty.

7. Fish Bowling Technique

Fish bowling technique is more structured and to-the-point in comparison to brainstorming technique. In this technique, the group of experts sits around a circle. A single chair is kept in the centre of the circle. One of the group member is invited to sit in the chair at the centre to give his views and opinions about the problem, and to suggest solution to the problem. The group members can ask him questions, but no cross-talk is allowed. When the presentation of the member in centre chair is over and his views are understood, he leaves the centre, and, the next member is invited to sit in that centre chair. He expresses his ideas as well as his views on the ideas expressed by the earlier member. The other members ask him questions regarding his views and ideas. When he vacates the chair, the next member occupies it. This process continues till all the participants have expressed their ideas, views and solutions to the problem.

8. Didactic Interaction Technique

This technique is applicable only in certain situations when a problem should result in a Yes-No solutions, for example, 'to buy' or 'not to buy'. Such a problem requires an extensive investigation and exhaustive discussion because a wrong decision can have serious repercussions. The group is split into two sub-groups. One sub-groups favours the 'Yes' decision, and the other favours the 'No' decision. The sub-group which favours the 'Yes' decision, has to list all the 'pros' of the problem solution. The other sub-group which favours the 'No' decision, has to list all the 'cons' of the problem solution. Then both the groups come together to discuss their views and findings. After the exhaustive discussion, both the groups switch their sides. They try to find weaknesses in their previous viewpoints. After discussing all the pros and cons, the decision is reached.

9. Stepladder Technique

Stepladder technique systematically adds new members into decision-making group and helps to increase the quality of the decisions. At the beginning, each of two members works independently on a problem. Then they come together and discuss their ideas and solutions. A third person works alone on the problem when the two person group works. Then the third person presents his ideas and joins the group. When the three person group discusses the problem and its solution, the fourth person works alone on it. Then, the fourth person presents his ideas and solution to the group and joins the group to discuss the possible solution. After each new individual is added to the group, the entire group works together to find a solution.

In stepladder technique, each person must be given enough time to work on a problem before he joins the group. He should also be given enough time to present his ideas thoroughly before the group. The final decision is made only after all the members are added to the group. By forcing each member to present his ideas without knowing what the group has discussed earlier, the new member is not influenced by the group. The stepladder group is expected to make better decisions than the conventional group meetings in which the members discuss the same problem all at once. Evidence suggests that this technique enhances the decision-making capacity of a group.

10. Synthetic Technique

Synthetic technique gives emphasis on generating creative solutions to the problems. The group members are encouraged to join together apparently irrelevant and different elements. They attempt to make strange things familiar and the familiar things to appear strange. Brainstorming technique is used to create climate in which large number of suggestions are generated. But, in synthetics technique, group attempts to find a solution by working at a problem in a new and previously unthought of ways.

11. Morphological Analysis Technique

The technique of morphological analysis is used to discover the fundamental patterns of relationships among the ideas. The group members arrange the ideas into a display which is called morphologram or a morphological chart. Morphologram consists of several columns. Each of these columns are labelled with one of the parameters of the problem. These parameters are constant but their value varies with the circumstances of its application.

D. Guiding Principles for Ethical Decision-making

Ethical issues in business are common and complex which involve the moral values, principles and standards of conduct and obligations for the individuals and groups in organisation. These ethical issues influence the decisions made daily in the organisations. If these issues involve the factors that confuse the distinction between 'right' and 'wrong', the decision-makers may experience ethical dilemmas. When there are no simple rules for ethical decision-making, the decision-makers have to develop their competency in applying ethical values and principles to decision-making.

There are no universally accepted rules, values and principles to resolve all the complex ethical issues in decision-making situations. There are many rules and principles that can provide ethical justification for a particular decision or behaviour. Some principles and rules justify the self-serving decisions whereas some other principles and rules justify only those decisions which are made after careful consideration of the rights of others. 'Hedonist' principle justifies whatever a businessman does in his own self-interest. 'Organisation interest principle' allows a person to make decision on the basis of whatever is good for the organisation. 'Might-equals-right' principle allows a person or group to do whatever they are capable enough to impose on others.

Principles of 'concern for others' consider decisions from the perspective of those who are affected by the decisions. For example, 'distributive justice' principle allows a person or group to act on the basis of treating individuals and groups equitably, rather than on the basis of caste, race, religion, gender, age, etc. The decision-makers act on the basis of 'how the general public are likely to respond to the "disclosure of the decision".

The 'golden rule' principle places the decision-maker in the position of someone who is affected by the decision thus, the distributive justice principle, disclosure principle and the golden rule principle are the principles of 'concern' for others. These principles are used in certain categories of decisions through laws and court rulings. Civil rights laws as well as labour laws forbid the managements of business organisations from considering the individuals on the basis of race, religion, gender, caste, etc. in decision to hire, select, recruit, promote or fire the employees.

Managers who adhere 'utilitarian' principle in decision-making, act on the basis of 'the greatest good for the greatest number of people'. They also verify whether their decision can cause greater harm than the good. Those who follow the means-end principle, act on the basis of whether the decision results in the overall good that justifies a moral transgression. Those who uphold the principle of 'professional standards', make their decisions on the basis of professional norms, standards and responsibilities. The professional standards principle, utilitarian principle and means-end principle are the three principles which are used to justify the decisions that balance the interest of multiple individuals and groups. Therefore, these principles are called balancing interests principles.

Ethical decision-making in business organisation is influenced in varying degrees by different factors. However, the top management should show their commitment to ethical decisions and behaviours of all the employees in the organisation. They must build values and ethics awareness. They should regularly communicate the ethical standards, operational principles and the shared values in their everyday business activities. A code of ethics should be officially declared, promoted and strictly followed. The code must define their ethical obligations in conducting business of the organisation. The process of performance appraisal should include the ethical issues. All the employees should be involved in identifying, understanding and solving of the ethical problems.

In ethical decision-making, who will receive the benefits or incur costs as a consequence of a decision is carefully determined. The utilitarian principle is a common approach to determine such costs and benefits. In order to assess the benefits and costs of a decision, the interests and values of a variety of stakeholders like shareholders, customers, suppliers, lenders, government agencies, local community and society at large, requires to be determined. 'Utilitarianism' gives emphasis on the provision of the greatest good to the greatest number of people in judging ethical value of a decision. A utilitarian manager studies the potential effect of alternative actions on the employees who will be affected by each alternative course of action before selecting the alternative that benefits the largest number of employees. However, critics believe that utilitarianism has been misused for too much short-term maximising of personal advantage.

Kant's moral theory and deontological principles consider duties to other people to be the core of ethical decision-making. Managers must do their duties to other people irrespective of whether they want to do it or not. Duties are considered as obligations that must be fulfilled. However, 'Mutual Benefits' principle and 'Modern Social Contract theory' emphasises that we are all dependent on one another for our well-being. Thomas Hobbes was the first philosopher to state that it is in everyone's best interest to trust one another for the purpose of mutually advantageous cooperation.

Managerial decisions are also guided by the 'Rights' principle. This principle calls on the managers to make the decisions which are consistent with fundamental liberties and privileges of the individuals in organisation, customers, shareholders and other stakeholders. Rights criteria provide protection to the whistle-blowers when they report illegal or unethical activities in the organisation to the parental body of the organisation or to the press or government agencies, on the basis of the 'right' to speech.

'Care' principle emphasises that individuals cannot exist in isolation from 'caring relationships with others'. 'Ethics of care' which is emphasised by feminist ethicists recently, emphasises that we exist in the web of relationships. Therefore, we should preserve and nurture those relationships with specific persons. Secondly, it demands that the decision-makers should exercise special care for those with whom they are concretely related by attending to their needs, values and well-being. Managers must respond positively to those who are dependent on their care.

'Justice' principle requires managers to enforce the rules impartially and fairly so that there is equitable distribution of costs and benefits. This principle looks at the issues from the perspective of the affected persons and groups. Business action, as far as possible, should be consistent with the moral rights of those whom it can affect and it should lead to a 'just' distribution of benefits and burdens. It should maximise social benefits and minimise social injuries.

'Virtue' principle emphasises on the character traits and virtuous nature of the decision makers. Managers should have the virtues like generosity, honesty, integrity, kindness, courage, thoughtfulness, loyalty, benevolence, and politeness. A person who has moral integrity can be counted on to make ethical decisions and to behave in a way that is constant and harmonious.

The ethical climate in the organisation, an individual's ethical attitude or personal code of ethics, organisation's code of ethics, culture of the organisation, formal policies, values, rules, regulations, laws, beliefs in abiding the laws, behaviour of the superiors in the company, professional norms, ethical standards, and ethical qualities of leadership also guide the managers to make the ethical decisions.

E. Ralph Potter's Model of Making Ethical Decisions

There are variety of ways to make justifiable ethical decisions. For ethical decision-making philosophers do not suggest that everyone should come to the same conclusion, but each person should be able to defend his decision-making process as having philosophic validity. Thus, all of them can come to differing but justifiable conclusions.

Harvard philosopher and theologian Ralph Potter has created a model for the process of decision-making which is called "The Potter Box". The series of boxes in 'Potter Box' are actually the series of logical steps to be taken by the people to find the way to deal with their ethical dilemma. They start by defining their ethical dilemma and then move through the other quadrants. The objective is not to force the choices, but to enable them to understand and ethically justify the choices.

After defining the ethical situation or dilemma, they look at the situation from points of view which are other than their own. As the case develops they recognise that additional insights may cause them to adjust their selections in other quadrants of the Potter Box.

Then they identify their values and beliefs that define what they stand for. Values are helpful in defending and rationalising their behaviour. Values are the standards of choice through which they seek meaning, satisfaction and worth. Some values are instrumental or desirable modes of conduct such as love, honesty, integrity, helpfulness, etc. Other values are terminal or end results like self-respect, equality, security, freedom, etc.

Thirdly, they identify the principles. They do not moralise or give dogmatic, ad hoc advice but use moral philosophy and give general consistent advice which is derived from the wisdom of the ages. Ethical principles are laid down by the philosophers. For example, Aristotle's Golden Mean, Kant's Categorical Imperative, Mill's Utilitarianism, Rawl's Vail of Ignorance, etc. Some of these guidelines may seem contradictory but most ethical people tend to follow one of these principles.

Finally, they are expected to choose their loyalty. They decide whom they are ultimately loyal, and to whom they are loyal at the intermediate steps, and who will benefit, and who will get hurt. They may have competing loyalties to themselves, to their firms, friends, colleagues, society at large and to their family.

EXERCISES

1. Write a detailed note on the meaning and process of ethical decision-making.
2. "Decision-making is a cognitive continuous process which is integrated in the interaction with environment". Explain.
3. "Ethical managers are those who make ethically acceptable decisions". Elucidate.
4. What are the phases in the process of ethical decision-making?
5. Elucidate various techniques to improve decision-making process.
6. Which techniques would you select to improve your ethical decision-making in various situations?
7. What are the guiding principles of ethical decision-making?
8. Explain Ralph Potter's model of making ethical decisions.
9. Write short notes on the following:
   - (i) Brainstorming
   - (ii) Group Decisions
   - (iii) Individual Decisions
   - (iv) Electronic Meeting
   - (v) Delphi Technique
   - (vi) Synthetic Technique
   - (vii) Fish Bowling Technique
   - (viii) Didactic Interaction Technique
   - (ix) Morphological Analysis Technique
   - (x) Nominal Group Technique
   - (xi) Stepladder Technique
10. Explain the universally accepted values and principles that you would use to resolve the complex ethical decision-making issues.

8

Ethical Communication

"In the beginning was the word, and the word was with God, and the word was God". —John 1-1

Learning Objectives

A. Meaning of the Concept
B. Characteristics of Ethical Communication
   (i) It is a Fundamental Responsibility
   (ii) It Reflects the Values and Ethical Choices
   (iii) It Occurs within a Context
   (iv) It Determines Ethical Response
   (v) It Insists on Active Listening
   (vi) It supports 'Honest Opinion'
   (vii) It is Concerned with Ethical Judgment
   (viii) It Delineates Professional Communication Standards
   (ix) It Designs Interpersonal Communication Standards
   (x) It is a Tool of Effective Decision-making
   (xi) It Covers Several Ethical Issues
C. Ethical Use of Language
   1. Introduction
   2. Influencing Receiver's Perception
   3. Use of Regional and Standard Dialects
   4. Mutual Linguistic Accommodation
   5. Blessing or Curse
   6. Conventional Arbitrary Symbols
   7. Avoiding Ambiguity, Verbosity, Abstractions and Incomplete Statements
   8. Abiding Language Rules
   9. Ethical Contexts of Verbal Messages

A. Meaning of the Concept

Ethical communication exhibits a sense of well-developed social responsibility. It avoids the tendencies of manipulating and exaggerating the details of information. It provides the factual, accurate, concise and complete message in sincere, honest and courteous manner. It does not hide any negative or unfavourable information for selfish purposes. It includes all required and relevant information. It is never deceptive. It always upholds truth, and never states opinions as facts.

B. Characteristics of Ethical Communication

(i) It is a Fundamental Responsibility

According to National Communication Association, 'ethical communication' is fundamental to responsible thinking, decision-making and the development of relationship and communities within and across contexts, cultures, channels and media'. It is essential to enhance human worth and dignity. It cultivates personal integrity, truthfulness, fairness, respect and responsibility for self and others.

Unethical communication threatens the well-being of individuals and the society in which we live. Managers who fail to provide ethical leadership and to establish systems that foster ethical conduct, share responsibility with those who knowingly benefit from corporate misdeeds. Unethical business practices reflect the attitudes, beliefs, values, language and behavioural patterns of unethical organisation's culture.

(ii) It Reflects the Values and Ethical Choices

Communication reflects the values and choices of the parties who are involved in the process of communication which always results in some consequences. Therefore, communication forms the basis of ethical makeup of interactions. Unethical communication is potentially harmful. It can thwart healthy human relationships and cause deep emotional wounds. It supports corruption, greed and oppression. It justifies injustice, genocide, conflicts and violence. On the other hand, the art of ethical communication is supportive to justice, truth, wisdom, compassion and love. Ethical communication has the power to heal, inspire, comfort and enlighten the people. Thus ethical communication reflects the values and ethical choices of the individuals and groups.

(iii) It Occurs within a Context

Ethical communication occurs within a context. The values, goals, emotions and perceptions of each individual shapes his or her approach in interpersonal communication situations. It requires understanding of what one intends to achieve through communication, how one decides to communicate, and what can be the possible consequences of communication.

(iv) It Determines Ethical Response

In any given situation, an individual or group has some moral options. Therefore, that individual or group has relative freedom to choose a particular option or a course of action. For example, an individual is often relatively free to choose how attentively he will listen to the other. He can decide how he should respond to other's statements and questions. He can decide whether to express hostility or to express love, sympathy and agreement. How an individual will respond is dependent on his preferences, abilities, cultural norms, customs, genetic makeup, attitudes, etc. The overall state of one's mind is a decisive factor that controls the cognitive or deliberative process across the contexts.

(v) It Insists on Active Listening

Communicators have an ethical responsibility to listen carefully and thoughtfully to others. Pseudo-listening, selective attention, insensitivity, defensive listening and ambushing can be unethical. People-oriented listeners are concerned about understanding and supporting people rather than in evaluating and judging them. They are more interested in creating and maintaining good relationships. But they are often unable to assess the quality and validity of information which the others give. They also become overly involved with the feelings of others.

Some listeners are more interested in the content and quality of message than in the message giver. They seek details, analyse the issues, sometimes challenge the ideas, and even become critical and hostile. Some listeners are neither interested in the relationships nor in the content analysis. They are concerned with the task at hand. They are interested to know what sort of action is required by the message. They keep a focus on the job and appreciate clear, complete and concise messages. Time conscious listeners often show disregard for the feelings of others. Their excessive focus on time hampers mutual understanding and thoughtful deliberation.

(vi) It supports 'Honest Opinion'

Charles H. Cooley introduced the notion of "looking-glass self" in 1902. He suggests that we put ourselves in the position of other people and then, in our mind's eye view ourselves as we imagine they see us. When messages come from 'significant others' or the people whose opinions we value, it contributes to the developing self-concept. A friend, a relative or a teacher whom we respect can leave a permanent mark on how we view ourselves. Thus it is clear that each of us has the power to influence other's self-concept.

An ethical problem arises in a case when our honest comment is likely to reduce another person's self-esteem, even though the comment is made with the best of intentions. It is a challenge to be honest and supportive in such case. It is necessary to preserve the face of others and to protect their dignity.

(vii) It is Concerned with Ethical Judgment

Ethical communication is concerned with the judgments regarding the degrees of virtues and vices in communicative interactions. Ethical guidelines in communication are often easier to talk about, but they are difficult to put into practice. Religious leaders and philosophers in all the cultures of the world have prepared the ethical guidelines which suit their socio-cultural needs, norms, customs, mores and traditions. These guidelines are used as ethical standards to evaluate behaviours and actions of their own as well as of the others. When we communicate with others we expect that the others believe in what we say, trust us, and adopt the behavioural patterns and actions we recommend to them. Therefore, our communication involves various ethical issues.

As social creatures, we all depend upon each other, and our relationships depend upon communication interactions. How to communicate, whether with a frown or with a smile, with truth or with falsehood, is decided by our free will. Ethical studies help us to think and to make decisions about that choice. Communication influences the behaviours of the people. It produces certain responses that results in change. It brings about behavioural change in the senders and receivers of message. They influence and enter into each other's life.

(viii) It Delineates Professional Communication Standards

In professional contexts, professionals are expected to be the role models to those around them. They are recognised for their skills of communication, for being audience centered, having ability to continually improve and adapt to the changing situations. They treat people with fairness, respect and dignity. In conducting an evaluation, making a selection and in making a decision, they give priority to the factors of ethical considerations. In their communications, they insist on integrity. They discern right from wrong and explain their reasoning for their decisions. They respect the boundaries placed around information which is regarded as 'secret' or 'private' information. They respect and adhere to the truth. They communicate in a dignified and respectful manner with others. The information imparted by them is authentic, reliable and appropriate. Their ethical considerations are based on their values and concepts of virtues. Values or moral principles and rules determine their ethical behaviour. Sometimes, these rules are presented as statements of what they believe, and intend to honour. Their organisational values include integrity, human dignity, teamwork, safety, reliability, truth, etc. These organisational values address both the experience of the employees and the experience of the customers. When they think of excellent leadership qualities, they include ethics in those qualities. Like all other leadership skills, they continually develop and maintain their ethics. In organisational context, they have shared understanding of what an appropriate communication means in a given situation.

They develop an ethical environment in the organisation that influences the communicative performances, moods, attitudes and decisions of the people. It influences the processes of discussions and deliberations that attempt to decide what is right or wrong. Typically outlined specific principles, guidelines, values, organisational goals and organisational mission, etc. support the ethical environment in the organisation.

(ix) It Designs Interpersonal Communication Standards

Interpersonal communication ethics is concerned with the ethical mandate to protect and foster the good of relationship between persons. It deals with the communicative exchange which is situated within ethical framework. However, to promote such relationship it does not presume any interpersonal agreement. It rejects the realm of 'self-approval' and the exaggerated need for 'relational approval' from the other that can lead to interpersonal 'colonisation'. It is concerned with a responsibility towards a notion of relationship that is neither owned by the self nor by the other.

Interpersonal communication ethics is based on the standards that call both the parties to accountability for the relationship. It requires necessary space for each communicative partner to contribute to the relationship. Interpersonal responsibility begins with each person's commitment to actively care for the interpersonal relationship. Therefore, interpersonal communication ethics is not about 'me' or 'you'. It is a co-constituted communicative benchmark that holds both the parties accountable for the relationship.

Interpersonal space or distance nourishes the relationship that keeps persons together interpersonally. This space is considered as an interpersonal responsibility, not a limitation or an obstruction. Interpersonal communication ethics holds the view that one cannot impose a particular type of relationship on another, nor can anyone demand a relationship from another. Something must be done for the good of the relationship, but cannot be demanded. First, the relationship cannot be demanded, but secondly, no one can demand that no demand ever be uttered.

(x) It is a Tool of Effective Decision-making

It is difficult to precisely define the nature and limits of a person's loyalty to ethical norms or to his organisation or to his subordinates or family members. Therefore, there are no easy solutions for many real-world ethical dilemmas. However, business people can use the process of internal dialogue to reach the difficult ethical decisions. They can ask themselves what kind of business climate or a kind of society will be created or destroyed by their decisions. They can think about what kind of business world would emerge if their decisions are repeated in similar situations by others. They should assess how their decisions will affect themselves and others. They can assess their gains and loss, and how they feel about it. They should objectively and accurately review the impact of their decisions on other individuals and society at large. They can ask themselves about the reasons for putting the welfare of others ahead of their own welfare, even though no businessman can be expected to be entirely altruistic. They should think about what leads them either to prefer or to keep aside their own interests. The internal dialogue on these questions can help them to reach difficult ethical decisions.

(xi) It Covers Several Ethical Issues

Ethical communication covers several ethical issues like:

1. **Defamation**. Defamation involves false and malicious statements that damages someone's name or reputation by saying something bad or untrue about that person or organisation. It is an ethical issue in organisational communication. Individuals or groups can be sued or defamation. Therefore, it is ethical as well as legal

issue. Oral defamation or slander violates the ethical principles of human dignity, respect and honesty.

2. **Invasion of Privacy**. Invasion of privacy refers to unprivileged, unreasonable and unconsented intrusion in the personal and private life of an individual. Right to privacy gives an individual a right to keep unwarranted intruders off his or her private life. Proliferation of computerised personal data often helps to make private information open to the public. The companies or individuals who violate the privacy of a person are ethically and legally guilty of invasion of privacy. A person's name, photograph or other identification cannot be used for commercial benefit without permission. An employee's right to privacy is violated if his or her private letters, e-mails, records and reports are read by other persons who are not entitled to read them.

3. **Harassment**. Harassing another person is an unethical and poor way of communicating feelings and negative attitudes. Ethically, it violates the principles of human dignity, fairness and respect for the others. It is an unethical behaviour which is intended to trouble or annoy someone or to cause someone problems. It also involves tormenting or irritating someone on a repeated basis. It can occur between superior and subordinate, between persons of different castes, religions and cultures or between colleagues. Sexual harassment is a form of sexual discrimination. Employees are granted legal protection from sexual harassment.

4. **Discrimination**. Discrimination occurs when the people become victims of others' prejudices. Prejudicial attitudes are harmful when they translate into actual verbal communication and actions. Everyone can be potential victim of prejudicial attitudes. Therefore, discrimination can be on variety of prejudicial basis. It can be based on age, physical condition, sex, race, caste, religion, national origin, etc. It involves deliberate exclusion of certain groups of people. It is both unethical and illegal.

5. **Plagiarism**. Plagiarism is also an unethical and illegal practice. It is a practice of copying or using someone else's ideas or work and pretending that he thought of it or created it. It occurs when a person quotes material without acknowledging its source. It is unethical because it denies the original author proper acknowledgement. Copyright gives legal protection from such practices.

C. Ethical Use of Language

1. Introduction

A most powerful stimulating device for changing minds is a word. Language is the specie's specific gift of God to mankind. It satisfies the basic needs of communicative functions like exchanging information, describing ideas, narrating events, giving and receiving orders and instructions, persuading, giving warnings, suggesting, making requests, discussing, negotiating, problem solving, expressing various feelings and emotions, giving advice, etc. The language reflects the user's attitude and influences the others in various ways. Sometimes consciously and sometimes unconsciously our speeches and writings shape other's ideas, attitudes, beliefs and values.

2. Influencing Receiver's Perception

Speech style, speech organisation and speaker's status influences the perception of the receiver. Unintelligible message of an apparently legitimate speaker is often judged as 'scholarly speech' in the speaker's area of expertise. Meaningless message in high level professional jargon or impressive sounding language can be regarded as 'stimulating', 'clear', and 'scholastic'. In academic writing, often a message loaded with pompous and unnecessary words and complex sentences is rated highly, whereas, the same message written in a simpler language, with shorter words and clearer sentences, is judged as less competent.

3. Use of Regional and Standard Dialects

Choice of words, phrases, speech rate, accent, age of the speaker create the positive or negative influence on the message. Speakers of standard dialect are rated higher than the speakers with other non-standard regional dialects. Inability or unwillingness to use the standard dialect fluently often results in serious consequences.

4. Mutual Linguistic Accommodation

Though freedom of speech is one of the most treasured civil liberties, some form of racist and sexist language is demeaning to the targets.

It shapes the attitudes of those who hear or read that language. The principle of free speech must be reconciled with the need to minimise the hateful and discriminatory messages. Language can be used for building and demonstrating solidarity with others. When people feel positive towards each other, their mutual linguistic accommodation becomes evident. Therefore, supervisors often adopt the language styles of managers.

5. Blessing or Curse

Language can be blessing to the communicator and receiver but sometimes it can also be something of a curse. Use of slang and jargon, use of equivocal words or language which has more than one correct meaning, use of relative words which gain meaning by comparison, use of overly abstract language, use of emotive language, deliberate use of evasive language or vague statements can have negative consequences.

6. Conventional Arbitrary Symbols

Hundreds of languages and thousands of dialects are used by humans on this planet. But the words used in all these languages have no meaning of their own. They just represent meaning. They are arbitrary symbols that stand for meaning. Therefore, meaning of a word conceived in the mind of a communicator can be different from that which is understood by the receiver. Our experience is associated with these symbols. This experience of conventional and arbitrary use of the symbols helps us to interpret and understand the symbols and their meanings in varying contexts.

7. Avoiding Ambiguity, Verbosity, Abstractions and Incomplete Statements

Problems arise because meaning in language is not in the words themselves but in the way we make sense of them. Often we mistakenly assume that others use the words for the same meaning and in the same way as we do. It is everyone's ethical responsibility to use appropriate words that are suitable to the varying contexts and receives. It is also necessary to avoid assuming that others will interpret words in the same way as we do. Thirdly, we can communicate reasonably well with one another if we try to avoid abstract terminology, ambiguous words, incomplete statements and inappropriate verbosity.

8. Abiding Language Rules

Language consist many types of rules. It is necessary to understand and follow these rules. Phonological rules prescribe how words should sound when they are pronounced. Syntactic rules show the way of how the words, phrases and clauses can be arranged. Semantic rules deal with the meaning or various shades of meanings of specific words. Semantic misunderstandings occur when words are interpreted in more than one way. Pragmatic rules show how people should use language in their communicative interactions. Understanding self-concept of the language users, context in which the language is used, perceived relationship between communicator and the receiver, and their cultural background decides the communicative effect of the language used. Pragmatic rules help to avoid offensive language, sexist speech, racist words and discriminatory messages.

Use of slang and jargon, use of equivocal words, use of disruptive language, use of confusing data, use of emotive language, use of evasive language to mislead others, use of euphemism or the use of pleasant term to substitute the less pleasant one etc. can create the communicative and ethical problems.

9. Ethical Contexts of Verbal Messages

Our verbal messages do not give only the intended messages but also reveal an additional information about our attitudes, values, morals and integrity. In other words, our spoken and written messages disclose our personal ethics. Therefore, it is necessary for every speaker to consider his or her listener's attitudes, feelings and values before preparing and presenting the message. A speaker has to use his communication strategies only after careful consideration of the listener's needs, roles, status and socio-cultural background. This provides an ethical context for designing the messages.

Having understood the ethical context, a speaker can select the relevant material or choose the information that will communicate his ideas fairly, concisely and accurately. It is an ethical responsibility of every speaker to avoid propaganda technique of card stacking or omitting relevant unwanted details of information. The information must be unbiased, correct and complete. It should be fair, clear and not likely to support one particular person, party or group which is involved in something.

The logical arrangement and reasoning of the message must be sound, sensible and reliable. The propaganda technique of exaggerating, filtering, and distorting information, must be avoided. The sources of the information must be recent and reliable. The information pertinent to the selected subject can be explored from different sources. A speaker has to verify whether he has done everything possible to prepare his message which is ethically valid and reliable.

10. Use of Language in Cross-cultural Messages

Our world has become a global village and the work force in business houses reflect the diversity of people from different cultures. They live and work together. They have different customs and ways of communication which naturally leads to miscommunication in the organisations.

Therefore, it is necessary to use the language which is clearly understood by others. Care should be taken to avoid offensive language and expressions. An awareness should be created about non-verbal means of communication in various cultures and their interpretations. Employees should be able to anticipate any possible misunderstanding that might occur, and should try to correct it. Ethical employees make efforts to avoid cross-cultural miscommunication. They also avoid gaining any advantage which is based on such misunderstanding. They make efforts to understand cultural symbols and their meaning of the other parties. They also try to understand the communicative responses expected by the employees of the other culture.

An ethical communicator considers the other employee's feelings, opinions and attitudes from his or her cultural perspectives. They attempt to understand the context of the message from the other person's position. They also help the other person to properly understand the context of communication and interaction. They are determined to be fair to all who are involved in the interactions and transactions.

The ethical communicators also take care of the visual dimensions of messages in different cultures. These visual dimensions are postures, facial expressions, eye contact, movements of body or gestures and use of space. The messages imparted by the use of these visual dimensions vary from culture to culture. For example, to be spontaneous and casual in postures is valued in North America, but in formal cultures like English, Japanese and German it can be interpreted as 'too loose', and it can lower the credibility of the speaker. In United States formal clothing is highly valued but in many other cultures it takes a very special occasion for men to wear suit. The Chinese, Japanese and Koreans try to hide the outward signs of facial emotions. Though smiling is an universal sign of happiness and friendliness, too much smiling is interpreted as a sign of an insincere person. Chinese and Japanese smiles can mask their emotions.

D. Ethics of Persuasive Communication

1. Ethical Persuasion

Persuasion is not something that the speaker does to the audience, but it is something that the audience and the speaker agree to do with mutual respect and understanding. It is a mutual interactive process. It is not by shouting down opponents, but by respectful hearing and openness to opposing arguments, that the speaker can change the opponent's mind. A person who does not want to influence other's lives, is a person who does not want to involve in the lives of other people. Persuasion can be used to convince the people to give up their bad habits, to protect the environment, to motivate for noble purposes, to get the job, etc. It is ethical if it conforms to the accepted social norms and standards. Ethical persuasion consist a speaker's plan in the best interest of the audience, and his motives are honest. His communication does not depend on false and misleading information to change the attitudes or behaviour of the audience.

2. Ethical Adaptation in Persuasion

Adapting to speaking situations is an ethical challenge when the speaker has to decide how much adaptation is ethical. Audience member's feelings, attitudes, beliefs and values are key elements in audience analysis. Attitudes, beliefs and values are structured in human consciousness like layers of an onion. Attitudes lie at the surface of the consciousness. Beliefs and values underlie the attitudes. An attitude is a predisposition of a person who responds to something or someone in a favourable or unfavourable manner. A belief is an underlying firm view about the truth of something. It is based on cultural training and socialisation of that person. A value is a firm and deeply rooted belief about a concept's worth. A speaker's inference about audience member's attitudes depend upon his ability to recognise the beliefs and values held by the audience. The positive and negative attitudes of the people are rooted in their beliefs and values.

To change a particular attitude, belief or behaviour, speaker has to use his skills of persuasion. It is the process of motivating someone to change the belief and behaviour through communication. Persuasion can be ethical when it is used to influence others' lives in worthwhile ways. Persuasion is not coercive. On the other hand, it makes a listener to willingly think or act in a different way. Attitudes and beliefs do not change instantly. Persuasion is a process which succeeds over time in a gradual manner. While establishing his goals, realistic speaker remembers that persuasion is incremental and gradual.

3. Unethical Persuasion

(i) Presenting Multiple Identities

People who pay attention to themselves are the high self-monitors. They have the ability to monitor their own behaviour. They observe other's reactions and adjust their communication to get the desired results. Generally, they are good actors who can create the impression they want. They can handle the social interactive situations smoothly. They are good 'people-readers' who can put others at ease. On the other hand, low-self-monitors straightaway express what they are feeling and thinking without paying attention to the impression they create, and the reactions they get from the others. They have simpler and focused idea of who they are, and what they want to be. They can be expected to act in more or less the same way in varying social situations. Their social interactions are less smooth. They lack flexibility. They are straightforward communicators.

Presenting multiple or different identities may not be considered as inherently dishonest act. But in many cases it is unethical and deceitful to present an identity that doesn't match one's private and real self. Presenting different identities is a strategic communication to influence others' perception of an individual who consciously seeks to present different public faces before other people.

(ii) Deliberate Misleading

Persuasive messages primarily consist of the propositions of facts in which various aspects of conflicting evidence are presented. The communication receivers are expected to choose the truth for themselves. Often the questions regarding the facts cannot be settled with simple 'Yes' or 'No' answers. Rather such questions are open for discussions, debate, deliberations, examinations, evaluations and careful interpretations. Unethical communication is giving false information, deliberate misleading and crooked information, ignorant misstatement about the facts, deliberate distorting, filtering and editing of the facts, suppression or hiding of the facts, deceptive and fallacious reasoning to misrepresent the factual information.

(iii) Dishonest Motives and Hidden Agenda

Unethical communicators withhold and suppress vital information to serve their self-interests. They do not disclose their private and dishonest motives, and special interests. They withhold the information about the 'purpose' of their speeches, written messages and presentations. They do not reveal the sources of the information. They omit certain evidences, or suppress some aspects of evidences, or present only one side of the coin. They use emotional appeals to substitute the lack of valid evidence. Emotional appeals are used to cover up the absence of sound reasoning.

Although it's true that not communicating enough is unethical, there are even times when too much communication is a mistake, and no communication is the best course. There are situations when too much communicating can make the problem worse.

4. Honouring the Audience

Slandering another person, caste, culture or religion is an unethical behaviour. A lack of respect for other people is insulting and unethical when we speak to the members of other castes, communities and cultures, it is necessary to respect their norms, customs and points of view. If we disagree with their norms and decisions, it would be ethical to point out weakness of those norms and decisions than to attack the people involved in those decisions. The speaker also must avoid the emotional appeals that are intended to frighten the audience or to mislead them.

Selected topic must be worthy of the time of the audience. A topic can be selected about the issues, subjects and controversies that affect the lives of the audience. It should be a topic that interests speaker as well as audience. Speaker has to know as much as he can about the culture, values, interests, attitudes, occupation, education, age and gender of the audience.

Having a good attitude towards the audience and also towards the ideas to be presented helps the speaker to make the speech pleasurable for himself and his audience. If he has the doubts about his speech and preparation, it can result in nervousness. Therefore, he has to come before his audience fully prepared. He must give justice to the subject and to his audience. If he looks directly to his audience, it adds to the liveliness of communication. It indicates that he respects the audience and cares to accomplish his communicative purpose. It also indicates that he is interested in them. It helps him to gain an insight into how his message is being received by the audience. Every successful speaker uses this information which is received by observing audience reactions to make necessary adjustments so that his speech meets the demands, interests and requirements of the audience.

Communicator must seek to elicit response from those who receive his message. Therefore, he has to determine the purpose of his communication. Every speech or writing should be an instrument of getting a reaction from the listeners or readers. It has to be an instrument of utility for change in thought, action or behaviour of the receiver. And, this change must be for the benefit of the receiver. It is also important to learn about the culture of the people to whom the speaker addresses. He must find out whether the changes he is suggesting are consistent with the norms, customs and values in that culture.

5. Language in Ethical Persuasion

Language is a powerful tool which can be used ethically or unethically, for good or for evil. Words should not be used to hide our thoughts and intentions. Emotional words and phrases should not be used to avoid the real issues and to appeal to a lower level of reasoning. Speaker must not use the inflammatory language to accomplish his purpose. It is necessary to find out who will benefit from the changes asked by the speaker. Will only the speaker profit from the changes or the listeners too will be benefited by them?

In persuasive messages, speakers often use fear appeals to replace the concrete evidence. It is misusing the fear appeals. Fear appeals can be legitimately and ethically used to show the hazards of 'drinking and driving' or 'unsafe sex and HIV infection', etc. But fear appeals should not include exaggerated claims. It must be ensured that the listeners have an access to fair and truthful information. Concealing information is a violation of ethical standards. Speaker has to regard others as he would like to be regarded.

E. Ethical Communication in Conflicting Contexts

1. Conflict of Values, Loyalties and Interests

Moral beliefs, values and ethical standards differ from culture to culture and person to person. Personal ethical values, organisational ethical standards and a set of public ethics may not complement each other. There can be tension between personal ethics of an employee and his obligation to remain loyal to the policies and practices of an organisation. When the values conflict, employees sometimes do not want to simply obey authority. When they face such ethical dilemmas, some employees choose to do nothing, some employees pass the moral decision-making to others, some employees simply quit, some employees decide to work further to change the unethical situation in the company's activities, and, some employees decide to blow whistle on the organisation's unethical practices. Thus conflicting values can lead to conflict in interactive communication.

Millions of dollars flow from the companies to the political action groups, candidates, parties and organisations. Each and every employee in the company is unlikely to agree with such affiliations of the company. They may have reservations about the company's allegiances. Some of the activities of the organisation can be found morally objectionable to the employees. Selling lethal arms to the terrorist groups or dictator's army can be regarded as unethical practices by the employees. Using industrial espionage and payoffs to gain unfair advantage over the rival companies is also an unethical practice which employees do not like.

Managers are often under pressure to communicate half-truths and even blatant lies to the clients and colleagues. To gain the investor's money and to produce the promised sales levels, the companies hide their sagging sales and tell the potential customers that the business is flourishing successfully. Employees may object to the company's harmful or potentially harmful actions. Many companies use difficult and ambiguous language to hide contingencies or information that a customer needs to know. Good companies follow good business practices and communicate with the customers in a timely, truthful and unambiguous manner.

Most of the decisions in the conflicting situations are influenced by the moral choices made by the managers. Therefore, these are the ethical decisions in which moral questions and ethical choices are involved. These decisions are not concerned with legal matters. For example, unexpected layoffs in which case law does not dictate the senior management to communicate its staffing plans including layoffs to the employees in advance. However, some moral decisions become legal issues. When a person acts on behalf of an organisation his ethical choices and actions become complicated. As a representative of his company his moral choices reflect on the ethical status, image and integrity of his organisation. Whatever he communicates or does on behalf of his company has legal obligations and legal consequences.

Therefore, a high level of ethical and legal awareness is required especially while writing proposals, letters, reports, memos, etc. which involve contracts, claims, commitments, interstate trade, assurances, warranties, formal charges, complaints, labour negotiations, personnel hiring and firing, etc. Companies and individuals fight for their survival, with every means at their disposal like legal rights and moral values.

2. Communication Styles in Conflict

In interpersonal communication, conflict arises when both the parties become aware that some disagreement exists. It is an expressed struggle between two parties who perceive that there is an interference from the other party in achieving their goals and objectives. This expressed struggle can be verbal or non-verbal expression of displeasure and disagreement. They perceive that one person's gain is the another person's loss. The parties can opt to see mutually satisfying solutions to their problems. Mutually incompatible and exclusive goals can lead to real conflict. The individuals involved in conflict can be non-assertive. Their non-assertiveness comes from their lack of confidence. They are unable and/or unwilling to express their thoughts and feelings. They know how to communicate in straight forward way but they choose to be non-assertive. Non-assertion is a common way in dealing with conflicts.

Individuals with non-assertive communication styles avoid confrontation even when the behaviours of others are displeasurable. Their approach to others is 'I am not OK' and 'You're OK'. Their non-assertion takes the forms of 'avoidance' or 'accommodation'. Accommodators deal with conflict by putting the other's needs ahead of their own. Avoidance may be the best approach when a conflict is minor or short-living. An individual may choose to keep quiet if the risk of speaking is too great.

On the other hand, communicators who choose the directly aggressive approach, embrace the conflict and make an outright attack on the others. They attack upon the position and dignity of the receivers. Verbal aggressiveness of communicator may help him to get what he wants in the short run, but the relational damage caused by it is not worth the cost. In indirect communication style, an individual tries to protect himself and save the face of receiver.

Assertive people believe that they have chosen the best ethical style of communication for facing conflict. They deal with conflict by communicating their thoughts, feelings and needs. However, they do not judge or dictate the receivers. It maintains the self-respect of themselves and also of those with whom they interact. Assertive communicators may not always get what they want, but they get the chance to assert themselves.

F. Ethical Implications of Messages

1. Multiple Ethical Implications

Every culture has various moral values and standards. As members of these cultures every person's mode of conduct is expected to be based on high moral standards. Our moral responsibilities are the social responsibilities. The speeches and communicative behaviour on mass media can influence the thinking and actions of millions of people. The art of rhetoric can be used either for good or bad ends. Therefore, ethical implications of the message must be considered carefully. The intentions and strategies for influencing the people must be analysed. The role, responsibilities, motives and tactics of the sender must be understood from ethical point of view. Our view of ethics is greatly influenced by our cultures. Therefore, cultural differences in perceiving ethical behaviours must be understood.

The motives behind giving the messages must be examined. An ethical communicator begins by examining his or her motives behind the message. Audience's or reader's perception of the message giver greatly hinders or assists the interpretation and understanding of the message. Prestige and moral standing of the communicator promotes acceptance of the message content.

The ideas and the thoughts of a communicator can be of benefit to others or it can be of benefit to himself only. Therefore, the ideas advocated by him must be reasonable and responsible from the receiver's point of view.

Therefore, all the sides of an idea or an issue must be investigated, analysed and examined thoroughly. Such an exercise is an important part of effective and ethical speech or writing. It is necessary to be morally thoughtful about what a person is going to talk or write to influence the thinking and action of the others.

It is not only the content of the topic but also the manner in which it is presented has to be examined. Message needs to be presented in an accurate and ethical manner. Not being accurate, complete and precise can mean imparting half-truths, outdated information and invalid statements. It can also mean withholding essential information from the audience and readers. The message should not only be accurate, but it should also be easily understood by the receivers. It is unethical to intentionally use the language which is not understood by the audience.

2. Ethics of Simplicity and Clarity

Using language that is purposefully obscure, abstract and complicated in order to keep the audience uninformed about some ideas or facts is an unethical communication. Speakers have to make their speeches simple and easy enough so that audience may pay attention with interest, understand the message clearly and remember it. Speakers who are generally experts on their topics, have to remember that they have to limit the amount of information which is presented before the audience at each sitting. Too much of information can lead to lack of attention, lack of clarity, message overload, anxiety, and a mental burden.

Simplicity in communication also results from the clarity of message organisation and its structure. An introduction that previews the ideas and limitations of the message to certain main points; the division, coordination and order of those points; and gives review of those ideas in the conclusion, helps the audience to understand, appreciate and remember the message. To enhance understanding, the speakers can use the familiar information to increase the understanding of the unfamiliar details in the message. Similarly, simple information can be used at the beginning to build up the understanding of complex information which is presented later. Simply repeating ideas in the same words might bore the audience, but it is necessary to remember that audience members are likely to understand the information which is repeated more than once. Use of simple and precise vocabulary, simple syntax, short sentences—enhances the simplicity and clarity of message.

3. Use of Insensitive and Derogatory Language

Our message influence other people and create change, therefore, we must follow some ethical guidelines in selecting our words and phrases. Our patterns of expression interfere with the effectiveness of communication. Inadvertently chosen words and phrases can divert the attention of the readers and listeners from the main ideas in the message. Certain words and phrases can lower the credibility of the message giver.

Some words and phrases are specific to a profession but these words are not common to the general audience. Therefore, speakers must avoid such technical 'jargon' language. Similarly meaningless and overworked terms, overuse of superlatives and exaggerations, bombardment of empty words like 'super special', 'extra special', 'magnificent and really great' etc. deserve little attention.

Some words that appear refreshingly novel for a time, but overuse of these words make them common place. These common place words, phrases and ideas are the clichés that lack originality and interest. They are used so much that they are no longer meaningful, interesting and effective. 'world-class', 'bottom line', 'time frame', 'state of the art', are the examples of such overused expressions.

Slang words and expressions are informal and are used by the people who know each other very well, but slang lowers a speakers status. Informal messages, derogatory language and taboo words indicate insensitivity of a speaker and his verbal bigotry. It is unethical to use the hateful and derogatory language. Words must be used carefully, correctly and ethically.

4. Message Evaluation: A Cautious Procedure

The purpose of the speech must be ethical, clear and easily recognisable. The subject must be worthy of time and energy of the listeners. The values stressed must be justified. The speaker must be realistic, objective and fair to the subject and the audience. He must take into consideration the age, sex, education, attitude and culture of the audience. His speech must be original and creative. He should separate facts from fiction. His personal opinions must not be confused with the facts and evidences. He should not make exaggerated and extravagant claims. His illustrations, statistics, analogies, examples and testimonies must meet the tests of evidence. The message must be well organised and arranged in logical order. The major parts of the message must be well balanced. The beginning of message must offer the preview of the rest of the message, and the end must sum up all the key points together. His language must be comprehensible, simple and clear. He should avoid slang, clichés, ambiguity, vagueness, and poor grammar. He must show genuine concern for the welfare of the audience. He has to demonstrate mastery over the subject. His words, actions, appearance and behaviour must contribute to his credibility and trustworthiness. He should not make personal attacks on the members of opposing groups. He must be ethical in his overall treatment of the subject.

Every word and idea of the communicator does something to the thoughts, feelings and attitudes of the receivers. Therefore, after having comprehended the message, receivers have to decide if they can use or reject it. The need for understanding and careful analysis of what we have heard or read should be obvious. The receivers have to work along with the senders of the messages at gaining meaning. It is often a great temptation to stop reading or listening when it requires efforts. We are continually bothered and constantly besieged by communicators to feel, think, agree and act in one way or another. Do we have to be an easy prey for the hucksters who try to sell useless or worthless things in a dishonest and aggressive manner, or for the propagandist who tries to persuade the people to support a particular idea or group by giving inaccurate information? We must think critically and evaluate cautiously all the messages of those who attempt to influence and control our behaviour.

EXERCISES

1. Explain the meaning and characteristics of ethical communication.
2. Describe various issues covered in ethical communication.
3. Elucidate on ethical use of language.
4. "Ethical communication depends on ethical use of language". Discuss.
5. Write a detailed note on the ethics of persuasive communication.
6. Comment on the difference between ethical and unethical persuasion.
7. Explain ethical communication in conflicting situations.
8. Discuss communication styles in conflicting situations.
9. What are the ethical implications of the messages exchanged in communication?
10. Write short notes on the following:
    (i) Honouring the Audience
    (ii) Deliberate Misleading
    (iii) Presenting Multiple Identities
    (iv) Ethical Persuasion
    (v) Ethical Use of Language
    (vi) Hidden Agenda
    (vii) Persuasion with Dishonest Motives
    (viii) Ethical Adaptation in Persuasion
    (ix) Communication Styles in Conflict
    (x) Conflict of Values and Loyalties
    (xi) Multiple Ethical Implications of Message
    (xii) Ethics of Simplicity and Clarity
    (xiii) Insensitive and Derogatory Language
    (xiv) Message Evaluation

9
Ethics in Global Business

"What we are trying relentlessly to do is to get that 'small company soul' and 'small company speed' inside our big company body"
—Jack Welch

Learning Objectives

A. Cross-Cultural Diversity
   1. The Concept
   2. Managing Cultural Diversity
   3. Self-Reference Criterion
   4. Cross-Cultural Reciprocity

B. Ethical Issues in Global Business
   1. Unethical Practices of Multinational Corporations
   2. Human Rights and Labour Standards
   3. Employee Privacy
   4. 'Outsourcing' in Global Business
   5. Migrant and Immigrant Workers
   6. Discrimination in Employment
   7. Corruption in Global Business
   8. Absolutism and Relativism
   9. Threats of MNC's Size and Power

C. Protective Measures and Mechanisms
   1. Shifting Exploitation Must Stop
   2. Need of Providing Safety Net
   3. Free Movement of Labour and Capital
   4. Responsibility Towards Environment Protection
   5. Regulation of Competition
   6. Benefits of Natural Resources
   7. Product Safety and Work Safety

8. Supporting UNGC Principles
9. Developing Human Resources of Host-Countries
10. Entrance Through Joint Ventures
11. Transfer of Technology
12. Harmful Products and Strict Liability
13. Tools to Infuse Prosperity in the Host Countries
14. Respect for the Rights of the Employees
15. Non-Involvement in Politics and Corruption
16. Helping the Governments and Communities

A. Cross-Cultural Diversity

1. The Concept

Many business organisations have dynamic environment of cultural diversity. People of one country have some common cultural characteristics that differentiate them from the people of other countries. These differences include the national origin, language, values beliefs, religion, social norms, customs, traditions, codes of behaviour, life styles, ideals, etc. When employees belonging to various cultural backgrounds work together in an organisation, it consist global cultural diversity or international diversity.

To manage successfully in an environment of global business, manager has to understand the common cultural characteristics of a particular country. It is a major challenge faced by the managements of global business organisations. Awareness of certain cultural characteristics of the people in other countries can reduce the misunderstanding and misinterpretations of words and concepts due to cultural connotative differences. Multinational companies, exporters, diplomats, tourists, sportsmen, etc. who work in diverse cultures, have to understand the cultural diversity which creates problems of cross-cultural differences in communication. In various areas of global business like global marketing practices, business negotiations, HRM, advertising, industrial relations, organisation structure, etc., managers are expected to be more dynamic today in managing their people and cultural diversity.

Different cultures have slightly different meanings of the concepts like trust, rights, equality, freedom, etc. and accordingly they place different emphasis on them. Americans give more importance to 'rights' than to 'equality'. China is often criticised for human rights violation. Japanese are accused for showing favouritism to Japanese firms. Japanese answer that they show loyalty to the companies in long established relationships. British protect their privacy. In India, asking personal questions is a sign of showing interest. In Europe and America, women in business have equal rights and opportunities, but women in middle east and other Asian countries still fight for equal rights and opportunities. Companies in Japan and Korea are closely linked with each other. They come to help each other in times of difficulty. Japanese 'Keiretsu', Korean 'chaebol', and Chinese 'guanxi' are the business societies or business groups which are built on long-term relationships.

A distinctive Japanese business practice is seen in 'Kaizen' or 'continuous improvement'. Everyone in the organisation has a responsibility of making continuous improvement in order to produce improved products at lower costs. It depends on vigorous group efforts, strong group commitment with a determination to benefit the whole organisation in which each employee's efforts are recognised and rewarded.

2. Managing Cultural Diversity

Managing cultural diversity properly is a challenging task. Multinational companies develop their global strategies to take advantage of cultural diversity in their organisations. They train and educate their employees for mind set and attitude formation about diversity. Managers are trained to enhance their understanding of cross-cultural interaction skills and global strategies in order to identify business opportunities and to use them. They are trained to understand the global perspectives of world market environment. Organisational culture is developed for valuing differences. Policies are developed regarding equal opportunities, sexual harassment and grievance systems. International business negotiation strategies are developed. Emphasis is given on win-win solutions, and on creating open and trusting business relationships.

To manage the cultural diversity, management avoids the policy of discrimination so that all the employees get the benefits of their performance, experience, skills, ideas and competencies. Discriminatory practices in recruitment, employee training and career development, etc. are avoided. Managers are prepared for foreign assignments through cross-cultural training. Ethics programmes are used to understand and acknowledge different value systems. Prejudicial mind set against other cultural group is eliminated. Human resource management systems are made bias-free.

3. Self-Reference Criterion

In business, 'self-reference criterion' is the idea in which business people perceive that "we" differ from "them". They perceive that other business cultures have different standards and modes of operation. They unconsciously refer to their own cultural values, customs, beliefs, knowledge and experiences when they confront the business situations. It also implies the ethical superiority in which "we" are considered superior to "them".

Ethical issues that arise in the global business situations differ from the domestic business situations. Ethical standards, values, norms and customs differ from company to company and country to country. Therefore, global issues in business ethics are often related to the cultural differences. Culture includes all the tangible and intangible concepts, values, laws, language, religion, technology, education, social and economic organisations, institutions, associations, education, politics, environment and traditions of the people in a particular region or country.

Each nation or region has a distinctive culture that consequently results in distinctive system of ethical standards. In all the business interactions and transactions they refer to these standards or criterion for decision-making. Therefore, while transacting business at global level, businessmen often encounter the ethical standards, values, criteria and ideas that are divergent from their own. Cultural differences also include language and semantic differences. Problems of translation add to the difficulties for the businessmen to communicate with the businessmen belonging to other linguistic community.

4. Cross-Cultural Reciprocity

Pluralism and cross-cultural differences worldwide often results in the conflict of standards. Therefore, both the business parties have to reconsider their policies and standards in the light of broader interest and desirable global relations. Cross-cultural communication can lead to a better understanding of the legal systems which helps to resolve the disputes between the business organisations. It can lead to a better understanding of common problems and systems of justice. Cross-cultural consensus is developed on many ethical issues. Racism, slavery, child labour, apartheid are universally considered as unjust.

However, ethical judgments are results of a country's own concept of justice. One society's point of view or ethical perceptions can lead to criticise or condemn the varying ethical concepts and practices of the other societies. Yet the business people of one country are not expected to directly interfere with the ethical practices followed internally by the business people of the other country. In different societies different systems can be just. Justice does not require that all the countries should adopt the view of justice of a particular country which is economically or politically stronger than the others. There is no single best ethical system which gives an ideal combination of ethical beliefs, values and practices for all the societies of the world.

For justice in international business transactions, a business transaction can be considered as just only if all those who are affected by it freely and reciprocally agree to it as just. For ethical progress in global arena, reciprocity, negotiation and compromise are the key words.

B. Ethical Issues in Global Business

1. Unethical Practices of Multinational Corporations

Multinational companies are often criticised for the reason that they operate their business to benefit themselves and to serve their own interests. They operate in several countries through their subsidiaries and branches. Industrialised countries like US, Japan, UK, Germany can easily control the foreign firms, but less developed or developing countries like Brazil, India, etc. are unable to do so. It is simply because some of the multinational companies have greater sales than the host country's GDP. There is no effective system to prevent the multinational companies from forming cartels. Cartels are the associations of manufacturers or suppliers that are formed to maintain high prices and restrict competition. They conspire to limit the production, create false shortages and drive up the prices.

Multinational companies operate internationally. Therefore, any government cannot check their books of account worldwide to prevent their unethical practices. Some multinationals support the authoritarian and oppressive governments that serve their interests. They use toxic and highly poisonous raw material. Union Carbide was responsible for killing several thousand people due to leakage of poisonous gas at Bhopal. Multinationals are also engaged in marketing dangerous drugs, hazardous produces and unsafe equipments. They exploit the natural resources, disrupt the culture, pollute the environment, compete unfairly, reap exorbitant profits, and impoverish the host countries.

2. Human Rights and Labour Standards

Concern about human rights abuses by multinational corporations is a major ethical issue. Multinationals have the obligation to respect the human rights of the workers, suppliers, customers, local communities, etc. Most of these rights are listed in the United Nation's 'Universal Declaration on Human Rights'. It includes the right to employment under fair and favourable conditions, right to an adequate standard of living, right to just wages and right to restrict multinationals in various ways to prohibit gross exploitation.

Companies often make some short-term decisions to boost profitability. They make opportunistic use of child labour, payment of lower wages, abuses against foreign workers in foreign factories, discrimination of minorities and women, sexual harassment, and abuses of other employee rights. Multinationals may not directly violate the rights of the employees and other stakeholders. But, they may indirectly violate the human rights by using labour contractors or suppliers or joint partners who violate the human rights. Multinationals have an obligation to ensure that these contractors, partners or suppliers do not violate the human rights. Multinationals also operate in the countries in which government violates the human rights. In such countries, multinationals may not be able to bring about change in government policies, but they should ensure that they will not violate the human rights in direct or indirect manner.

United Nations has developed 'Global Compact' which expects the companies to adhere to the human rights and labour standards. Global corporations now support and advance the principles of UN's Global Compact in their business abroad. They commit themselves to the ten principles of human rights, environment protection, labour standards and anti-corruption as a part of their corporate culture and business operations. Amnesty International has established Human

Rights Guidelines for companies. These guidelines are the principles concerning the link between business and human rights.

Vast amount of personal information is collected by government agencies and businesses in recent years. Employees would scarcely intrude openly into the private lives of the employees, but they use less obvious ways of acquiring such information. New technologies have enabled employees to watch more closely than ever before. Hidden cameras and microphones can also be used to observe the employees and their movements without their knowledge.

3. Employee Privacy

Employee privacy refers to protecting an employee's private life from intrusive actions. AIDS testing, genetic testing, drug testing, and information technology are the major areas in which such intrusive actions take place. Technological advances and use of electronic communication in the companies provide the employers with opportunities to monitor the employees and to obtain data about them. Companies monitor the e-mails and faxes of the employees. They track the web-use of the employees. They use the video cameras to keep an eye on employee's movements and activities. Phone calls of employees are also recorded.

Drug testing assumes legitimacy if the drug testing is relevant to the job, but if the information obtained from drug testing is irrelevant to the job of the employee, it is considered as invading the private life of the employee. Genetic testing helps the company to identify and delete the employees who are susceptible to certain genetically based-illness. It can also be used to discriminate against some employees.

4. 'Outsourcing' in Global Business

The issue of outsourcing work in international business has become a contentious subject. Multinational companies are outsourcing their work to the countries where they can find cheaper labour. It is economically and ethically acceptable to many people. But when a company moves its factory from one place to another, many workers lose their jobs and towns lose their part of financial footing and support. When company moves from one country to another to lower the labour costs and enhance profitability, many people criticise such action as unethical, because the country loses industry, jobs and national tax base. It harms the country by adding to the unemployment, but on the other hand, it creates jobs for the people in the host country where unemployment is a serious problem.

In the ethical context, evaluation of outsourcing in international business should be in the broadest possible perspectives. It is necessary to consider all those people who are affected by the action. If it serves the interests of both the countries and helps them to prosper, it is definitely an ethical action. Recently, the fear of the people in industrialised countries has increased because high-tech jobs are exported to the countries like China and India, which has resulted in substantial increase in the computer related jobs in these countries. Accounting and other white-collar work has also been outsourced to these countries. It is often argued that the key ingredient in determining the fair wages is the market. From utilitarian point of view outsourcing seems to do more good for larger number of people.

5. *Migrant and Immigrant Workers*

'International Convention on the Protection of the Rights of All Migrant Workers and Members of the Families' was established by United Nation in 1990. It defines a migrant worker as 'a person who is to be engaged, is engaged or has been engaged in a remunerated activity, in a state of which he or she is not a national'. Migrant workers are workers who move from one place or country to another to find work. They often move with their families, from one job to the next, as they have no permanent home. Primarily they do the agricultural and seasonal works.

Migrant's work is manual and the pay is poor. They usually do not get the safeguards which the organised and permanent workers get from the employers. They do not get the health insurance or retirement benefits. Their annual earnings are usually below the poverty line. If their children go to school, it is sporadic and irregular.

Like migrant workers illegal immigrants also work on farms, construction work and in other areas. They are hired in cash without any records. Immigrants come because they find work. Therefore, business houses, individuals and corporations who employ them are also involved in illegal immigration. It is necessary that all the worker's rights must be respected. The employers must abide the minimum wage law, and all the workers must get the benefits they deserve. Migrants and immigrated workers must not be exploited by the employers. Their children must get the educational and health facilities. They should not be alienated.

6. Discrimination in Employment

Discriminating on the basis of sex, age, race, religion or disabilities, in hiring, firing and promotion of the employees, is a global ethical issue. Though law prohibits practices of discrimination, it is still a reality in the world. Workers who are discriminated on various grounds, get least desired and lowest-paying jobs. They are not given citizenship even though they live in that country for decades. They do not get promotion in the job. They face difficulties in getting the job. They do not get job-security. In some countries women are positively discouraged from seeking employment or entrepreneurship.

If such discrimination is curbed, it not only helps the business to get specific benefits, but it can significantly help to reduce employee turnover. It can further reduce the costs of hiring and training the new employees. It can raise the morale of the workers, and improve the productivity. Company can enjoy the goodwill and support of the people. It enhances the company's overall reputation. Therefore, companies have to discourage, prevent and curb the discriminatory acts in employment, medical care, housing, education and other areas of public life.

Generally, discrimination in employment arises from the employer's decisions about hiring, pay, fringe benefits, promotion and the other terms and conditions regarding employee's economic interests. If these decisions are reasonably job-related, they can be just, but if they are made on the basis of race, caste, religion, sex, age, nationality, physical disabilities, they are ethically unjust.

7. Corruption in Global Business

In global business transactions, multinationals face a common and controversial issue of bribery which is universally condemned. It induces foreign official to do an act which is unlawful and dishonest to his official duty. It is a payment made with an intention to corrupt that official. The payment is made with an intention to cause that official to betray a trust and to be disloyal in his performance of the duties. For example, a government official who has to make decisions regarding the purchase of warship according to a given criteria, is influenced to purchase a warship built by a particular multinational company by bribing him. However, there are certain kinds of payments which are legally permitted. These are called 'facilitating payments' or 'grease payments; which are made to expedite the routine government action by lubricating the rusty machinery of government services. These payments do not coax anyone to violate a trust. Entertaining a foreign purchase official in the course of doing business is considered as an expenditure for legitimate expenses. But, if a government official is violating a duty or trust and a multinational agency is inducing him for such violation by offering bribe, it is a legal offence, that requires a particular punishment. A systematic and widespread corruption through foreign bribery inhibits the growth of fair global market, because bribery does not give open access to all competitors on equal terms.

8. Absolutism and Relativism

There are two answers to an ethical question, 'When in Rome, do what?' An absolutist answers that business ought to be conducted in the same way all over the world, an absolutist does as he would do it at home. On the other hand, a relativist holds the view that business ought to be conducted abroad according to what is legally and morally accepted in a given country. He answers, 'When in Rome, do as the Romans do'.

Moral absolutist respects the eternal moral values and principles that are applicable at all times and at all the places in the world. He claims that all moral norms are always and everywhere the same. An alternative to absolutism is relativisim which claims that morality is not eternal or universal. Multinational companies cannot always depart from the ethical standards of their country in doing business abroad. Similarly, if the country of a multinational company permits violations of human rights, bribery, workers working in unhealthy and unsafe working conditions, exploitative wages, racial discrimination, sexual discrimination, etc. it need not, and cannot follow the same unethical practices in its business abroad. If a foreign country is significantly different, then the ethical standards of business which are appropriate at home, are not possibly applicable there. For example, pharmaceutical companies in the developed countries adopted double standards in promoting drugs in developing countries. They give more indications for use and fewer warnings about the side effects of their drugs.

9. Threats of MNC's Size and Power

Multinational companies transfer jobs overseas where employees are paid lower wages. They also use the labour saving devices that increase the unemployment. They misuse and misallocate the scarce resources. They create gap between the rich and the poor countries. Their size and financial power enables them to exploit both human and natural resources. They pay low prices for the minerals, oil, timber and other natural resources which are purchased by them in large quantity. Then, they sell the products made from those resources at much higher prices. They exploit the labour markets of the host countries by paying inadequate wages. Sometimes, they pay higher wages than the local employers can afford to pay. But as compared to the wages in their own country, the wages paid by them are much lower in the host country. The most productive and skilled workers in the host country leave their jobs in the local businesses and go to work for the multinationals. Multinational corporations can borrow money from the local financial institutions in huge volume. Thereafter, very little is left for the local institutions and organisations to borrow from the financial market. Multinational corporations use the advanced and high-productivity technologies. The local business houses cannot afford to use such technologies. Due to advanced technology, multinationals require fewer employees than the local businesses to produce the same product. As a result of it, multinationals are more productive and more competitive. They earn more profits and they can afford to pay higher wages to their workers than the local firms. Some multinational corporations have strong ethical values. They try to be good global citizens.

C. Protective Measures and Mechanisms

1. Shifting Exploitation Must Stop

The economic interests of the nations are influenced not only by the economic activities in their own country, but also by what goes on in the global economic arena. During colonial period, developed countries could reduce the level of exploitation of their own workers by shifting those aspects of exploitation to their colonies. Today advanced industrialised and capitalistic nations of the world are able to flourish because their MNCs exploit the resources and people of the developing and underdeveloped countries of the world. In order to face this challenge, the governments of nations involved in international economic interactions have to take measures which are necessary to keep competition fair, to protect the interests of the workers and consumers, to protect the natural resources, especially of the poor and developing countries, for the future generations, and to provide safety net to those who without their own fault cannot compete with the mighty multinational corporations of the developed countries.

2. Need of Providing Safety Net

Moral obligations should not stop at the borders of the developed nations. A nation does not have a moral society if it does not respond to the needs of the developing and underdeveloped economies, and lets the people of poor countries die of starvation. Some countries and people have so much wealth and use so much of the world's natural resources, that the others are left with so little. There is no system of international redistribution of wealth like that within an individual country—the wealthy are taxed for equal distribution of nation's income. There is a need of such a system at international level. The framework of globally acceptable international business should be based on various laws, conventions, shared values, and norms of formal and informal organisations and mechanisms like legal systems, social systems, political systems, environmental groups, consumer forums, labour unions, etc. But at international level, such effective institutions are absent. Though international law covers some areas of conducting business, it is not always enforceable against powerful nations. UN and its commissions have no power to enforce its guidelines governing international trade and commerce. There is no international police force which is capable of enforcing even agreed-upon rules that govern the trade between nations. Multinational corporations operate on the agreements, goodwill and moral persuasion.

3. Free Movement of Labour and Capital

Both Capital and labour must be able to move freely in a free-market system. But in the international business, though now-a-days capital moves relatively freely, labour does not move with that ease from one country to the another. National borders are becoming tighter and the migration of labour is restricted. Labour is cheaper and plentiful in the underdeveloped and developing countries, because workers cannot move to the other countries to seek job. On the other hand, multinational companies of the developed countries move the work to the poor countries where work is considerably cheaper. If the developed countries advocate free market economy, they should allow the workers to move freely all over the globe.

Multinational corporations have to follow the ethical codes to guide their business activities. They have to adopt a corporate mission statement and implement the voluntary codes of conduct. They should uphold the universal standards of business ethics and values.

4. Responsibility Towards Environment Protection

MNC's business activities must show that they are responsible towards environmental protection. There are numerous examples that have shown that MNCs have not followed safety regulations and have not shown concern for public health and environment protection. They should not denude forests, strip-mine the land and pour toxic substances into rivers and streams.

MNCs should use natural resources of the host country in an appropriate manner. They should not dump toxic waste in the poor countries. Their producing centres should not produce carbon-dioxide which causes global warming.

5. Regulation of Competition

Multinational Company (MNCs) should not drive out competition from the market of the host country.

Multinational corporations give rise to huge merged conglomerations that reduce competition and free enterprise. They raise capital in host countries but export the profits. They erode the traditional cultures, limit the wages of the workers, exploit the natural resources of the host countries, and ultimately challenge their sovereignty. Therefore, competition must be regulated to ensure healthy competition between companies for the ultimate benefit of consumers and the economy.

6. Benefits of Natural Resources

MNCs should use the natural resources for the production of goods which are meant for the domestic consumption in the host country. If these products are exported, they should provide the benefit of foreign exchange to the host country.

7. Product Safety and Work Safety

MNCs should follow the standards of product safety and work safety. Some MNCs sell certain harmful products in other countries, but they do not sell such products in their advanced industrialised nations. For example in US, cigarette sales is declining due to stricter tobacco regulations. But these tobacco companies have increased their efforts to market cigarettes and other tobacco products in other countries, especially in underdeveloped and developing countries. Nestle Corporation had aggressively promoted its infant formula in 1970s. In its marketing strategy, mothers were discouraged from breast feeding by portraying the practice as primitive. Bhopal Gas Tragedy was a result of Union Carbide's utter neglect of safety standards.

8. Supporting UNGC Principles

MNCs should support the United Nation's Global Compact principles in their business abroad. They should commit to the principles of human rights, anti-corruption, labour standards and environment protection in their day-to-day operations. UNGC is UN's initiative to encourage business worldwide to adopt sustainable and socially responsible policies, and to report on their implementation. It is the world's largest corporate citizenship initiative with two objectives: (1) to mainstream the ten principles in business activities around the world, and (2) to catalyse actions in support of broader UN goals such as the 'Millennium Development Goals (MDGs).

9. Developing Human Resources of Host Countries

MNCs should develop the human resources and managers of host countries, especially of the developing countries. Knowledge and skills are the key sources of competitive advantage. The HRD professionals of the MNCs have to demonstrate their ability to 'deliver value' by developing the managers and human resources of the host countries. MNCs should not merely function as a channel for information and knowledge, but they should contribute to the development of the labour force in the host countries by developing learning abilities, professional skills, and various competencies in the workforce of the host countries. Training programmes should be conducted for the improvement of local managerial (personnel) skills and capabilities.

10. Entrance Through Joint Ventures

MNCs should enter the host country mostly through joint ventures with local business firms. Joint venture is a business agreement in which the parties agree to develop a new entity and new assets by contributing equity. They exercise control over the business and consequently share revenues, expenses and assets.

11. Transfer of Technology

MNCs should transfer technology to the developing countries. Transfer of technology is closely related to knowledge transfer. It is the process of transferring knowledge, skills, technologies, manufacturing methods, manufacturing samples and facilities among the governments and other institutions. It ensures scientific and technological developments of the users who can further develop and exploit the technology into new processes, products, services and other applications.

12. Harmful Products and Strict Liability

MNCs should avoid marketing products which are harmful to the health of the people in the host countries. Many products can injure and even kill the people. Therefore, manufacturers have a responsibility to ensure that a product is safe before it is placed and

muster rolls of the establishment, and (iii) he should have completed not less than one year of continuous service under the employer.

The employers have certain duties in regard to the lay-off. The lay-off must be for the reasons specified in Section e (kkk). The employer must maintain a muster roll of workmen and to provide for the making of entries therein by workmen who may present themselves for work at the establishment of the appointed time during normal working hours, notwithstanding that the workmen have been laid off. The compensation for lay-off must be according to the Section 25C of the Industrial Disputes Act.

The temporary lay-offs occur mainly because of slack periods when the decreased workloads do not require a large work force. Workers are recalled when the work resumes to its normal levels. It is a cost-cutting measure for the management, but it turns workers into cyclical employees. Business organisations make adjustment to variations in market demand for its products through temporary lay-offs.

When a firm goes out of business or transfers to a distant location, lay-offs can be permanent. Blue-collar employees sometimes receive offers to transfer to another plant of the same organisation. However, older employees are typically reluctant to move away to some other locations. Lay-offs involve loss of income, therefore the employees and trade unions are prone to restrict the firm's freedom of decision regarding lay-off.

EXERCISES

1. What is the role of ethical human resource manager?
2. Write a detailed note on ethics in human resource management.
3. How does 'Reward System' reinforce ethical behaviour of the employee?
4. Explain the ethical dilemmas in recruitment and selection.
5. Discuss the ethical issues in performance appraisal.
6. Write a note on prejudicial attitudes and job discrimination in business organisations.
7. Express your views about the protection of privacy of the employees.
8. Comment on the unwarranted and intrusive actions of HR managers in the private life of the employees.
9. What are the advantages and disadvantages of "Whistle Blowing"?

10. Explain the ethical responsibilities of HR managers regarding health and safety of the employees.
11. Write a note on the significance of fair and just disciplinary system in business organisation.
12. Discuss the ethical aspects of 'employee dismissal' and 'lay-offs'.
13. Write short notes on the following:
    (a) Job Discrimination
    (b) Privacy of Employees
    (c) AIDS and HIV Testing
    (d) Drug Testing
    (e) Whistle Blowing
    (f) Lay-offs of Employees
    (g) Reward System
    (h) Disciplinary System
    (i) Ethical Dilemmas in HRM

11

Ethics in Marketing

"It is not necessary to advertise food to hungry people, fuel to cold people, or houses to the homeless".—J.K. Galbraith

Learning Objectives

A. Introduction
B. Ethical Issues of Marketing Personnel
C. Ethical Challenges for Marketers
D. Unethical Market Exclusion
E. Unethical Practices in Advertisements
F. Deception in Marketing
G. Marketing to Children
H. Marketing to Minorities
I. Portrayal Women in Marketing
J. Unethical Behaviour of Salespersons
K. Unethical Practices in Marketing Mix
  1. Product and Services
  2. Price
  3. Promotion/Advertising
  4. Discrimination
  5. Packing
L. Norms and Values for Ethical Marketing
M. Dave Kahle's Ethical Guidelines

A. Introduction

A marketer can uphold the honour and dignity of marketing profession by being honest to the employees, customers, suppliers, distributors and the public in general. However, marketing ethics refers especially to the area of interaction of a business firm with the customers. Firm's ethical behaviour in marketing determines whether the customers will stay with the firm or it will lose them. When customers decide that they can no longer trust the organisation, they will not support it by purchasing its products or by investing in its stock. Therefore, the business organisations have to build and maintain the trust of the customers by conducting ethical transactions.

Marketing professionals have to decide appropriateness of their actions on the base of ethical considerations, rather than merely on the legal guidelines. They have to consider customer's expectations from the marketing firm. Marketers have to be accountable and responsive to the customers by providing better 'quality' goods at reasonable 'price' with 'courtesy' and timeliness. They should not create artificial scarcities. They should not practice discriminatory pricing and make false claims about their products. They have to recognise consumer's right of speedy redressal of grievances. They have to be sensitive to the needs of society, and should respect the right of public information on activities of the organisation.

Business ethics examines various ethical rules, principles and problems within business context. It also deals with obligations, special duties and responsibilities that apply to the people who are engaged in business. Whereas, marketing ethics is concerned with the issues and problems in the domain of marketing. Marketing professionals are often singled out for unethical advertising, sale on promotion of products and services that damages the environment, deceptive advertisements, promotion of shoddy products etc. Therefore, to win and maintain customer's relationship and to fulfil social responsibility, marketing has to be sensitive to the needs of the society.

B. Ethical Issues of Marketing Personnel

Marketing managers have ethical responsibilities. He has to guide his subordinates in ethical issues and help them to resolve their ethical dilemmas. His failure in shouldering this responsibility can result in the fall of performance of the salespersons. Its long term implications for the organisation can be negative image of the organisation in the market, legal hassles in the court of law, customer dissatisfaction, lost customers, conflict between sales personnel and management, and ultimate decrease in the sales and profit. The pressure which the marketing managers exert on their sales persons to achieve the sales targets must not go beyond the limit because it forces them to act unethically. Marketing manager is expected to inform the salespersons about their career options in the organisation.

When customers complain or raise issues regarding the ethics of personnel, the marketing manager should not blindly support his subordinates. He should provide training and develop the necessary skills in the sales personnel so that they behave ethically and politely with the customers. Salespeople often do not provide adequate information about the products or services to the customers. They try to sell high-priced products to obtain higher commission, even though there may be other products available in the market at a lower cost. Sales people must be guided to be ethical in their sales approach. Offering gifts to the customers is a practice followed by many companies to build up the customer loyalty. However, sales persons often offer gifts to their prospects so that they can be converted into customers.

To obtain information about competitions, the salespeople should not be encouraged to follow the unfair and unethical means. The sales manager should make efforts to ensure that healthy competition prevails in the market. He and his subordinates should not disclose information about the company's pricing, credit terms, lines of business etc. to the competitors. Sales manager should not encourage his subordinates to give or receive gifts from suppliers and dealers of the company. He and his subordinates should not communicate information about company's pricing, credit terms, lines of business etc. to the suppliers and the dealers. He should follow ethical practices in all the matters of company. He should not quit the company to join a competitive firm.

C. Ethical Challenges for Marketers

There are divergent interest groups that pose variety of ethical challenges for the marketers. Employers expect them to raise sales and profits. Suppliers expect continued business, society expects them to be honest and responsible, and the customers expect to satisfy their needs. Most firms have a code of ethics for their employees to address the ethical issues. But the ethical failures take place due to conflicting goals. To deal with the ethical challenges, organisations communicate their ethical standards and expectations to the employees. They appoint the ethics officer to respond to the inquiries and complaints. They reward and appreciate the ethical behaviours and decisively deal with the unethical behaviour.

Building public's trust and creating a strong ethical climate within a marketing firm is a real challenge before the marketers. Marketing and sales professionals often rank poorly in the ratings of the most trusted professions. There are marketers who give importance to the long term trust of their customers. For them this low ranking is disappointing.

There is a popularist anti-marketing stance which holds the view that any kind of marketing is inherently evil. This view is based on the argument that marketing infringes upon the buyer's right to self-determination. Beside damaging the personal autonomy of the buyers, marketing causes harm to competitors, manipulates social values, promotes consumerism and over focuses on materialism.

D. Unethical Market Exclusion

'Selective marketing' or excluding the potential customers from the market, is used to discourage the demand from undesirable market sectors. Such disenfranchisement of an undesirable market sector is an unethical practice. An example of an unethical market exclusion is the pharmaceutical industry's exclusion of developing countries from AIDS drugs. There are the examples of marketing which unethically target the elderly. It is believed that the elderly hold a disproportionate amount of the world's wealth, and therefore, they are the target of financial exploitation. Children are a lucrative market. They are not able to resist or understand the marketing tactics at younger ages. "Cheap Loan" providers and "Gold Loan" providers are also seen as loan sharks who unethically exploit the economically disadvantaged people, especially in the developing countries.

Markets are segmented before they are targeted. Most widely used factors for segmentation are the demographic factors like age, race, sex, religion, education, nationality, location, etc. To delineate more homogeneous or smaller market segments, composite classification systems are brought into play, for example, 'family life cycle' and 'social class'. Family life cycle combines marital status, presence of children, age of children and age of parents to form different segments.

The number of 'people within each age group', or 'the people at various levels of income', or 'the people who have obtained education at various levels', or 'the people belonging to various occupational groups', or 'the people belonging to various caste communities, racial communities, and religious communities', or 'the people belonging to various national and cultural communities', or 'the people associated with given territory or location', or 'the people belonging to different stages of family life cycle' (bachelor stage, newly married couple with no children, married couple with youngest child under six years, married couple with youngest child above six years, older married couple with .... etc.), 'the people belonging to various social classes' etc. forms the basic data which is used to isolate the segment and then to 'target' it with various marketing strategies.

E. Unethical Practices in Advertisements

False advertising not only offends against morality but also against the law. In 1950s, tobacco was advertised as promoting health. Sexual innuendo is often found in the content of the advertising. It is also regarded as a form of sexual harassment. Violence is used especially for children's advertising and advertising which is likely to be seen by the children. The advertising of condoms is acceptable in the interest of AIDS-prevention, but by some people these advertisements are regarded as promoting promiscuity. In negative advertising, the advertisers highlight the disadvantages of the products of their competitors rather than the advantages of their own products. When approaches are unsolicited, direct marketing with TV commercials, direct-mail etc., push the borders of ethics. Anti-competitive practices, planned obsolescence, pyramid scheme, vender lock-in/vendor lock-out, viral marketing/guerrilla marketing, 'embrace, extend, extinguish', 'search engine optimisation', spamdexing, spyware/adware, etc. are the known unethical or controversial marketing strategies.

Unethical advertisements conceal some important information that can affect human life. Degrading rival products or spreading negative publicity of the competitors through ad-war, or giving misleading information about the products and services etc. are the unethical practices in advertising. Some advertisements give false promises such as warrantee or guarantee with no intention to perform. Advertisements which make exaggerated or tall claims are unethical. For example, medicines, especially creams for fair skin. Erratic or sensuous advertisements with obscene, immoral sex projections are ethically unacceptable. Ethical advertisements are those which keep social morality, contain truth and observe the relevant laws and norms.

F. Deception in Marketing

Deception in marketing can occur in the form of misrepresentation or misleading practice while working with any element of the marketing mix. When a product or service does not give expected value, or when customers believe that they should get more value from a product or service than they actually receive, the marketing practice is supposed to be deceptive. In case of deceptive pricing practices, customers believe that the price they have paid for some unit of value in a product or service is higher than what it deserves. Deception can be in the form of making false price comparisons, providing misleading suggested selling prices, omitting important information or making low price offers if other items are purchased. Promotion practices are deceptive when seller does not disclose information regarding pyramid sales. They do not provide factual information about how a product is made or about how it performs. They use bait-and-switch selling techniques in which they offer to sell a product at a lower price to attract the customer. Then they encourage the customer to purchase the expensive items. Deceptive packaging constitutes intentionally mislabelled packages regarding contents, weight, size, etc. False or exaggerated claims regarding product or services are deceptive. Not honouring warranty obligations or failing to render promised services are also the deceptive practices.

G. Marketing to Children

Children are vulnerable to the impressive images and psychological appeals used for marketing various products. They are targeted for marketing certain products. Their knowledge about those products, media, marketing strategies, etc. is not adequate, therefore, they are more vulnerable to marketing appeals than the adults. Ethical questions arise when the children are exposed to unethical marketing messages and tactics. Use of the internet, direct marketing to children, presenting objectionable materials to underage consumers etc. raise ethical issues. In some countries marketing to children is closely controlled and regulations are imposed to limit different ways of marketing that can be directed to the children. Children influence their parent's buying decisions in addition to their own purchasing power which is found to be considerable. Therefore, advertising industry spend huge money on advertising to children. Nowadays, parents buy more for their children because of the smaller family size, dual incomes and due to postponing having children until later in life. Therefore families have good deal of disposable income to be spent for the children. Children and teens are increasingly becoming targets of the strategies of marketers. This has resulted in the enhancement of negative impacts of marketing to the children.

The matter of advertising directed to children is most passionately criticised. It is clear from the onset that the controversy swirls around television advertising which appears during the children's programmes. The advertisers use 'multisensory experiences' that includes words, voices, sound effects, pictures, etc. to induce consumption of candy, chocolates, sweet drinks, expensive toys and other assorted products and services which are considered as undesirable. The advertising directed to children is simply wrong. There should be total ban on television advertising directed to children who are too young to understand the selling purpose or to evaluate the commercials.

H. Marketing to Minorities

Markets are divided into segments in which people share some common characteristics. Marketing tactics are designed to exploit the minority market segments. Negative or stereotypical representation of minority, associating questionable products with a particular minority segment, and demeaning portrayals of a race etc. are the tactics used to manipulate a minority market. When higher prices are charged for the products or services sold to the minorities, when high pressure selling is directed to them, or when poorer services are provided to the minority customers, the ethical questions arise.

African-American, Hispanic or Latino American, and Asian American are the minorities targeted by the marketers in United States. In the African-American images in advertising the caricature of "Aunt Femima" was famous. African American women shown in advertisements were dark, heavy, subservient, and they were stereotyped as belonging only in the kitchen. Complaints about use of the stereotype began in mid-80's. It was found that children who watch advertisements that routinely stereotype people of colour have less favourable attitudes towards those who are shown as 'different'. Often minority children were given passive and ignorant roles. Some of the worst stereotypes which were opposed include—'Lively Latins', 'Pigtailed Chinese', 'Subservient Blacks' 'Mexican Bandits', 'Frito Bandito'. They were dropped after many years of complaints from Hispanic groups. Some stereotypes like Asians as 'Computer Geeks', 'African American' girls as 'Dance Girls' still remain.

I. Portrayal Women in Marketing

In marketing efforts, women have been portrayed in a variety of ways. When the images of women are portrayed as formulaic, overly conventional or oversimplified, they are viewed as stereotypical. Demeaning stereotypes include those women who are presented as less intelligent, submissive, unable to make decisions, submissive to men, unable to assume leadership roles, and dressed with short and revealing clothes in order to appeal to the sexual interests of men. When projected images are considered demeaning or harmful, they are offensive and detrimental.

Some ads imply dolls are for girls and chemistry sets are for boys. Sexual stereotypes in advertisements portray women as weak, silly and overemotional. Ethical advertising pictures both the sexes as attractive, intelligent and physically able. Some advertisements reinforce the "dumb-blonde" cliché that portray the women as 'stupid', who are unable to balance their cheque books, or unable to manage a household without the help of outside experts, particularly male ones. Some ads use belittling language, for example, 'gal Friday', 'her kitchen' but 'his car', 'men's discussion' but 'women's chatter' etc. Contemptuous phrases like, "the weaker sex", "the war department", "the little woman" etc. are also used. Many advertisements consistently show women waiting on men, for example, women nurses or secretaries serving coffee etc. to male bosses or colleagues.

J. Unethical Behaviour of Salespersons

Some salespersons cheat the management by stopping some of the sales orders in the current month in order to pass them on the next month, so that they can meet the targets of the next month. They misuse the company's assets such as the company vehicle, sales expenses, money spent on the entertainment of customers, bribing the customers, giving gifts to get large orders, offering free samples, etc. Some salespersons take undue advantage of the lack of supervision to take on multiple jobs to add to their regular income.

Encouraging salespersons of the same company to compete against each other is an unhealthy practice. Some salespersons even cheat the fellow by snatching business from their account. Some of them show fake sales to win the sales contest. They dump the stock on the customer and assure that they will take it back later, if it is not sold. Salespersons are revenue generators of the firm, therefore, they face pressures from the sales managers to achieve sales targets. This compels the salespeople to adopt unethical sales practices.

Situations in which salespersons face unethical course of selling are numerous, for example, salesperson asks customers for information regarding competitors; he offers promotional and other gifts to the buyer; he tries to belittle a competitor's salesperson in order to get customer's orders; he gives special treatment to certain customers due to the recommendations of sales manager; he offers free trips, luncheon and dinner to the prospective buyers; he offers to sell the product at a premium price; he quotes different prices to different customers; he tries to get information from the buyer about the competitor's quotation in order to quote less price, etc.

K. Unethical Practices in Marketing Mix

1. Product and Services

In this component of marketing mix, the unethical practices include selling unsafe and shoddy goods, mislabelled products, giving inadequate warranties, selling products that cause environmental pollution, selling counterfeit brand goods as originals, etc.

Ethical responsibility for this component includes responsibility to ensure product safety, to disclose all product risks, and to identify the factors that might change the performance of product.

2. Price

In this component, the unethical practices include price discrimination for preferred groups, price differentiation, excessive mark-up prices, unfair pricing, loss leader pricing, bait and switch, predatory pricing, deceptive pricing (buy one, take one free) price fixing etc. Marketers must not involve in such practices. They must disclose all prices associated with purchase including service, installation and delivery.

3. Promotion/Advertising

Unethical practices in this regard include exaggerated claims, deceptive advertising, tele marketing, captive audience (TV commercials shown to school children), persuasive role model (celebrity speaks for liquor), tasteless advertising (indecent sexual promiscuity) etc. Marketers are expected to avoid misleading and deceptive sales tactics. They should not manipulate consumers to buy.

4. Distribution

Unethical practices in distribution include fraudulent sales and direct marketing which involves misleading claims of product performance. Suppliers must not coerce their intermediaries to take the unwanted products. They must not create false shortage to raise the prices of their products.

5. Packing

Unethical practice in packing include 'deceptive quantities' in which product quantity is decreased while maintaining same price and package.

L. Norms and Values for Ethical Marketing

American Marketing Association Commits itself to promote the highest standard of professional ethical norms and values for its members. Norms are established standards of conduct, and values represent the collective conception of what people find desirable, important and morally proper.

According to the general norms, marketers must do no harm. They should do the work for which they are appropriately trained and experienced. They should actively add value to their organisation and customers. They should adhere to all applicable laws and regulations. They must foster trust in the marketing system. This means that products which they sell are appropriate for their intended and promoted uses. Marketing communications about goods and services should not be intentionally deceptive or misleading. They should build relationships that provide for the equitable adjustment and/or redress of customer grievances. They should strive for good faith and fair dealing. They must embrace, communicate and practice the fundamental ethical values.

The basic values for the marketers are intentionally aspirational and include honesty, responsibility, fairness, respect, openness and citizenship. Marketer's 'honesty' means to be truthful and forthright in their dealings with customers and the stakeholders. They have to tell the truth in all situations. They have to offer the products of value that do what they claim in their communications. They have to honour their explicit and implicit commitments and promises.

The value of marketers '**Responsibility**' means they have to accept the consequences of their marketing decisions and strategies. They have to make strenuous efforts to serve the needs of the customers. They should avoid coercion with all stakeholders. They should acknowledge the social obligations to stakeholders, and they should recognise their special commitments to economically vulnerable segments.

'**Fairness**' in marketing means to try to balance justly the needs of the buyers with the interests of the sellers. Marketers have to avoid false, misleading and deceptive promotion. They should reject manipulations and sales tactics that harm the customer trust. They must not engage in price-fixing, predatory pricing or bait and switch tactics.

Value of '**Respect**' means to acknowledge the basic human dignity of all stakeholders. The marketers have to value individual differences, avoid stereotyping customers or depicting demographic groups like gender, race, etc. They should listen to the needs of the customers and make all reasonable efforts to monitor and improve customer satisfaction. They should acknowledge the contributions of others, such as employees, co-workers, consultants, intermediaries, suppliers, distributors, etc.

'**Openness**' in marketing means to create transparency in all marketing operations. They have to strive to communicate clearly with all their constituencies. They have to accept the constructive criticism from their customers and other shareholders. They have to explain the product or service risks, and other foreseeable eventualities. They should fully disclose list prices, available price deals and adjustments, and the terms of financing.

The value of **'Citizenship'** in marketing means to fulfil the economic, legal, philanthropic and societal responsibilities towards the stakeholders. Marketers have to strive to protect the natural environment in the execution of marketing campaigns. They have to give back to the community through volunteerism and charitable donations. They should contribute to the overall betterment of marketing and its reputation.

M. Dave Kahle's Ethical Guidelines

Dave Kahle (2004) gives ethical guidelines for salesperson in "the Ten Commandments for the Ethical Salesperson". These guidelines are as follows:

First, a salesperson should always remember not to lie to a customer under any circumstances. Truthfulness adds to the credibility of a salesperson.

Secondly, a salesperson should sort out any misunderstanding that may affect the sale. The misunderstanding may pertain to the company, product or competitors of the company.

Third, a salesperson should always work hard for the company that has employed him. It is impossible to monitor a sales persons job constantly. Some salespeople may take advantage of this situation, and avoid the work by remaining at home.

Fourth, it is necessary for a salesperson to focus on developing a long-term relationship with the customer even if it means foregoing some short-term gains.

Fifth, a salesperson should never promise beyond what he can deliver. Despite the temptations to grab customer's business from a competitor who is indulging in overpromising, the salesman should never make promises that cannot be fulfilled.

Sixth, a successful salesperson should cultivate the habit of returning to society something of what he has received from it.

Seventh, an ethical salesperson should never forget to recognise and to acknowledge the timely help and support extended by people both in office and elsewhere.

Eight, a salesperson should constantly learn new ways and means of improving his performance both for his own benefit as well as that of the organisation.

Nine, a salesperson has to learn some important tricks of the trade. He has to learn not to give up at any stage.

Ten, a salesperson should desist from speaking ill of others, especially in front of customers. He should never speak ill of the competitor.

EXERCISES

1. Explain the significance of ethics in marketing.
2. What are the ethical responsibilities of marketing managers?
3. Discuss various ethical issues regarding marketing personnel.
4. What are the ethical challenges for marketers?
5. What is 'Unethical Market Exclusion'?
6. Comment on unethical practices in advertising.
7. Discuss various forms of deception in marketing.
8. Write a note on marketing to children, minorities and women.
9. How are the women portrayed in marketing?
10. Write a note on the unethical behaviour of salespersons.
11. Describe unethical practices in marketing mix.
12. Discuss the values and norms for ethical marketing.
13. Explain Dave Kahle's guidelines for ethical marketing.
14. Write short notes on the following:
    - (i) Ethical challenges for marketers.
    - (ii) Selective marketing.
    - (iii) Unethical advertisements.
    - (iv) Deception in marketing.
    - (v) Marketing to children.
    - (vi) Marketing to minorities.
    - (vii) Portrayal of women in marketing.
    - (viii) Unethical behaviour of salespersons.
    - (ix) Norms and values of ethical marketing.
    - (x) Dave Kahle's ethical guidelines.

12

Ethics in Accounting and Finance

"When money speaks, truth is silent" —Proverb

Learning Objectives

A. Professional Objectives and Responsibilities
B. Creative Accounting and Imaginary Numbers
C. Integrity of Financial Reporting and Auditing
D. Causes of Unethical Behaviour in Accounting
E. Ethical Role and Responsibilities in Auditing
F. Unethical Practices in Financial Services

A. Professional Objectives and Responsibilities

Accounting keeps systematic records of financial transactions. This systematic record protects the business properties from unwarranted and unjustified use. The manager or proprietor gets information regarding various matters from accounting. The amount of the proprietors funds invested in the business, the amount which the business has to pay to the others, the amount which the business has to recover from the others, the amount which the business has in the form of fixed assets, cash in hand, cash at bank, and stock of raw materials, finished goods, work in progress, etc. are the essential details of information imparted to the decision-makers through accounting.

Accounting helps to ascertain the net profit earned or the loss suffered on account of carrying the business. It serves as barometer for ascertaining the financial health and position of business. It provides the information to the concerned authorities to facilitate rational decision-making.

Financial management aims at maintaining adequate liquid assets of the firm to meet its obligations. Finance manager has to maintain a balance between liquidity and profitability.

Profit maximisation is an important objective of financial management. However, profit maximisation at the cost of moral or social obligations is considered as a short-sighted policy. Wealth maximisation is considered the main aim of financial management. This aim is consistent with the aim of maximising the economic welfare of the shareholders of a company. Therefore, finance manager is expected to follow policy which increases the earning per share in the long run.

In order to maximise wealth, the firm has to avoid the projects that involve high profits together with high risks. It should pay regular dividends to increase the firm's reputation and consequently to raise the value of firm's shares. The firm should maintain the growth in sales by developing new markets. It should maintain the value of its equity shares at reasonable levels.

The management cannot ignore its social responsibility. It should protect the interests of the consumers, pay fair wages to the workers, maintain proper working conditions, involve in the environmental issues, provide educational and physical facilities to the workers. Such social actions are in the interests of the shareholders in the long run. Financial management should ensure fair return to the shareholders. They should build up reserves for growth and expansion. They should make efficient and effective utilisation of finances. Financial management is responsible for maintaining financial discipline in the organisation.

B. Creative Accounting and Imaginary Numbers

The managers and the auditors of the firms like Enron, Adelphia, Tyco, Xerox, Quest, Sunbeam, World.Com, Arthur Anderson, Global Crossing, Rite-Aid, etc. were involved in corporate accounting scandals. They won the award for developing a mathematical concept of 'imaginary numbers'. The 2008 Ig Nobel Prize award, a parody of the Nobel Prize, was presented to the CEOs, corporate directors and the auditors of the firms that were involved in accounting fraud. The 'imaginary numbers' were behind the concept of 'Creative Accounting'. The term 'creative accounting' was taken from Mel Brook's film 'The Producers' which is based on the theme of financial scandal. The firms like Enron, world-com, etc. artificially propped up their financial statements in order to assure their stockholders that they still had a viable company which ultimately collapsed financially like a house of cards.

Accountants can depict a picture which can either be enlightening or misleading. They can carry out various manoeuvres, even within the framework of law, which can be regarded as ethically unacceptable. Such 'cooking the books' or 'creative accounting' is often legal but morally dubious practice. Two poets or two civil engineers can describe the same landscape differently. Similarly, two accountants can present the accounts of the same firm in two entirely different ways. A firm may sell-off some of its capital and treat the proceeds as profits. Reputed firms quite typically place hypothetical monetary value of intangible assets (goodwill) in their annual accounts. If a company has built up enough goodwill among customers, it is often worth more than the physical assets. If a buyer is given credit, it is possible for a vendor to consider that sale as a loss of goods and hence a debit. If the companies can enjoy the right of deciding how to organise their own affairs, they can decide how to present their accounts. It is believed that no standard accounting scheme can be devised because the affairs of different firms are all very different. A system of accounting which is appropriate for one firm, can be quite inappropriate for the another. Hence, many firms feel the need of 'creative accounting' and 'imaginary numbers'.

Finance and accounts has functional responsibility to act in public interest, and until recently global surveys had ranked these professionals very high in professional ethics. But the world has witnessed various accounting scandals during last decade. It has put a serious question mark on the role of finance and accounting professionals. They failed in providing right information for decision-making both within and outside their respective organisations. In various accounting scandals around the world, the accounting information used by the finance departments was false and manipulative. There were some accounting professionals who were directly involved in fraudulent activities, but there were large number of other accounting professionals who did not challenge what they had already known.

C. Integrity of Financial Reporting and Auditing

Accurate financial reporting is required to enable the investors and other stakeholders to make investment, credit and financial decisions related with the firm. It helps the stakeholders to determine the level of cash flow. Above all, it helps to identify the economic resources and obligations of the firm. However, accountants can interpret financial reporting in different manners. Their ability to make valid judgments about the economic reality of the financial statements is influenced by economic, political cultural and psychological factors. Therefore, absolute objectivity in accounting profession is not feasible. Every individual makes a judgement of economic reality on the basis of individual perspective. Thus, two accountants with exactly the same information, may make two totally different decisions based on their personal perspective. Financial information can be developed and interpreted in an inherently subjective manner. If objectives of financial reporting are based on normative values, it cannot be accurately verified or validated from an empirical evaluation. Therefore, financial information can be open for different interpretations. Such interpretations can be unethical and illegal.

Astounding waves of accounting scandals have naturally raised the fingers of doubt towards the auditors who should not have allowed the firms to make up the 'imaginary numbers' year after year. The internal and the external auditors have the responsibility to find out the problems, to identify the frauds and to bring those frauds to the notice of the stakeholders. If accepted accounting principles and auditing standards are followed, the auditor's report expresses his opinion about the fairness of the financial statements. Auditors, who are considered as the 'gatekeepers' for the stakeholders, have a responsibility to ensure the integrity of financial reporting.

There must be transparency and accuracy in all the information produced by the firms. For this purpose, they should encourage the collaboration and integration among the different units of the firms, so that these units communicate with each other. Transparency of the financial information and transfer of relevant information can allow the employees to identify and report the unethical behaviour. In the process of corporate governance, the employees must be well informed about the financial issues; and, the board of directors must be able to interpret the financial information that impacts the operations of the company. Errors in financial reporting must be identified and corrected. Beside financial information, non-financial information regarding the company performance in customer satisfaction, loyalty of the employees, productivity levels, operational quality, overhead, etc. must be reported. There must be an efficient system of checks and balances in place to minimise the chances of errors. A reliable and consistent communication system should be developed to provide all the needed information to the investors and other stakeholders.

D. Causes of Unethical Behaviour in Accounting

Companies pay to get audited by the accounting firms, therefore, the companies can exercise powers over the auditing firms. Consequently, the acceptance of company's 'overaggressive accounting' by the external auditors becomes a strong possibility. Accounting firms are always concerned about retaining their clients. They compromise on their level of independence from the firm. They do not challenge key information that may upset and annoy the client. As a result, both the accuracy of the financial statements and objectivity of the auditor are lost.

Company managements always put pressures on the external auditors to sign a 'clean audit' because they want their financial statements to show how efficiently the executives manage their firms. If the auditor pleases the firm, he gets financial incentives because the firm is a revenue-generating client for the auditors. On the other hand, if the auditor abides by all the standards and guidelines, he makes overall evaluation of the integrity of the financial statements.

The management of a firm always wants to present 'clean' financial statements to the shareholders because shareholders do not like the negative issues associated with the financial statements. The shareholders select and assign the payment levels to the external auditors via the board of directors. Therefore, the auditor also has duty to the shareholders to review and evaluate the financial transaction of the firm in an objective manner. However, if an auditor has financial interest in the firm, he can get benefit by violating professional standards established by accounting organisations.

A finance and accounting professional has an obligation to follow certain fundamental principles, however his responsibilities to an employing firm and his professional obligations to comply with the fundamental principles can be in conflict. His responsibilities to the employing organisation can bring pressure upon him to act in ways that can directly or indirectly threaten compliance with the fundamental principles. There can be explicit or implicit pressures from a director, manager, supervisor or other individuals from the employing organisation to act contrary to laws, regulations and professional standards in order to facilitate unethical and illegal earnings. For example, when Sherron Watkins sent a message with detailed information of the accounting fraud to ENRON's top executive Kenneth Lay, instead of taking note of that 'accounting hoax', the management demoted Sherron. Like Sherron, hundreds of finance and accounting employees of Enron knew about the happenings but they preferred to be silent observers. Like Enron, many other companies like Xerox, World.Com, Global Crossing, etc. created the accounting entries or 'imaginary numbers' to make their financial statements look attractive and thereby invited further investments from unsuspecting investors.

Manipulating accounting entries to depict good profitability by many companies like Enron, World.Com, etc. could help those companies to raise further capital from the market. The downfall of these companies was because they gave emphasis on the short-term results. Most of the compromises are small at the start, however, later they are transformed into large problems. When Enron was doing well, there were no question marks on its financial statements, but when it took downward turn, the finance and accounting officers made compromises over fundamental principles and code of conduct. The compromises were effected to depict a financial position that would keep the investors satisfied in the market. All this resulted in mammoth crisis and ultimate downfall of a giant company. Therefore, business organisations should develop an environment where even small ethical lapses are taken seriously so that they do not recur in the future.

The accounting professionals who work as consultants or auditors usually do not comply with the fundamental principles in the circumstances when they have a close business relationship with a client, or they have a concern about the possibility of losing a client, or they have a hope of potential employment with a client, or they have some financial interest in a client, or they jointly hold a financial interest with a client.

When an accounting professional works as an employee, he may not adhere to the fundamental principles because he gets incentive compensation arrangements, or he makes inappropriate personal use of corporate assets, or he has a serious concern over the employment security, or he has some pressure from outside the employing firm.

When accounting professionals work as external consultants or auditors they may not adhere to legal and ethical principles in certain circumstances. When they have close or immediate family relationship with a director or officer of the client, or they have close or family relationship with an employee of the client, or their former partner is a director or officer of the client, or when they accept gifts or preferential treatment from a client.

E. Ethical Role and Responsibilities in Auditing

From 1970s, the independent auditors were allowed to solicit the clients. It created a bidding war by the audit firms for clients. During 1980s–1990s these firms began to offer a risk-based audit model. This model was designed to enable the independent auditors to focus more time on the high-risk areas of business firms. The auditors assess the level of risk of the chance of fraud by the client. If the risk of fraud is found to be low, an auditor may not administer the same number of tests as he would do on a client firm which is considered as a firm with a high risk of fraud. It was found that the auditors rely more consistently on what the clients tell them.

The Sarbanes-Oxley Act of 2002 establishes a new authority to set auditing standards. In the light of the ethical scandals that have arisen in the past decade, this act established new regulations for the public companies. Corporations are required to provide more enlightened financial reporting to the users of financial statements. Publicly listed companies must have an audit of their financial statements. It must be conducted each year. An auditor is nominated by the company's audit committee, and this nomination is to be approved at the annual meeting of the shareholders. The audit firm sets the ground rules for the audit and gives an engagements letter to the company. Audit firm reviews the previous year's reported financial statements. If auditor is new, he meets the previous auditor. In an attempt to find the spots of fraud the audit firm has to perform a risk assessment test and inspect the company's computers and accountants. The auditor inspects even the non-routine transactions that occurred during the year, and tests the accounting and inventory systems. The auditor calls randomly selected sample of customers who owe the company money. He inspects notes included with the financial statements. He can demand that adjustments be made in the financial statements. If the firm refuses, he can give a qualified opinion about the statement.

Auditors have to understand how a firm is affected by the changes in the business environment. They have to identify key risk areas which involve significant estimates and judgments. They have to approach the audit with objectivity and scepticism. Audit committees have to evaluate a culture and environment of the firm that promotes high-quality financial reporting. Auditors make management aware of identified audit differences on a timely basis. They have to foster ongoing communications with management and audit committee. When they face grey area, they perform appropriate procedures to corroborate management's explanations, and consult with others whenever needed.

According to Working Group Report on Companies Act, the audit committees should be set up through the voluntary initiative of the industry associations. Although it has clearly stated the need of the audit committees, it did not legislate audit committees. It expected the listed companies which satisfy the criterion to have the audit committees, to form such committees by the fiscal year 1998-99. All the listed companies with a turnover of more than Rs. 100 crores or paid up capital of Rs. 20 crores whichever is less were expected to set up the audit committees within two years.

According to recommendation of the Confederation of Indian Industry (CII) for responsible corporate governance in India, an audit committee should be set up of at least three members who are preferably drawn from company's non-executive directors (NEDs). The NEDs should have adequate knowledge of finance accounts and the basic elements of company law. These members of the audit committee should be willing to spend more time on the company's work as compared to the other NEDs. The audit committee should help the company board to fulfil its functions, particularly related to corporate accounting and reporting practices, financial and accounting controls, financial statements and proposals that accompany the public issue of any security. The committee should, thus, provide effective supervision of the financial reporting process.

To ascertain the quality and veracity of the company's accounts, and the efficiency of the auditors themselves, the audit committee should periodically interact with the auditors. The management must ensure that the members of the audit committee that consist of non-executive directors get full access to the financial data of the company and its associated and subsidiary companies. Generally, the non-executive directors suffer from the informational deficiency. There is a lack of complete information and knowledge regarding various issues. They suffer due to the poor quality of disclosures that are made by the management. Therefore, in the best interest of the good governance certain key information must be placed before the audit committee. The audit committee should have full access to the data on contingent liabilities, debt exposure, current liabilities, investments and loans. Such an access can help the audit committees to shoulder their responsibilities in an efficient manner.

Therefore, some of the information which should be made available includes—annual operating plans and budgets, updated long-term plans and its details, overhead budgets, capital budget, manpower, quarterly reports of a company and its operating divisions or segments, internal audit reports, reports regarding theft and dishonesty of a material nature, details of any joint venture or collaborative agreement, any transaction involving substantial payments towards goodwill or intellectual property, show cause and prosecution notices from revenue authorities which are considered to be materially important, any serious or fatal industrial accident, labour problems, pollution problems, any default in payments, any issue of public liability or product liability, appointment or removal of the chief financial officer and the company secretary, recruitment and remuneration of senior officers, quarterly details of foreign exchange exposure and the steps taken to limit the risks of adverse exchange rate movement. Such key information should be furnished by management to the audit committee in the best interest of the good governance.

F. Unethical Practices in Financial Services

Finance covers a broad range of activities, but the two major aspects are the 'financial markets' like commodity market, currency markets; and the 'financial services' industry which includes financial planners, stock brokers, tax advisors, insurance agents, commercial banks, investment banks, mutual fund companies, insurance companies and both the private and public pension funds.

Ethical violations in finance can be attributed to the inconsistency in modern financial economic theory and the widespread use of a principal-agent model of relationship in financial transactions. The financial-economic theory underlying the modern capitalist system is based on the rational-maximiser paradigm. It holds a view that individuals are self-seeking and that they seek to maximise their own interests when they behave rationally. This behavioural assumption runs contrary to the ethical ideas of trustworthiness, loyalty and stewardship. The most frequent occurring ethical violations in financial operations are as follows:

Deception is quite common in financial operations and services. Brokers, insurance agents and other sales people are deceivers when they do not explain to their clients all the relevant information truthfully in an understandable manner. These salespeople have developed a new vocabulary that misleads and conceals rather than reveals. They avoid speaking of their commissions, even though commissions are the source of their compensation. Commissions on mutual funds are called "Front-end" or "back-end loads". The commissions of insurance agents can approach 100 per cent of the first year's premium, but they rarely disclose this fact. Insurance agents often represent their life insurance policies as "retirement plans" and refer to the premiums as "deposits".

Promotional material for a mutual fund or insurance policy is often misleading because it is used for misinterpreting the facts. When it is used for emphasising the strengths of the fund or policy and to minimise the weaknesses, it serves the agent's purpose of misleading the investor. Figures of past performance are often carefully selected and displayed in a way to mislead the investors. Essential information is not revealed. The projected hypothetical returns do not show all the changes. It is also found that deception by a financial service provider is similar to that of deceptive advertising of financial products like mutual funds and insurance policies.

When a broker has an intention to generate commission rather than generating benefits to client through inappropriate and excessive trading for a client's account, it is called 'churning'. Churning occurs when a client gives over the control of an account to the broker who assumes the responsibility to serve the interests of the client. Churning is indicated by excessive trading that consistently favours trades that yield higher commissions, no matter the amount is gained or lost.

Insurance agents, brokers and other salespersons cheat innocent investors by recommending unsuitable securities and financial products. Recommending stocks when bonds would be more suitable for investor's objectives, or selecting lower-rated bonds when higher rated ones are more suitable for investor, are some of the examples of unsuitability. Unsuitable diversification can also leave the portfolio vulnerable to changes in market. Investments are deemed unsuitable if they involve excessive risk. But few risky investments in a well-balanced conservative portfolio can be appropriate. The brokers, insurance agents and other salespeople have an obligation to recommend only the suitable financial products.

The regulations of financial markets have a purpose to protect not only the individual investors but also the general public. There are many possible ways in which the investors can be treated unfairly by the operations of the financial markets. The 'frauds' are the wilful misrepresentation of material facts that cause harm to the persons who unreasonably rely on the misrepresentation. Investors are vulnerable to frauds because the value of financial instruments depends on the information which is difficult to verify. The important information remains in the hands of the issuing firms, and the investors have to depend upon whatever the information is made available to them. 'Manipulation' involves buying and selling of securities for the purpose of creating misleading impression about their price in order to induce the investors to buy or sell the securities.

'Insider trading' is perhaps the most publicised behaviour by the traders in financial markets. It is trading in the securities of corporations to take advantage of material non-public "inside" information. This trade is motivated by the possibility of generating extraordinary gain with the help of 'inside' information about the company which is not available to the public. A person who is engaged in insider trading violates some legal duty to the company and its shareholders.

EXERCISES

1. "Accountants can depict a picture which can either be enlightening or misleading". Discuss.
2. What is 'creative accounting'?
3. What is the importance of integrity in financial reporting and auditing?
4. What are the causes unethical behaviour in accounting?
5. Explain the ethical role and responsibilities in auditing.
6. Write a note on unethical practices in financial services.
7. Write short notes on the following:

(i) Imaginary numbers
(ii) Ethical Responsibilities in Accounting and Finance
(iii) Creative Accounting
(iv) Integrity in Financial Reporting
(v) Accounting Scandals
(vi) Integrity in Auditing
(vii) Deceptions in Financial Operations
(viii) Insider Trading

13

Environmental Ethics

"Nature is a revelation of God". —H.W. Longfellow

Learning Objectives

A. Nature and Perspectives of Environmental Ethics
   1. Anthropocentric Ethical Perspective
   2. Intrinsic and Instrumental Values
   3. Prudential Anthropocentrism
   4. Consequentialist—Utilitarian Approach
   5. Deontological Approach
   6. Biocentrism
   7. Individualism and Environmental Holism
   8. Virtue Ethics

B. Environmental Degradation
   1. Introduction
   2. Human Responsibility of Environmental Degradation
   3. Natural Hazards
   4. Anthropogenic Hazards and Pollution
   5. Air Pollution: Nature, Causes and Effects
      (a) Nature and Causes of Air Pollution
      (b) Effects of Air Pollution
      (c) Other Major Effects of Air Pollution
   6. Ozone Depletion: Nature, Causes and Effects
   7. Green House Effect or Global Warming
   8. Acid Rain: Nature, Causes and Effects
   9. Water Pollution: Nature, Causes and Effects
   10. Soil Pollution: Nature, Causes and Effects
   11. Marine Pollution: Nature, Causes and Effects
   12. Noise Pollution: Nature, Causes and Effects
   13. Biodiversity: Nature, Significance and Threats

A. Nature and Perspectives of Environmental Ethics

1. Anthropocentric Ethical Perspective

Anthropocentric or human-centred ethical perspectives assign a significantly great amount of intrinsic value to human beings than to any non-human things. Anthropocentrism always justifies the promotion and protection of human interests at the expense of non-human things. In 'Politics' Aristotle says, 'nature has made all things specifically for the sake of man'. He maintains that the value of non-human things in nature is merely instrumental. A cruel treatment of other species or animals is not considered as wrong deed except when such a treatment leads to unfavourable consequences for mankind. Environmental ethics poses a challenge to this traditional anthropocentrism.

2. Intrinsic and Instrumental Values

In environmental ethics, intrinsic value of anything is the value of that thing as an 'end in itself'. On the other hand, instrumental value of anything is its value as 'means' to further some other end. Certain fruits have instrumental value for birds who feed on them. Feeding on the fruits is a 'means' to survival for the birds. Anthropocentric view does not agree that fruits have value as ends in themselves. A teacher has an instrumental value for those learn. In addition to this value, that teacher as a person has an intrinsic value. A plant may have instrumental value because it provides herbal medicine for human beings. The same plant also has a value in itself which is independent of its instrumental value for furthering some other ends. This value of the plant is its intrinsic value. This value generates a direct moral duty on the part of moral agents to refrain from damaging the existence of the plant.

Environmental ethics challenges the assumptions of anthropocentrism. It questions the anthropocentrist's assumed moral superiority of human beings to other species on the earth. It develops rational arguments for giving any intrinsic value to the non-human contents of natural environment.

3. Prudential Anthropocentrism

Prudential anthropocentrism advocates that our moral duties towards the environment are derived from our duties to mankind. The practical purpose of environment ethics is to provide moral grounds for protecting the earth's environment. Environmental devastation can damage the well-being of human beings now or in the future. Well-being of the human species is dependent on a sustainable environment. Anthropocentrism is a form of human chauvinism which is simply based on blind class loyalty or prejudice. It unjustifiably discriminates against those who are outside the privileged class. Anthropocentrism is a main tradition western approach of moral thinking which is unable to allow all the other living things and all the landscapes to have intrinsic value. Environmental ethics maintains that such a tradition requires overhaul of a significant kind. Earth as a whole is an object of moral concern for environmental ethics which argues for our moral obligations towards all the species, communities and ecosystems on this planet.

Species are intrinsically more valuable than individual specimens. The trees, forests and other natural objects should have at least the same status in law as corporations. These natural things should become beneficiaries of compensation if they suffer compensable injury through human activity.

4. Consequentialist—Utilitarian Approach

Consequentialist ethical theories maintain that the rightness or wrongness of an action is determined by its 'good' or 'bad' consequences. For example, utilitarianism which is a paradigm of consequentialism, regards pleasure, or satisfaction of desire, interest and preference as the only intrinsic value in the world. On the other hand, pain or frustration of desire, interest and preference is regarded as the only intrinsic disvalue. Utilitarian maintain that right actions are those which produce the greatest balance of pleasure over pain. The question of to whom a pleasure or pain belongs is irrelevant in the assessment of the rightness or wrongness of actions. Therefore, the interests of all the sentient beings who are capable of experiencing pleasure or pain, including all the non-human ones are equally considered. The animal liberation movement is considered comparable to the movements of women and people of colour.

Environmental philosophers attribute intrinsic value to the natural environment and ecosystem, but utilitarian in general attribute intrinsic value to the experience of pleasure or pain. They do not give any intrinsic value to the beings who have such experience. The non-sentient objects in the environment like plant species, mountains, rivers and landscapes are of no intrinsic value to the utilitarian. Non-sentient objects in the environment are given instrumental value which is based on the satisfaction of sentient beings. For the utilitarian right actions are those that increase the overall balance of interest satisfaction over frustration and pain. For them, the killing of elephant for ivory, which causes pain and suffering to non-human animals is right after all. Such a practice is right because it might produce a lot of interest-satisfaction for human beings.

5. Deontological Approach

Deontological approach to ethics denies the utilitarian claim that morality of an action depends on its consequences. Deontological theory maintains that actions are morally right or wrong independent of their consequences. From the deontologist perspective there are distinct moral duties and rules—like 'not to kill or harm the innocent', 'to respect the rights of others', 'not to lie', etc. Deontologists are mostly concerned with rules and duties and obligations. They are non-consequentialist. They argue that it is not necessary that an actions rightness or wrongness should depend upon the consequences. They claim that the morality and ethics are to be understood as systems of rules which are meant to govern and guide conduct.

In justifying an alleged moral rule, duty or its corresponding right, a deontologist may appeal to the intrinsic value of those beings to whom it applies. They argue that the animals with 'intrinsic' or 'inherent' value, have the moral right to respectful treatment. It is our general moral duty not to treat the animals as mere means to other ends, and not to harm them. Certain practices like experimentation on animals, commercials or sports hunting, etc. is a gross violation of the moral right of intrinsically valuable animals to respectful treatment. Such practices are intrinsically wrong regardless of whether or not some good consequences are gained from them. All those animals and other non-human species have intrinsic value who have sense—perceptions, desires, motives, memory, beliefs, a sense of the future and a psychological identity.

6. Biocentrism

Biocentrism is an ethical stance which asserts the value of non-human life in nature. Biocentricity predicts that there is no life whatsoever in the observable universe anywhere, that is unrelated to Earth's life. Biocentrist argues that each individual living thing in nature—whether it is an animal, a plant, or a micro-organism—is a "teleological-centre-of-life". It has a well-being of its own which can be damaged or enhanced. Individuals who are teleological-centre-of life have equal intrinsic value or inherent worth. This inherent 'value' or 'worth' entitles them to moral respect. The intrinsic value of non-human living things generates a *prima facie* moral duty for us to preserve and promote their goods as ends in themselves. Any practices that display a lack of respect for them are intrinsically wrong. However, some critics point out that HIV has a good of its own, but it does not mean that we should assign any positive moral duty to the realisation of that good. There is also a hierarchical view that while all living things have a good of their own intrinsic value, some of them (humans) have a greater intrinsic value.

7. Individualism and Environmental Holism

Ethics of animal rights and biocentrism are both individualistic in their approach. Their moral concerns are directed towards individuals only. Their moral concerns do not cover ecological wholes such as species, population, biotic communities and ecosystems. Preservation of these collective ecological entities is a major concern for environmentalists. The goals of animal right's movement, such as reducing animal suffering and death, may conflict with the goals of environmentalists. For example, to preserve the integrity of an ecosystem, may require culling of some feral animals (culling of camels in Australian desert region) that threaten the fragile habitats in the ecosystem. Therefore, there is a dispute about whether the ethics of animal rights is a proper branch of environmental ethics.

Land-ethical holism considers a thing is right when it tends to preserve the integrity, stability and beauty of the ecosystem as a whole. Ethical holism criticises individualistic approach because it fails to accommodate conservation of ecological wholes. In ethical holism earth's biotic ecosystem is the only locus of intrinsic value. The value of its individual members is dependent on their contribution to the larger community. Ethical holism holds a view that an individual member of a biotic community can be sacrificed if it is needed for the protection of the holistic good of the community. But, in order to be consistent, the same rule also applies to human individuals because they are also the members of a biotic community.

8. Virtue Ethics

Virtue ethics speaks a quite different language from the other two-deontology and consequentialism— which consider the thin concepts such as goodness and rightness. Virtue ethics proposes the thick concepts such as justice, kindness, honesty and sincerity to understand morality. Virtue ethics views the motivation and justification of actions are both inseparable from the character traits of the acting person or group. Virtue ethics may seem anthropocentric as its central focus is human flourishing. Aristotle states that a flourishing human life requires friendships and one can have real friendships if one really loves, respects, cares and values for one's friends for their own sake, not merely for the sake of benefits of friendship. A flourishing human life also requires a moral capacity to love, respect, care and value for the natural non-human ecosystem as an end in itself.

B. Environmental Degradation

1. Introduction

Modern technology and rapid growth of population and industrialisation has polluted our environment and depleted our natural resources. William Shaw describes the effects of our environmental recklessness in following words: "human beings have scarred the globe, contaminated the natural environment, and gobbled up the earth's resources... Our rivers and lakes are dirty, and our air is unclean. The planet is warming, its protective ozone fraying. Lush forests are disappearing, and with them countless species of plants and animals. As our numbers have multiplied, half the world's wetlands have disappeared. Eighty per cent of its grasslands now suffer from soil degradation; 20 per cent of its dry lands are in danger of turning into deserts, and groundwater is seriously depleted".

2. Human Responsibility of Environmental Degradation

Phenomenal increase in population, urbanisation and industrialisation has put tremendous pressure on natural resources. Environmental degradation is overall lowering of environmental qualities because of adverse changes brought in by human activities in the basic structure of the components of the environment to such an extent that these changes adversely and critically affect all living organisms in general and man in particular. On the basis of various factors responsible for the lowering of environmental quality, the environmental degradation is of two types: (1) extreme events and hazards, and (2) pollution. On the basis of causative factors, the extreme events and hazards are of two types—Natural hazards and Anthropogenic hazards.

3. Natural Hazards

Natural hazards are terrestrial natural hazards, atmospheric natural hazards, and cumulative atmospheric hazards. Terrestrial natural hazards include volcanic eruptions, earthquake, etc. Atmospheric natural hazards include tropical cyclones, lightening, forest fires, etc. Cumulative atmospheric hazards include floods, draught, etc. Though man is responsible for creating atmospheric, hydrospheric and lithospheric imbalance, some hazards like volcanic eruptions and earthquakes are purely natural. When the volcano Mount St. Helens erupted in May 1980, it damaged 220,000 acres of timberland and emitted enormous amount of sulphur and ash in the air.

4. Anthropogenic Hazards and Pollution

Anthropogenic hazards are the result of human activities. These hazards are caused by cumulative and even by sudden effect of human activities. These are divided into three groups—physical hazards, chemical and nuclear hazards and biological hazards. Large-scale landslides (e.g. Kedarnath, Himachal Pradesh in June 2013), deliberate forest fires, etc. are some examples of physical hazards. Sudden outburst of lethal gases (e.g. Bhopal Gas Tragedy in December, 1984), nuclear explosions (Hiroshima and Nagasaki in August, 1945) etc. are some examples of chemical and nuclear hazards. Explosion of human population, outbreak of epidemics, etc. are the examples of biological hazards. Human activities are responsible for all the above anthropogenic hazards.

Human activities are responsible for pollution. It is an undesirable contamination of the environment. It is divided into four sub-groups—

Air Pollution, Water Pollution, Land Pollution and Sound Pollution. Pollution occurs when short-term economic gains are obtained at the cost of long-term ecological benefits for mankind and other biotic communities.

5. Air Pollution: Nature, Causes and Effects

(a) Nature and Causes of Air Pollution

Air pollution began with industrial revolution at the beginning of nineteenth century and increased as industrialisation expanded. Air pollution affects animal and plant life and causes catastrophic global damage in the form of global warming and depletion of ozone layer. Air pollution became a serious problem in London during Industrial Revolution due to abundant use of coal in industries. 'London Smog' occurred in 1952 which resulted in more than 4000 deaths in the city. With the development of transportation systems based on large-scale use of diesel and petrol, air pollution increased rapidly in the twentieth century.

The atmosphere is normally composed of 79 per cent nitrogen, 20 per cent oxygen and 1 per cent as a mixture of carbon dioxide, water vapour and traces of several other gases such neon, helium, methane, krypton, xenon and hydrogen. In pure air, the proportion of different constituents is fixed and definite. Air is polluted when some gases like sulphur dioxide, nitrogen oxide, carbon monoxide, emission from volcanoes and swamps, etc. are added to the air. There are five primary pollutants that together contribute to about 90 per cent of the global air pollution. These are carbon oxides (CO and CO_2), nitrogen oxides, sulphur oxides, volatile organic compounds (mostly hydrocarbons) and suspended particulate matter.

Carbone monoxide is a colourless, odourless and toxic gas produced when organic materials like natural gas, coal or wood are burnt incompletely. The single largest source of carbon monoxide is the vehicular exhausts. The number of vehicles are increasing all over the world. Sulphur oxides are produced when fossil fuels containing sulphur are burnt. Nitrogen oxides are found in vehicular—exhaust. Hydrocarbons are a group of compounds that consist carbon and hydrogen atoms. They either evaporate from fuel supplies or are emitted from the fuel that does not burn completely. Particulates are small pieces of solid material like smoke particles from fires, dust particles, aerosol (sprays from pressurised cans), mist (sulphuric acid mist), particulates from burning garbage or cigarette smoke, fumes (zinc or lead fumes), smog (a mixture of smoke and fog) etc. which are dispersed in the atmosphere. The effects of particulates of asbestos are carcinogenic (causing cancer). Lead is a major air pollutant which is largely unmonitored and emitted by vehicles.

Industrial exhaust releases the chief air polluting agents like CO, CO_2, SO_2, NO, N_2O, NO_2, CL_2, F_2, NH_3 and particulate matters. These gases are released by paper and pulp factories, chemical factories, steel plants, petroleum refineries, sugar factories, etc. Domestic burning releases CO_2, CO, SO_2 etc.

Sewage gas, seepage from natural gas and oil fields, biological decomposition of organic matter release the organic substances like C_2H_6, CH_4, $C_6H_5NH_2$, C_2H_4 etc. War-explosives release poisonous gases.

'Chlorofluorocarbons (CFCs) are released into atmosphere from air conditioners, systems of cold storage, refineries, etc. Photochemical oxidants are formed by certain photochemical reactions. 'Photochemical smogs' contain different gases like SO_2, NO, N_2O, unburnt hydrocarbons, dust and moisture. A significant quantity of carbon monoxide gas and unburnt hydrocarbons are released from aircrafts and jets.

Agricultural chemicals like pesticides, fungicides, insectides, herbicides are also released into air as pollutants. Agricultural fertiliser manufacturing plants like ammonium fertiliser plants release ammonia gas in air.

(b) Effects of Air Pollution

Exposure to air pollutants can cause diseases such as asthma, chronic, bronchitis, and lung cancer. Exposure to carbon monoxide for several hours can cause collapse, coma and even death. Carbon monoxide remains attached to haemoglobin in blood for a long time and reduces the oxygen carrying capacity of blood. This impairs thinking and perceptual system and causes headaches, drowsiness and nausea.

Sulphur dioxide causes a condition similar to bronchitis. It causes swelling of nasai system. Prolonged exposure can cause lung cancer.

Nitrogen oxides can cause serious health hazards like inflammation of lung tissues, respiratory diseases like—lung cancer, pulmonary haemorrhage, and destruction of oxygen transport efficiency of blood. It can aggravate asthma or chronic bronchitis, and also increase susceptibility to respiratory infections.

Hydrocarbons have carcinogenic effects on lungs. Benzpyrene induces cancer. Methane at higher level causes narcotic effects.

Suspended particulates in the air can cause bronchitis and asthma. Asbestos particles cause lung disorder and cancer. Lead containing particles affect the brain of children. Lead interferes with the development and maturation of red blood cells. Prolonged exposure to particulates damages lung tissue, and develops chronic respiratory diseases and cancer. Volatile organic compounds like benzene, formaldehyde, etc. and toxic particulates like lead and cadmium can cause mutations, reproductive problems or cancer.

Prolonged exposure of plants to CO (carbon monoxide) can cause leaves drop, leaf curbing, reduction of leaf size, etc. It also inhibits cellular respirations in plant by reacting with cytochrome oxidise. SO_2 (Sulphur dioxide) affects plant growth and nutrient quality of products. It kills leaf tissues which causes leaf necrosis. Its chronic exposure to plants causes bleaching of plant pigments. It decreases pH of leaf tissues. It causes chlorosis and dwarfing. Nitrogen oxide at higher concentration causes loss of photosynthetic activity and chlorosis. Hydrocarbons retard the growth of plants. Hydrocarbons along with ozone causes chlorosis. Ethylene hydrocarbons damage leaf tissues and flowering plants. Acetylene and propylene bring about early maturity of plants. Deposition of particulates on soil makes the soil unsuitable for plants. Its deposition on leaves decreases the rate of photosynthesis by preventing CO_2 absorption. Gaseous pollutants enter the leaf pores and damage the leaves of crop plants. Chronic exposure to air pollutants can break down the waxy coating of leaves that helps to prevent excessive water loss. It can also lead to damages from diseases, pests, draught and frost. It interferes with photosynthesis and plant growth. It reduces nutrient uptake. It causes the leaves to turn yellow or to drop off altogether.

(c) Other Major Effects of Air Pollution

- Increased level of carbon dioxide (CO_2) causes greenhouse effect.
- Chlorofluro carbons (CFCs) and nitrogen oxides cause ozone layer depletion and ozone hole.

- Scattered atmospheric particulates absorb sunlight and reduce visibility.
- Particulate matter causes corrosion of metals, and erosion and soiling of monuments (Taj Mahal), buildings, sculptures and ancient paintings, and painted surfaces of buildings.
- Oxides of sulphur and nitrogen combine with water particles in the atmosphere and cause acid rain.
- Particulates serve as carrier for micro-organisms and spread diseases and epidemics.

6. Ozone Depletion: Nature, Causes and Effects

Ozone is a form of oxygen with three atoms instead of two. The upper stratosphere is called 'ozone layer' which consists of considerable amount of ozone. The layer also has a mixture of other common atmospheric gases. In the densest ozone layer which is between 20 to 25 km. above the earth's surface, there will be only one ozone molecule in 100,000 gas molecules. Even small changes in ozone concentration can produce dramatic consequences on the life of earth.

In 1985, large-scale destruction of the ozone which was called 'Ozone Hole' came in limelight. Research findings convincingly established that chlorofluorocarbons caused ozone depletion. CFCs are extremely stable, non-flammable and harmless to handle. Therefore, it is used in many industrial applications like refrigerators, aerosols, air conditioners, and fire extinguishers. Many cans of room freshners, perfumes, etc. that give out sprays and foams, use CFCs. Halons are used as fire-extinguishing agent. When CFCs and Halons are released they go up into upper atmosphere and deplete ozone layer over south pole and also over the countries like Australia, South Africa, parts of South America and New Zealand.

Our atmosphere's stratospheric ozone layer shields life on earth from most ultra-violate (UV) radiation. Ozone depletion has serious effects on the life of plants and animals. Its effect on human health includes aging of the skin, skin cancer, cataract, sunburn, etc. It weakens the immune system by suppressing the body's resistance to certain infections. It reduces the nutrient content and growth of the plants. Plant and animal planktons (zooplanktons) are damaged by UV radiation. Planktons form the basis of marine food chain. Any change in their number can have disastrous effect on aquatic life.

7. Green House Effect or Global Warming

"Green House Effect" is also known as "Global Warming" or "Carbon dioxide Enrichment". The average global temperature is constantly increasing in recent decades. Global warming is accelerating due to enormous emission of Green House Gases. About 75 per cent of the solar energy which reaches the earth is absorbed by the earth's surface. It increases the temperature of earth. Rest of the solar heat is radiated back to the atmosphere. Some of the is heat is trapped by the green house gases (GHGs), mostly carbon dioxide which is released by various human activities. This causes global warming. Earth's average surface temperature is about 15°C which is 33°C higher than it would be in the absence of the green house effect. It means, without green house gases, average temperature of earth's surface would be –18°C and it would result in devastating most of the life on earth—because most of the earth's surface would be frozen.

Human activities during last few decades have polluted the atmosphere to such an extent that carbon dioxide has increased by 35 per cent since pre-historic times. This has caused more heat to be trapped in the lower atmosphere. This is green house effect or global warming. GHGs include CO_2, CFCs, CH_4 (Methane), N_2O (Nitrous Oxide). These gases are released into atmosphere by burning fossil fuels, industrial activities, thermal power stations, vehicles, aircrafts, use of CFCs and halons in coolants, refrigerants, etc. and domestic waste, sewage, etc.

GHE or global warming is causing melting of glaciers and polar ice caps, and raising the level of sea-water. GHE has already increased changes in rainfall pattern. It has decreased snowing period. Cereal production has decreased due to reduction in soil moisture. It has caused fluctuations in rainfall leading to floods and draughts.

8. Acid Rain: Nature, Causes and Effects

Acid rain is one of the most serious consequences of pollution. It is caused by the presence of various pollutants like nitrogen oxides. Sulphur oxides and halogen molecules in the atmosphere. These pollutants are discharged into air by human activities and natural processes. The natural sources of these pollutants are volcanic eruptions, burning fossil fuel, forest fires, decomposition of organic matters, etc. Human activities like burning fuels, automobile exhausts, thermal power plants, petroleum refineries, industries and smelting plants release large quantities of these pollutants.

Acid rain is a serious threat to farm lands, forests, grasslands and water bodies like rivers, lakes, ponds and reservoirs. Acid rain is any precipitation such as rain, fog, mist or snow which is more acidic than normal.

The chemical pollutants mentioned above react with water particles and other chemicals in the air to form sulphuric acid, nitric acid and other pollutants like sulphates and nitrates. These acid pollutants are carried by air currents and spread in the atmosphere. Finally, they return to the ground in the form of acid rain, fog or snow.

Nutrients in the soil are dissolved and washed away by the acid rain. Acid rain also dissolves natural toxic substances like mercury and aluminium. These dissolved toxic substances pollute water and poison the plants and animals. It creates holes in the waxy coating of leaves and affects photosynthesis. It makes water bodies like lakes, rivers, wetlands acidic. Many species cannot tolerate acidic water. It adversely affects entire food chain. It seriously affects soil fertility. It damages buildings and structures of stone and metals.

9. Water Pollution: Nature, Causes and Effects

Approximately one per cent of the total quantity of water in hydrosphere is available to the human beings and all the other biotic communities on this earth. Population explosion, unplanned urbanisation and rapid industrial growth generate water pollutants. These are urban pollutants, industrial pollutants, domestic wastes, agricultural pollutants and natural pollutants. The urban pollutants mainly contain the chemicals from automobile exhaust, chemicals from urban sewage, pathogenic organisms, heavy metals, effluents with oils, greases, and nutrients and solids from domestic wastes. Industries release various industrial pollutants like sulphides, chlorides, carbonates, nitrates of heavy metals like mercury, lead, zinc, arsenic, etc. and radioactive wastes. Agricultural pollutants contain chemical fertilisers, pesticides, insecticides and herbicides. The natural pollutants include decomposed—organic matter, volcanic dusts, sediments due to weathering and debris of landslide, etc.

Water pollution has detrimental effects on mankind and all the other living organisms. Polluted water spreads dreaded diseases and epidemics like, typhoid, dysentery, tuberculosis, jaundice, cholera, etc. Water contaminated with toxic chemicals causes death of aquatic plants and animals. Water contaminated with asbestos fibres causes cancer. Water polluted with mercury causes minamata disease. Polluted water decreases agricultural productivity and soil fertility. It kills soil micro-organisms. Basic salts in polluted water increases alkalinity of soil. Concentration of organic and inorganic pollutants in water bodies causes eutrophication which results in uncontrollable and rapid growth of plants and animals in water. Water pollutants pollute underground water, and water in rivers and lakes.

10. Soil Pollution: Nature, Causes and Effects

Initially soil is made up of rock which is transformed by climatic conditions like rainfall, wind, etc. and also by vegetation and various micro-organisms. Soil formation also depends on plants, climatic factors and age of land mass. Soil is a weathered layer of the earth's crust which plays an important role of producing food for humans, plants and animals.

Soil gets polluted by a number of ways. Industrial waste is a major cause of soil pollution. Chemical industries, pulp and paper mills, sugar factories, metal processing industries, textile mills, etc. dispose their industrial waste in soil. Municipal solid waste including bio-medical waste is disposed off for land-fill. Fly-ash from coal fired thermal power plants pollutes soil. Oil spillage from fuel storages and maintenance of vehicles also pollutes the soil. Urban wastes consists of both domestic and commercial wastes which are also referred as 'refuse'. Agricultural pollutants include chemical synthetic fertilisers, herbicides, pesticides, and excessive use of endosulphur, DDT, BHC etc. Unscientific use of irrigation facility causes soil to become saline.

Mining and radioactive substances are also the major causes of soil pollution. During mining fertile topsoil is removed and discarded. Explosion of nuclear devices, nuclear wastes and atmospheric fallout from nuclear dust causes soil pollution. Acid rain also pollutes soil. Discarded plastic bags clog the drains and also choke ponds, streams and rivers. Plastics have adverse effects on soil fertility. PVC can cause skin diseases and cancer. It harms respiratory system and destroys fertility of the animals. Increasing volume of electronic waste, or 'e-waste' is becoming a serious environmental hazard.

If industrial and urban wastes are not recycled or properly

disposed off, it can be potential environmental hazard. Lead, cadmium, mercury, chromium, etc. from e-waste are highly toxic and dangerous to human health. Toxic metals in industrial waste (Hg, Pb, Cd, As, Cr, Cu, etc.) kill bacteria and beneficial micro-organisms in the soil. Dumped urban waste spread several chronic diseases. Urban sewage is an excellent medium for the growth of pathogenic bacteria, viruses and protozoa.

NPK fertilisers can reduce the protein contents of corn, maize, gram and wheat crops. Chemical fertilisers inhibit the synthesis of Vitamin C and carotene in vegetables and fruits. Nitrogenous fertilisers can induce stomach cancer. Crops, vegetables and fruits from fertilised land are prone to pests, diseases and insects. Pesticides in the soil sometimes appear in the fruits, vegetables and other farm products. It's entry into human body can cause deformities in foetus, nervous disorders, liver and stomach cancer, etc. Organophosphate pesticides can cause extreme muscular weakness, tremors and dizziness. Pathogenic bacteria in soil act as a carrier of chronic diseases like cholera, typhoid, amoebic dysentery, polio, hepatitis, leptospirosis, etc.

11. Marine Pollution: Nature, Causes and Effects

More than two third of the earth's surface is covered by oceans. Oceans maintain atmospheric, biological and chemical balance of our planet. Half of the world's population gets its protein from fish. The decline in the oceanic life in recent years is largely due to human activities which affect the marine environment. Almost all pollution load from main land and coastal areas enters the marine environment and gets dumped into the seas. It severely degrades the habitats of marine organisms. Marine pollutants are responsible for the mass death of fishes, corals and mammals.

Marine pollution changes the physical, chemical and biological properties of sea water. It causes harm to marine life and hazards to human health. Liquid waste coming from human settlements, industries, mining activities, oil spills and dumping of solid waste, are the causes of marine pollution. Domestic source of marine pollution includes disposal of municipal sewage, domestic waste and effluents from coastal mega cities, small towns and scattered settlements all along the sea coasts. Industrial pollutants include various organic and inorganic chemicals, heavy metals such as lead, cadmium, mercury, PCBs, synthetic detergents and foaming agents which are discharged directly or indirectly into the sea.

Under sea nuclear weapon testing, nuclear accidents in ocean and sea-coast, release radioactive waste in the ocean. Radioactive waste which is generated from nuclear reactors, is opposed to be dumped on land. It ultimately reaches the sea water which is considered as more convenient dumping ground.

Oil spills are the major pollutants of marine ecosystems. Ship accidents, leakages of oil from oil tankers and pipelines, washing of oil tankers and vehicles, drilling and transportation of petroleum products, wastes from oil refineries and petroleum plants etc. are sources of oil pollution in the marine environment. The thermal and nuclear power plants which are located near coastal areas require a large amount of water for cooling purpose. They discharge their heated waste water into the coastal waters which is a breeding ground for diversity of marine life. It changes the water temperature and badly affects the breeding process. These power plants also add heavy metals to marine ecosystem.

Excessive use of chemical fertilisers and pesticides ultimately reaches to the sea along with run-off water and river flows that also carries the heavy metals and various toxic substances into the sea. It poisons sea food and causes minamata disease. Minamata is a neurological illness which causes weakening of muscles, loss of vision, paralysis, coma and death. Sewage affect and reduce the diversity of sea-life. It brings pathogenic organisms such as viruses, bacteria, protozoa, etc. into the sea-water. These cause diseases in fish, shellfish and other aquatic organisms. Humans who consume such sea-food suffer due to enteric diseases. Detergents, sewage and agricultural run-off with chemical fertilisers and pesticides also creates eutrophic condition which reduces diversity of natural organisms. Oil pollution reduces light penetration, depletes dissolved oxygen and suffocates aquatic life.

12. Noise Pollution: Nature, Causes and Effects

'Noise' is a word derived from the Latin 'nausea' which means a condition of feeling sick and the feeling that one is going to vomit. Noise of an unwanted, unpleasant and annoying sound causes discomfort. It is a disagreeable and wrong sound in the wrong place and at the wrong time. A loud sound which prolongs for a longer period of time is noise for all. Decibel (dB) is the unit of sound intensity. It is used to indicate how loud a sound is. Continuous exposure to sound above 80 decibels can be harmful. It can lead to hearing impairment.

Roaring of sea, thunder, cyclone, etc. are the natural sources of noise. Man-made noise includes the sounds of jet engines, industrial machinery, steam and diesel engines, aeroplanes, loudspeakers and sound systems used in social functions, trains, and traffic noise of moving trucks, buses, cars, two wheelers like scooters, motorbikes, etc., neighbourhood noise like loud TV, stereo, jazz music, radio sets, etc.

Auditory effects of noise pollution includes auditory fatigue and deafness. The non-auditory effects include contraction of muscles and blood vessels, high blood pressure, nervous breakdown, tension and even insanity; damage to liver, kidney and brain; headache, loss of working efficiency, difficulty in concentration, sleeplessness, nausea, vomiting, emotional disturbances; injurious effects on growing foetus; negative effects on animal behaviour and physiology, adverse effects on feeding and breeding habits of animals, etc. High levels of noise develop cracks in the buildings.

13. Biodiversity: Nature, Significance and Threats

The term 'biodiversity' refers to the differences in genes among the individuals of a species, and the variety and richness of all the plant and animal species in a region. The biodiversity is broadly described at three levels-genetic diversity, species diversity and ecosystem diversity. Genetic diversity refers to the diversity in the organisms within a species. Species diversity is used to classify millions of different plant and animal forms on earth. Based on this level of diversity, India is considered "mega-diversity" country. Ecosystem diversity includes living organisms like plants, animals, microorganisms, etc. and non-living things like air, soil, water minerals, etc. in a given area. Biodiversity is a product of continuous process of evolution and natural selection.

Value of biodiversity depends on its consumptive use, productive use, social value, ethical value, religious value, aesthetic value and option value. Human beings are totally dependent on other species for food, medicine, etc. Biodiversity provides raw material for domestic and industrial use. Society depends on local biodiversity for their daily needs and survival. It is believed that each species is a unique creation of nature, and has every right to exist and to be respected. This belief is also found in almost every religion. The beauty of nature has created a special place in human life. Ecosystem adds to beauty and richness of life on the earth. Once a species is extinct or ecosystem is damaged beyond repairs, it cannot be recreated; it is gone forever. Biodiversity gives us immense options to meet our varied demands.

Habitat loss, poaching of wildlife, and man-wild-life conflicts are the threats to biodiversity. Man has overused and misused most of the natural ecosystems. The unsustainable resource use has turned the productive grasslands and forests into wastelands and deserts. Mangroves are cleared for fuel wood and prawn farming. Wetlands are drained for agricultural use. This has destroyed the habitat essential for breeding aquatic species. Large areas of wilderness habitats, diverse tropical forests and coral reefs are destroyed. Such human activities have eliminated millions of species from earth. Population explosion and increase in the livestock population has increased pressure on grasslands and forests.

Illegal hunting or poaching of wildlife has increased because of the commercial value of the bones, horns, skin and other organs of wild animals. Body parts of the wild animals also have the medicinal value in international markets. On the other hand, pace of deforestation has increased. Loss of wild habitats, rapid growth of human population and short-term economic development contribute to rapid destruction of biodiversity. Man and wildlife has been co-existing from primitive period. But conversion of vast wilderness areas into agricultural land, and rapid industrialisation has taken major toll of wildlife by destroying wildlife habitat and polluting the environment. Construction of large dams, mining activities, man induced landslides, soil erosion, deforestation and desertification also threaten biodiversity.

EXERCISES

1. Write a detailed note on the nature and perspectives of environmental ethics.
2. Elucidate on human responsibility for environmental degradation.
3. Enumerate and explain major aspects of environmental degradation.

4. Discuss anthropocentric ethical perspective.
5. Explain intrinsic and instrumental values in environmental ethics.
6. What is prudential anthropocentrism?
7. Discuss utilitarian and deontological approaches to environmental ethics.
8. What is biocentrismn?
9. Comment on individualism and environmental holism.
10. Write a note on he nature, causes and effects of air pollution.
11. Explain the nature, causes and effects of water pollution.
12. Discuss the nature, causes and effects of noise pollution.
13. Write a note on the nature, causes and effects of soil pollution.
14. Write short notes on he following:
    i) Biodiversity
    ii) Marine Pollution
    iii) Acid Rain
    iv) Global Warming
    v) Ozone Depletion
    vi) Green House effect
    vii) Natural Hazards
    viii) Anthropogenic Hazards
    ix) Virtue ethics
    x) Biocentrism

14
Environmental Protection

"To pay homage to beauty is to admire Nature; to admire Nature is to worship God". —R.W. Emerson

Learning Objectives

A. Corporate Proactive Environmental Programmes
   1. Nature of Proactive Programmes
   2. Motives for Proactive Environmental Strategies
   3. Corporate Environmental Protection Strategies
      (i) Porter and Van der Linde's Strategies
      (ii) Renato Orsato's Strategies
      (iii) Corporate-Functional Strategies
   4. Implementation of Corporate Environmental Strategies
   5. Justifiable Distribution and Utilisation of Natural Resources
   6. Rights of Non-human Species

B. Environmental Protection: Measures and Remedies
   1. Need and Urgency of Environmental Protection
   2. Collective Responsibility
   3. Controlling Population Growth
   4. Integrated Land and Water Management
   5. Minimum Use of Pesticides, Insecticides, Herbicides, etc.
   6. Waste Control Programmes
   7. Prevention and Control of Pollutants
   8. Minimising Noise Pollution
   9. Environmentally Compatible Transportation
   10. Regulation of Tourist Activities
   11. Sustainable Management of Agriculture and Irrigation
   12. Animal Husbandry Policy
   13. Forest Conservation and Afforestation Programmes

14. Prevention of Environmental Hazards in Energy Generation
15. Industrial Growth with Environmental Guidelines
16. Regulating Mining and Quarrying Activities
17. Environmental Laws, Rules and Regulations

A. Corporate Proactive Environmental Programmes

1. Nature of Proactive Programmes

An increasing number of companies all over the world are introducing proactive environmental programmes. They integrate environmental issues into their business processes and strategies. Establishing environmental departments, reducing the amount of waste, saving electricity and other forms of energy, recycling the waste material for new use, developing an environmentally sensitive organisational culture, and spreading environmental philosophy to the buyers, suppliers and other stakeholders, are some of the proactive environmental programmes of the companies.

Business organisations have an environmentally proactive strategy if they formulate a long-term plan of environmentally friendly activities. Some researchers are of the opinion that proactive environmental strategies have a positive influence on the company performance. But these strategies are also considered as something that produces extra costs rather than higher profits. Secondly, there are not only green consumers, but consumers with different interests and motives.

2. Motives for Proactive Environmental Strategies

'Regulation' or governmental legislation is the most basic motive for the environmental concern of the companies. Lawmakers are the powerful people who exert their powers to regulate business activities like controlling the maximum allowed emissions or other forms of pollution, regulating packaging content, product design and distribution channels, etc. All the industries do not attract the same amount of government regulation.

'Public concern' is an external force which is exerted by different interest groups such as environmental activists. Expected competitive advantage is a motive that arises from the belief that a firm can outperform its competitors by differentiating products and services or by significantly cutting costs. 'Top management commitment' is an internal force in the companies. Top management shows its environmental commitment by appointing senior managers who are responsible for overseeing environmental strategies of the company.

3. Corporate Environmental Protection Strategies

(i) Porter and Van der Linde's Strategies

Porter and Van der Linde have examined the relationship between the natural environmental and competitive advantage. They argued that natural environment should be viewed as a potential area to develop and maintain competitive advantage, and it should not be considered as a cost of production. Firms should focus on environmentally friendly strategies, so that they are able to market their goods as eco-friendly which helps them to differentiate their products. Firms should focus on the efficiency issues in the production process to reduce the amount of waste generation and production costs.

(ii) Renato Orsato's Strategies

Renato Orsato presented competitive business strategies which can be used by the firms to convert the natural environment into a competitive advantage. Orsato's four strategies are: 'Ecoefficiency', 'Beyond Compliance Leadership', 'Ecobranding' and 'Environmental Cost Leadership'. In ecoefficiency strategic focus, companies can gain an environmental competitive advantage through 'productivity'. If the firm enhances its resource productivity, it can get the benefits in material savings, and better use of the by-products.

The firms provide proof to their stakeholders regarding their commitment to natural environment in their second strategy 'Beyond Compliance Leadership'. Having 'Environmental Management System's (EMS) certification, having a formal environmental code of conduct, having ISO 14000 certification, investing in environmental improvement programmes, etc. are such proofs.

In the 'Ecobranding' strategy, firms use their proactive environmental commitments to differentiate their products and services. This strategy allows the potential customers to consider the natural environment while purchasing the products and services. They provide reliable information about the product's environmental performance to the customers who clearly see the environmental benefits with the purchase of the firms products and services.

In the fourth, 'Environmental Cost Leadership' strategy, firms embrace proactive environmental ideals and reduce the overall costs of production. They focus on radical product innovation like 'using fewer materials to yield cost savings', 'material substitution', etc.

(iii) Corporate-Functional Strategies

According to S. Bannerji *et al.*, (2003) corporate environmentalism has two dimensions: environmental orientation regarding importance of environmental issues facing their firm, and environmental strategy or the extent to which environmental issues are integrated with a firm's strategic plans. Bannerji *et al.*, address strategies on two organisational levels—the corporate level and functional level. Corporate environmental strategies address the extent to which environmental issues are incorporated into firm's decisions on starting new businesses, plant locations, choice of technology and research and development investments.

Functional level strategies deal with strategic questions within different business functions. These strategies discuss about the environmental concerns in the business functions such as purchasing, production, marketing and personnel.

Purchasing environmental strategy stimulates recycling, reuse and resource reduction. The production environmental strategies address product planning, disclosure policy and pollution prevention programmes. They also include capacity planning and scheduling, process design, workforce management, inventory management and quality management. Marketing environment strategy include all the activities that generate or facilitate any exchange intended to satisfy human needs and wants. It emphasises that these activities should not have any negative impact on environment. Personnel environmental strategy is concerned with training employees and building their awareness about environmental issues.

4. Implementation of Corporate Environmental Strategies

In implementation of corporate environmental strategy, the companies are involved in the following activities:

(1) They integrate environmental issues in their strategic planning process.
(2) Where possible, they link environmental goals with their other corporate goals.
(3) They develop new processes and new products that minimise negative environmental impact.
(4) Environmental issues are always considered when they develop new products.
(5) Their quality is measured in terms of the environmental impact of their processes, products and services.
(6) Environmental protection remains the driving force behind their strategies.

In implementation of functional environmental strategies, the companies are involved in the following activities:

(1) They educate their staff on the ways of protecting natural environment.
(2) They encourage employees to recycle waste within the company.
(3) They raise employees' awareness about environmental problems by using internal newsletter.
(4) They always reward the employees with new ideas that contribute to the protection of the environment.
(5) Their employees are encouraged to use environmentally friendly modes of transport to work.
(6) They make continuous efforts to decrease the proportion of waste in their production.
(7) Where possible, they use renewable energy sources.
(8) They always recycle the waste they generate.
(9) Reduction of environmental pollution is the main goal of their manufacturing process.
(10) Their marketing strategy is strongly influenced by environmental problems.
(11) Their ads emphasise the environmental aspects of their products and services.
(12) Their product-market decisions are always influenced by environmental concerns.
(13) Their marketing activities emphasise the concern for environmental protection.

(14) They adapt packaging so as to reduce the negative environmental impact.
(15) Their main goal in purchasing is concern for the environment rather than cost reduction.
(16) Whenever possible, they purchase environmentally friendly material.
(17) They use specific standards for the environmental evaluation of their suppliers.
(18) They manage to raise the proportion of the recycled materials in their purchases to a very high level.

5. Justifiable Distribution and Utilisation of Natural Resources

There are global, national and local concerns regarding just distribution and justifiable utilisation of natural resources. Some individuals use the resources many times more lavishly than the other individuals. Unequal distribution of wealth and access to land and natural resources is a serious environmental concern. Sustainable development for urban, rural and tribal communities should be based upon equitable sharing of resources. A report on the 'Status of India's Environment' by Anil Agarwal emphasises the fact that India's environmental problems were caused by the excessive consumption patterns of the rich that left the poor poorer. According to him environmental destruction is largely caused by the consumption of the rich. The worst sufferers of environmental destruction are the poor.

It is often said that the forests are degraded due to fuel wood collection by poor rural and tribal communities, but they conveniently forget that the rich use much greater quantities of timber. Biomass-based industries like rubber, paper, sugar, cotton textiles, jute, food processing, tobacco, packaging, plywood, etc. need land, energy, water and other natural resources which should not be used excessively or wasted carelessly. So-called educated, rich and urban people need environment education more than the rural and the tribal people. Educated urban dwellers utilise much larger quantities of natural resources and energy than the traditional villagers and tribals.

Economically advanced and industrialised nations of north America and Europe use greater amounts of energy and resources per individual and also waste more resources than the people in the poor and developing countries. Having exploited and exhausted their own natural resources, the industrialised north American and European countries now buy resources from economically deprived nations at a low cost. This depletes the natural resources of the developing countries. However, over 90 per cent of the population growth in the world is taking place in the developing countries which are not in a position to cope with the resource crisis.

Sustainable development is the development which is equal for all. It is based on equity, justice and optimal use of the natural resources as a common property. It also guarantees that the future generations get access to "social capital" and natural resources to create life which is at least equal to that of the present generation. United Nations World Commission on Environment and Development proposes certain priorities necessary to sustain human into the distant future. These priorities include, achieving population control, decreasing inequality, poverty and debts in developing countries, developing sustainable agriculture, protecting wilderness and genetic diversity, protecting ocean and coastal resources, protecting fresh water quality, improving energy efficiency, developing renewable energy resources, controlling greenhouse gases and other air pollutants, protecting ozone layer, minimising wastes, reducing military spending and diverting funds for sustainable development.

6. Rights of Non-human Species

Equitable distribution and utilisation of natural resources by present generation, and preserving resources for future generations of mankind is not enough. Is man a single species entitled to use and exploit the earth's resources? Plants and animals also have a right to live and share the natural resources. Various species who have taken millions of years to evolve, must not be pushed to extinction. All the wild and domesticated animals and different plant species have a right to life and dignified existence upon this earth. Nature always maintains balance in different ecosystems. Terrestrial ecosystems consists the ecosystems like coastal area, desert, hills, mountains, grassland, alluvial plains, rain forest, deciduous forest, alpine and glacier zones, thorn forest, temperate rain forest, tropical rain forest, tropical seasonal forest, temperate forest, savana, taiga, tundra zones, etc. Aquatic ecosystems consists lakes, open sea, coastal water, coral habitats, rivers, ponds, reservoirs, swampy regions, oceans, etc. Man alone has caused serious damage to these ecosystems. Man alone is responsible for the recent rapid decline in the number of species on earth. Man has endangered the existence of wild plants and animals, and has brought them close to the brink of extinction. Animals and plant species have a right to the dignified existence. Their life, well-being and liberty must be respected. To respect the rights and dignity of non-human species is a corporate environmental responsibility.

B. Environmental Protection: Measures and Remedies

1. Need and Urgency of Environmental Protection

Though population is an important resource of development, it is also a major source of environmental degradation. Population growth is exceeding the threshold limits of the support systems. There is a need for rigorous drive for population control. Hundreds of millions of men, women and children are suffering from under-nutrition. A growth in the population of domestic animals has resulted in a loss of area under pastures and grassland. Only 3.5 per cent of our geographical area has remained under grassland.

In India 180 million hectares of land requires special treatment to restore its fertility and productivity. The degradation of soil is caused by water and wind erosion, river action, salinity and alkalinity. Our forest resources are dwindling because of over exploitation for commercial and household needs, over-grazing, encroachments, unsustainable farming practices, and development activities like roads, construction of buildings, power projects, irrigation projects, etc. According to Botanical and Zoological Surveys of India, over 1,500 plant and animal species are endangered.

India's unique wetlands were rich in aquatic and bird life, but now they are facing the problems of pollution and over-exploitation. The major rivers in the country are highly polluted. Coastal vegetation of mangroves and sea grasses is rapidly getting denuded. Extensive deforestation is leading to erosion of valuable topsoil. Agricultural land is damaged as a result of soil degradation. Some areas of agricultural land are facing the problem of rising water table and water-logging because of poorly planned and ill-executed irrigation system. Marine ecosystems are affected by indiscriminate exploitation of coral reefs.

Global warming, rising ocean levels, incursion of salt water, periodic floods, landslides, melting of glaciers, altered temperature and precipitation are some of the results of global atmospheric changes. We are facing serious problems of pollution and unsanitary conditions. Urban slums are expanding and megacities are emerging. Millions of people have no access to basic civic amenities. Incidence of malaria is high, safe drinking water is still a luxury, and liver ailments and gastro-intestinal diseases are common.

2. Collective Responsibility

Environmental protection is a collective ethical responsibility. Various regulatory and preventive measures must be taken to prevent and control pollution, to conserve forests and wildlife, to prevent soil erosion and soil degradation, to form and implement policies, laws, regulations for environmental protection and to form various institutions, departments and boards to shoulder the responsibilities.

3. Controlling Population Growth

There is an urgent necessity to control the unabated population growth. It requires stern legislative measures and incentives. Female education, employment and social security programmes need more social and political support. The means of family planning and health care facilities must be easily accessible and available. Added incentives should be provided in terms of taxation and other benefits for family planning.

4. Integrated Land and Water Management

In the context of recurring droughts and floods, conservation and use of land and water should be considered together. An integrated land and water management is needed for sustainable development. Land near the water bodies must be protected and construction works thereupon must be prevented. Improvement in traditional rain water harvesting and storage should be encouraged. Stringent measures must be taken to prevent and control pollution due to indiscriminate disposal of effluents, solid wastes and hazardous substances in land and water. Legislative measures are necessary to check overexploitation of surface and groundwater. It is necessary to build up a network to assess the quality of water and soil throughout the country. Special programme can be undertaken for afforestation, conservation of soil and prevention of soil erosion. An extensive campaign should be undertaken for the works like contour trenching, contour bunding, construction of small storages, catchment treatment and protection of vegetal cover in the catchments and watersheds. Measures should be taken for water conservation and recycling. Conservation of wetlands is necessary for ensuring sustainable ecological benefits. Municipal and industrial wastes generated from urban areas should be intercepted and diverted from the water bodies.

It is necessary to properly survey the contaminant water sources. The waste sludges from factories, washing and dumpings of tailings, toxic and hazards effluents from industries, toxic effluents from urban areas, inorganic nutrients from agricultural fields, discharge of organic wastes from hills, etc. should be properly treated before their entry into lakes and rivers. The use of bio-fertilisers should be given preference over the use of chemical fertilisers. It is also necessary to minimise the use of pesticides, insecticides, herbicides and rodenticides.

5. Minimum Use of Pesticides, Insecticides, Herbicides, etc.

A study by the Food Safety and Standards Authority of India under the Union Agriculture Ministry has found that common food items contain banned pesticides in quantities a thousand times more than the permissible limits. The findings were based on random samples—collected across the country. From the vegetable basket brinjal tops the chart with the level of banned pesticide "Heptachlor' at 860 per cent above the legal limits, followed by Cauliflower (Aldrin-320%), cabbage (Cypermethrin-95%), Okra (Cypermethrin-55%). According to survey, both apples and oranges were found to have banned pesticide level of 140 per cent above permissible limits, followed by banana (Chlorodane-54%). Wheat and rice too had these dangerous chemicals. While the level of Aldrin in wheat is 21,890—times more than the permissible level, that of Chlorfenvinfos in rice was measured at 1,324 per cent above the allowed limits. Pesticides are neurotoxins and can affect vital organs like kidney and liver as well as endocrine system (*TOI*, Nov. 14th 2013).

6. Waste Control Programmes

Improper disposal of solid wastes creates conditions for a wide range of diseases like cholera, typhoid, conjunctivitis, hepatitis, entamoebiasis, poliomyclitis, roundworms, hookworms, etc. Therefore, open dumping on the land surface near pond, river, lake and sea without proper treatment should be discouraged. Solid wastes can be treated and allowed to be decomposed and recycled in a specially made oxidation pond or sanitary landfills. It can be treated by incineration or in a chemo-mechanical regeneration system. Sometimes municipal waste is subjected to open dumping followed by open burning. Such open burning produces a lot of dangerous gases like SO_2, NO_x, PAN, etc. Waste control programmes should be developed by the government in cooperation with municipalities, industries and local organisations.

7. Prevention and Control of Pollutants

There are six major categories of pollution—air or atmospheric pollution, water pollution, soil pollution, or land pollution, noise pollution, thermal pollution and pollution by radioactive substances. There are various types of pollutants. Biological pollutants include pathogenic organisms, products of biological origin, and parts of biological origin. Chemical pollutants include pesticides, herbicides, insecticides, toxic metals, particulates, gaseous pollutants, hazardous organic and inorganic chemicals, acidic substances, carcinogenic substances, petroleum hydrocarbons and toxins. Physical pollutants include radiation (ionising and non-ionising), thermal (heat), sound waves, etc. Pollution can be monitored and prevented at sources. The best available practicable technical solutions must be encouraged, developed and applied to prevent and control pollution. It is necessary to ensure that the polluter pays for the pollution and for the control arrangements.

To control industrial pollution and pollutants, it is necessary to use various devices like 'Gravity Settling Chambers', 'We Scrubbers', 'Cyclone Separators', 'Electrostatic precipitator', etc. for particulate pollutants. The gaseous pollutants can be controlled by the processes like adsorption, absorption, combustion, condensation, etc. Mining activities, industrial areas, nuclear testing must be kept away from forests and residential areas. Alternative energy technologies should be encouraged, developed and used. Legal provisions should be used to control pollution. Exhaust emissions of vehicles must be timely checked. Fuel efficiency of vehicles must be ensured.

Various scientific and technical methods can be used to treat wastewater and sewage wastewater abatement process with physical abatement, biological treatment and chemical treatment. Public awareness and people's participation is essential for controlling all types of pollutions.

8. Minimising Noise Pollution

Necessary steps should also be taken to minimise the level of noise pollution. The noise pollution by industries, and community can be controlled and lowered down by using improved techniques, sophisticated machinery, sound proofing, using sound absorbers, using protective devices like ear plugs, ear muffs, etc., planting trees along the highways, streets and industries, incorporating silencers in the vehicles, maintaining speed limits, banning air horns, operating radio, TV, music system, loudspeaker at threshold intensity, creating awareness about harmful effects of noise pollution, implementing stringent laws to control noise pollution.

9. Environmentally Compatible Transportation

Environmentally compatible transportation systems should be developed to prevent pollution. Mass transportation systems should be improved in order to reduce fuel consumption, traffic congestion and pollution. Hazardous substances can be transported through pipelines. Transport system based on bio-energy and other non-polluting energy sources should be developed. Traffic flow should be improved through proper maintenance of roads and traffic regulations. Smoke emission standards should be enforced for containing vehicular exhausts at the manufacturer and user level. Use of lead in motor spirit should be phased out.

10. Regulation of Tourist Activities

There should be strict regulation of the tourist activities in sensitive areas such as hill slopes, sanctuaries, islands, national parks and coastal stretches. Indiscriminate growth of tourism should be restricted. Development of tourism should be in harmony with the environmental conditions. It should not affect the lifestyles of the local people. Promotion of tourism should be based on careful assessment of support facilities.

11. Sustainable Management of Agriculture and Irrigation

For environmental conservation and sustainable management of agriculture and irrigation, the methods of sustainable farming, especially organic and natural farming should be developed and promoted. A national policy should be developed for the use of pesticides and insecticides. An integrated pest management and nutrient supply system should be developed. The agricultural inputs like agro-chemicals should be efficiently used. Diversion of prime agricultural land for other purposes should be restricted. Cost-effective and efficient methods of water conservation and use should be evolved. Environmentally compatible cropping patterns and use of bio-fertilisers and bio-pesticides should be promoted. Crop rotation patterns should be encouraged.

Measures should be taken to enhance the efficiency of water use, water conservation, and water recycling. Alternate irrigation systems such as water harvesting, and conservation of run-off rain water should be developed. Water-logging and leaching should be prevented. Optimal utilisation of water resources should be ensured. Focus may be given on decentralised network of small irrigation and water projects with minimum environmental disruption. There should be continuous evaluation and monitoring of all the projects in agriculture and irrigation.

12. Animal Husbandry Policy

Animal husbandry policy should be developed for containing unsustainable growth in livestock population. Stall feeding and rotational grazing can be promoted. Grazing lands should be restored and protected. Distribution of animals like goats under IRDP should be consistent with the availability of pastures. Incentives can be given for growing fodder crops and also for establishment of fodder banks.

13. Forest Conservation and Afforestation Programmes

Conservation of existing forests and raising the forest cover requires essential life support system and concerted efforts. Diversion of forest lands for non-forest uses should be restricted. Where such diversion is unavoidable, compensatory afforestation should be undertaken. Productivity of forests should be increased with efforts to meet the essential national needs, and the forest produce should be efficiently utilised. Afforestation on common lands by the local communities should be encouraged. Land owners and farmers can be motivated to resort to tree-farming. Local people and dedicated NGOs can be involved in the afforestation programmes. Forest produce should be supplied to the industrial consumers only at its true market value, and not at concessional rates. Alternative sources of energy and fuel efficient stores should be developed and promoted.

14. Prevention of Environmental Hazards in Energy Generation

Pollution and environmental hazards in energy generation and use requires to be prevented and controlled. Measures should be taken to popularise environmentally benign energy systems. Biogas plants based on cow-dung, vegetable wastes and human excreta should be set up on large scale. Concerted efforts are needed for development and promotion of non-conventional renewable energy generation systems, especially the solar energy systems. Incentives should be given for use of non-conventional energy sources. The use of energy efficient devices should be promoted in all sectors including households, transportation, industry and agriculture for energy conservation. Location of energy generation projects should be based on environmental considerations including loss of biodiversity, pollution and displacement of people.

15. Industrial Growth with Environmental Guidelines

Industrial growth should be integrated with environmental considerations. Locations of industries should be according to environmental guidelines for siting of industry. While deciding upon site, priority should be given to compatible industries so that wastes from one industry could be used as raw material for the other. Incentives should be given to environmentally clean technologies, reuse of wastes and recycling. Effluent tax should be introduced and 'polluter pays principle' should be followed. Small-scale industries can be given fiscal incentives for reduction of wastes and for pollution control. Reduction of automobile emissions should be encouraged. Pollution control norms should be enforced in various industries, particularly in the highly polluting industries. Collective efforts are needed for installation and operation of common effluent treatment facilities in industrial estates. Environmental cells should be set up in industries for compliance of environmental laws and also for implementing environmental plans. Environmental audit system should be introduced to focus on environment related policies, plans and activities.

16. Regulating Mining and Quarrying Activities

Environmental repercussions from mining and quarrying operations should be prevented. Adequate ecological restoration and rehabilitation of the abandoned mined areas must be ensured in a phased manner. Systematic extraction of minerals along with environmental conservation should be ensured. Environmentally safe disposal of the by-products of mining is necessary. The mining and quarrying activities in sensitive areas such as hill slopes, areas rich with biodiversity and areas of natural springs should be banned or restricted.

17. Environmental Laws, Rules and Regulations

Increasing pollution and environmental degradation have alarmed the human community and threatened the existence of all the other biotic communities on the earth. All the countries in the world are now participating in the process of evolving a global environmental governance to monitor, prevent, control and resolve the environmental problems. They are forming the policies and strategies for environmental protection, and drafting the legal provisions to be implemented in this regard. Abiding by them is our collective ethical responsibility.

Arhus Convention (1998), Espoo Convention (1991) Convention on Long-Range Transboundary Air Pollution, Geneva (1979), Chicago Convention on Civil Aviation (1981), Framework Convention on Climate Change, UNFCCC, New York (1992), Kyoto Protocol (1997), Vienna Convention for the Production of Ozone Layer (1985), Montreal Protocol on Ozone Layer (1987), CEC Water Convention, Helsinki (1992), Convention on the Control of Transboundary Movements of Hazardous Wastes and their Disposal, Basel (1989), Convention on Civil Liability for Damage Caused during Carriage of Dangerous Goods by Road, Rail and Inland—Navigation Vessels, CRTD, Geneva (1989), Convention on the Transboundary Effects of

Industrial Accidents, Helsinki (1992), Convention on Hazardous Chemicals and Pesticides in International Trade, Rotterdam (1998), FAO International Code of Conduct on Distribution and Use of Pesticides, Rome (1985), Stockholm Convention (2001), Waigani Convention on Hazardous and Radioactive Wastes (1995), Minamata Convention on Mercury, Minamata (2013), London Convention on Marine Pollution (1972), International Convention on Civil Liability for Oil Pollution Damage, Brussels (1984, 1992), OPRC-HNS Protocol, London (2000), UN Convention on Law of the Sea, Montego Bay (1982) etc. have formed official agreement between countries, organisations and groups of people for protecting environment at global level.

In Indian Constitution, there are two articles related to protection of environment. Article 48A says, "The State shall endeavour to protect and improve the environment and to safeguard the forests and Wildlife of the country". Article 51A (g) is regarding the fundamental duties of citizens—"It shall be the duty of citizen of India to protect and improve the natural environment including forests, lakes, rivers and wildlife and to have compassion for living creatures". The major environmental Acts and rules are as follows:

The Air Act (1981, amended up to 1987) for Prevention and Control of Air Pollution: The Environment (Protection) Act, 1986; Environment (Protection) Rules 1993: Environment Standard; The Water Act, 1974, for Prevention and Control of Water Pollution (amended up to 1988); The Water (Prevention and Control of Pollution) Cess Act, 1977 (as amended up to 1991); The Forest (Conservation) Act, 1980 (amended up to 1992); Forest (Conservation) Act, 1980 (amended up to 1992); Forest (Conservation) Rules, 1981; The Wild Life (Protection) Act, 1972 (amended up to 1991); Wild Life Rules (1983); Mines and Minerals (Regulation and Development) Act, 1957; Mineral Conservation and Development Rules, 1988; The Biodiversity Act, 2002; Biodiversity Rules 1999; Biomedical Waste Management and Handling Rules, 1998; Hazardous Microorganisms and Genetically Modified Organisms (Manufacture, use, Import, Export and Storage) Rules, 1999; Coastal Zone Regulations, 1991; The Public Liability Insurance Act, 1991, etc. It is the legal and ethical responsibility of all individuals, groups, organisations, industries, government agencies and society at large, to honour, implement and to abide by all of these laws, rules and regulations in order to protect our environment from pollution, degradation and depletion.

EXERCISES

1. Write a detailed note on corporate proactive environmental programmes.
2. Describe the nature and motives for proactive environmental programmes.
3. Comment on various corporate environmental protection strategies.
4. Discuss various activities involved in the implementation of corporate environmental strategies.
5. Express your views on justifiable distribution and utilisation of natural resources.
6. Write a note on rights of non-human species.
7. Discuss various measures and remedies for environmental protection.
8. Write short notes on the following:
   (i) Controlling Population Growth
   (ii) Waste Control Management
   (iii) Prevention and Control of Pollutants
   (iv) Integrated Land and Water Management
   (v) Pesticides, Insecticides and Herbicides: Misuse and Effects
   (vi) Minimising Noise Pollution
   (vii) Regulating Tourist Activities
   (viii) Sustainable Agriculture and Irrigation Management
   (ix) Animal Husbandry Policy
   (x) Industrial Growth with Environmental Guidelines
   (xi) Regulating Mining and Quarrying Activities
   (xii) Environmental Laws, Rules and Regulations

15

Corporate Governance

"Make it difficult for people to do wrong, and easy to do right".
—Anonymous

Learning Objectives

A. Meaning of Corporate Governance
B. Significance of Corporate Governance
C. Basic Ingredients of Corporate Governance
D. Mechanisms and Controls of Corporate Governance
  1. The Board of Directors
  2. Internal Auditors and Control Procedures
  3. Monitoring by Large Shareholders
  4. Balance of Power
  5. Remuneration
  6. Proxy Voting
  7. Takeover or Hostile Takeover
  8. Financial Structure
E. Principles of Corporate Governance
  1. Rights and Equitable Treatment of Shareholders
  2. Role and Responsibilities of the Board
  3. Transparency and Disclosure
  4. Interests of Other Stakeholders
  5. Integrity and Code of Ethics
F. Models of Corporate Governance
  1. Anglo-American Model
  2. Coordinated or Multi-Stakeholder Model
G. Theories of Corporate Governance
  1. Agency Theory
  2. Ownership Theory
  3. Stewardship Theory
  4. Stakeholder Theory

A. Meaning of Corporate Governance

Corporate governance refers to the system structure and process by which companies are directed and controlled. It is a deliberate and sustained effort on the part of corporate entity to strike a judicious balance between its own interests and the interests of various other people like shareholders, employees, suppliers, customers and society at large. It is a formal system of accountability of the corporate management to corporate stakeholders by attempting to maintain balance between its economic goals and social goals. It is governing and control by the corporate managers with the objective to run the business of their company successfully and to take care of the interests of all its stakeholders.

> *"Corporate governance is to conduct the business in accordance with owner's/shareholders desires, which generally, will be to make as much money as possible while confirming to the basic rules of the society embodied in law and local customers".* —Milton Friedman
>
> *"Corporate governance deals with laws, procedures, practices and implicit rules that determine a company's ability to take managerial decisions vis-à-vis its claimants—in particular, its shareholders, creditors, the state and the employees in general".*
>
> —Confederation of Indian Industry (The CII Code definition)
>
> *"Corporate governance is the system by which companies are directed and controlled. Board of Directors are responsible for the governance of their companies. The shareholder's role in the governance is to appoint the directors and the auditors and to satisfy themselves that an appropriate governance structure is in place. The responsibilities of the board include setting the company's strategic aims, providing the leadership to put them into effect, supervising the management of the business and reporting to shareholders on their stewardship. The board's actions are subject to laws, regulations and the shareholders in the meeting".* —The Cadbury Committee

Corporate governance is considered as the system and process by which companies are controlled and directed. It involves the roles and relationships between and among the company's board of directors, managerial hierarchy, shareholders and the other stakeholders. These roles, relationships and regulatory mechanisms are directed towards the achievement of the company's goals. The external stakeholder groups affected by corporation's policies and activities are the shareholders, debtholders, suppliers, customers, creditors and the communities. The board of directors, executives and other employees are the internal stakeholders of a corporation.

In large size corporations, there is a separation of ownership and management, and the shareholders have no adequate control. The upper management may have very different interests, and considerably more information about the corporate activities than the shareholders. Therefore, principal-agent conflicting issues often arise between upper-management (the agent) and the shareholders (the principals). Rather than overseeing management on behalf of shareholders, the board of directors often become insulated from the shareholders. Therefore, in contemporary business corporations, an important theme of corporate governance is the nature and extent of accountability of people in business.

B. Significance of Corporate Governance

Corporate governance represents a framework of values and ethics. The business decisions are taken under such ethical framework.

Corporate governance is expected to ensure the clarity and integrity of financial reports.

Corporate governance focuses on the structure or framework for creating long-term trust between and among the concerned parties.

Corporate governance rationalises the management and monitors organisational performance in order to successfully encounter challenging domestic and global situations.

Corporate governance helps to gain a reasonably good degree of stakeholder confidence that contributes to the proper functioning of a market economy.

Corporate governance can improve the process of strategic thinking by inducting independent directors who can bring with them the innovative ideas and experience.

Corporate governance is based on the principles of transparency and accountability. These principles are crucial to the legal credibility and integrity of the market system.

C. Basic Ingredients of Corporate Governance

The board of directors of a company, and its auditors have a definite role to protect the interest of all the stakeholders in every business decision. They have to set up a proper organisational structure, its systems, norms, procedures and processes for direction, supervision and accountability of the organisation.

The quality and competence of directors are the important ingredients of corporate governance. Policy formation, decision-making, implementing decisions and responsiveness depends on them.

Transparency is a key element of good corporate governance. It is a shared way of corporate functioning. It requires timely disclosure of right information with integrity.

Corporate governance requires conforming to the laws, rules and spirit of codes. The process of governance requires greater simplicity and a system of checks and balances.

Clarity in the responsibilities of directors, chairman and managing director is needed to enhance the accountability.

Good corporate governance involves adequate reporting to the shareholders and the other stakeholders. For this purpose company has to publish periodical reports.

Above all, the accountability of the board of directors to the ultimate owners, shareholders and the other stakeholder is the important ingredient of corporate governance.

D. Mechanisms and Controls of Corporate Governance

Corporate governance mechanisms and controls are designed to minimise the inefficiencies that result from the moral hazards and adverse selection.

1. The Board of Directors

The Board of Directors provide the first mechanism which monitors the management. The board maintains checks and balances on management. Cadbury Committee recommends an independent member as a Chairman of the Board and a formal selection procedure for non-executive directors.

The board of directors have legal authority to hire, fire and compensate top management. Regular meetings enable the board to identify, discuss and avoid the potential problems. Executive directors possess superior knowledge of the decision-making process. They evaluate the management on the basis of the quality of its decisions.

2. Internal Auditors and Control Procedures

Internal auditors test the design and implementation of internal control procedures. They also test the reliability of financial reporting. Internal control procedures are the policies implemented by the board of directors, audit committee, management and other personnel.

3. Monitoring by Large Shareholders

In respect of their large investment in the company, these stakeholders have the right degree of control and power to monitor the decisions and performance of the management.

4. Balance of Power

Separation of power is developed in the companies where separate divisions check and balance each other's actions. The simplest balance requires that the President is different person from the treasurer. When one group proposes administrative changes, another group reviews and opposes the changes and third group takes care that the interests of all the stakeholders are adequately served, the balance of power is maintained.

5. Remuneration

Performance-based remuneration is given in the form of cash or non-cash payments. The non-cash payments are shares and share options, superannuation and other benefits. This proportionate remuneration relates to individual performance and his salary. Performance-based remuneration are the incentive schemes. These schemes can be reactive if these schemes do not provide any mechanism to prevent mistakes or opportunistic behaviour.

6. Proxy Voting

Proxy voting is a mechanism with a purpose to have a better

management. But this mechanism faces the free-rider problem. Shareholders own the company in terms of the residual control rights. But, they may get very little or no incentives for monitoring the management. When shareholders are large in number but do not have sufficient influence to exert pressure individually, they face a significant "free rider problem". An individual shareholder can incur the cost for monitoring, but the benefits of the improved company performance accrue to all shareholders. Therefore, nobody wants to bear the cost of investigating the company's underperformance and launching the proxy fight.

7. Takeover or Hostile Takeover

In principle, the mechanism of takeover or hostile takeover does away with incentive and free-rider problems. It aligns the interest of the management and the other stakeholders of the company. It allows an individual who identifies an underperforming factor to obtain a large reward. It is argued that the regulations which protect the managements from hostile takeovers lower disciplinary role of takeovers. Therefore, it may prove to be counterproductive in the end. However, hostile takeovers have raised doubts about whether it really improves the economic performance in the long run.

8. Financial Structure

Corporate financial structure is a mechanism which acts as a source of discipline on corporate management. The debt obligations of a company force the management to keep the part of the revenues to make repayments. These obligations also constrain the management's opportunities to invest in the wrong projects in the terms of economic performance. Due to close relationships with companies, banks can detect early the underperformance and risks of a company. They can demand enforcement of harsh restructuring plans with credible threats to shut down the credits channel if the company does not implement the restructured plans quickly.

E. Principles of Corporate Governance

Cadbury Report (1992), the Principles of corporate Governance (OECD, 1998 and 2004), and the Sarbanes-Oxley Act (2002), are the three major documents released since 1990 that refer to the principles of the corporate governance. These reports present general principles of corporate governance for the guidance of corporate businesses which are expected to operate to assure proper governance.

1. Rights and Equitable Treatment of Shareholders

Rights of the shareholders should be given due respect. Organisations should help the shareholders to exercise those rights. They can help the shareholders to exercise their rights if they openly communicate information about the business activities to the shareholders. Shareholders should be encouraged to participate in general meetings.

2. Role and Responsibilities of the Board

The board has to review, and if required, challenge the performance of management. For this purpose the board needs sufficient relevant knowledge and skills. The board also needs its adequate size, commitment, and appropriate level of independence.

3. Transparency and Disclosure

Organisations have to clarify the roles, responsibilities and performance of the board and management, and make it publicly known so that a level of accountability is provided to the stakeholders. Procedures should be properly implemented to independently verify and safeguard the integrity of the financial reporting of the organisation. Disclosures concerning the organisational and business activities should be timely and adequate in order to ensure that the investors get the clear, correct and factual information.

4. Interests of Other Stakeholders

Organisations should recognise the obligations to non-shareholder stakeholders. These are the legal, contractual, social and market driven obligations. The non-shareholder stakeholders include customers, investors, suppliers, creditors, employees, local communities, policy makers and the government agencies.

5. Integrity and Code of Ethics

Organisations should develop a code of ethics for their directors, executives and all the other employees. They should try to promote ethical decision-making and morally responsible conduct in the organisational activities. In choosing corporate officers and board members integrity is to be considered as a fundamental requirement.

F. Models of Corporate Governance

There are different models of corporate governance around the world. This difference is due to various forms of capitalism in which they are embedded. The 'Anglo-American Model' tends to dwell upon the interests of the shareholders. 'Coordinated Model' or 'Multi-stakeholder Model' recognises the interests of the customers, employees, investors, suppliers, creditors, managers, local communities and the government. Multi-stakeholder or coordinated model is associated with the Continental Europe, Japan and India.

1. Anglo-American Model

Anglo-American model of corporate governance gives priority to the interests of the shareholders. It is based on single-tiered Board of Directors which is dominated by the non-executive directors. These non-executive directors are elected by the shareholders, therefore, it is also known as the 'unitary system'. In this system, boards include some executives who are ex-officio members of the board. Non-executive directors outnumber the executive directors. Non-executive directors hold the key posts including audit and compensation committees.

United Kingdom and United States differ in one basic respect with regard to corporate governance. In United Kingdom, the CEO generally does not also serve as the Chairman of the Board. In United States dual role is a norm. The CEO also serves as Chairman of the Board. In United States, corporations are governed by state laws, while the exchange of securities in corporations is governed by federal legislation.

2. Coordinated or Multi-Stakeholder Model

Continental European countries like Germany, Netherlands, etc. have a two-tiered board of directors. This system is considered as a means of improving corporate governance. In two-tiered board, the Executive Board is made up of company executives. The Executive Board generally runs day-to-day operations. The Supervisory Board is entirely made up of the non-executive directors who represent the employees and shareholders. The supervisory board reviews major business decisions, determines the compensation of the members of executive board, and hires and fires them.

In India, SEBI Committee on Corporate Governance defines corporate governance as "The acceptance by management of the inalienable rights of shareholders as the true owners of the corporation and of their own role as the trustees on behalf of the shareholders. It is about commitment to values, about ethical business conduct and about making a distinction between personal and corporate funds in the management of a company". (Report of the SEBI Committee on Corporate Governance, 2003). Indian approach is drawn from the Gandhian Principle of Trusteeship and the Directive Principles of the Indian Constitution.

G. Theories of Corporate Governance

1. Agency Theory
2. Ownership Theory
3. Stewardship Theory
4. Stakeholder Theory

1. Agency Theory

Agency theory of corporate governance argues that the owners hire management to run the affairs of the organisation. They are the principales who have the ownership rights. They have the rights to resolve the conflicts which occurs inside or outside the organisation. On the other hand, managers are agents who work in the interest of the owners. The owners hire the agents.

The board controls and directs the management. It acts as arbitration between management and principals. It is responsible to ensure that decisions are always made in the best interests of the owners. It is intermediary between management and shareholders. It intermediates independently between those who contribute the resources and those who allocate and utilise the resources. Those who contribute the resources are the owners and those who allocate and utilise the resources are managers or the agents. Managers have to utilise the resources in such a way that the interests of the owners are met optimally.

The board oversees the operations of the agent, and may even hire the external monitors. The board acts in the best interests of shareholders. It can fire the CEO if he acts against the interests of the shareholders and the company.

According to Eisenhardt (1989), 'Agency theory is directed at the ubiquitous agency relationship, in which one party (the principal) delegates work to another (the agent), who performs the work'. Pure agency theory is characterised by the conflict between the principal and the agent. Conflict occurs due to varying interests of principals and the agents. Contractual view of the firm assumes that the conflicts can be resolved by having appropriately designed contracts. But perfect contracts are not possible in practice.

2. Ownership Theory

Success is often measured in terms of how much one owns. The distinction between those who own and those who do not is moderated on the basis of information received by them. An informed person always on average makes some gains, while an uninformed person on average loses and fails to make any gains. Often, the information can be incomplete, imperfect and incorrect. The value of ownership is moderated by complete and perfect information.

In financial terms, capitalist experiments with private ownership has led the world to go through a series of financial crisis. In case of 'Lehman Brothers', 'AICE' etc. all the gains are privatised and all the risks and debts are socialised through state. Ownership, whether well-informed or uninformed, privately held or publicly held, raises the question of distributive justice. Ownership and the desire to own is often responsible for many of the scandals, social evils and wars. Ownership is often viewed from an instrumental point of view. The concept of ownership is naturally held in relation to the end one seeks.

Ownership is based on the answer to the question, "who has the legal ownership of the information?" (Stanwick *et al.*, 2011). Legitimate owner is the 'ultimate decision maker' pertaining to the information. An individual has ownership of his or her own personal information from a privacy perspective. From a property rights perspective, an organisation has to verify whether the management is the sole owner or some other party/parties are the owners of the information regarding the operations of the organisation.

Harvard Professor Robert Nozik's (1974) theory of economic justice, which he calls the "entitlement theory", maintains that the people are entitled to their holdings (goods, money, property) as long as they have acquired them fairly. However, he does not specify fully what constitutes a just original acquisition of holdings.

Ownership of private property is central to capitalism. Capitalism requires private ownership of the 'major means' of production and distribution. Private hands control the economic assets and productive resources. 'Capital, as an economic concept, is closely related to private property', says William Shaw (2002). Individuals and corporations acquire various means of production and assets to produce and sell the goods and services in order to earn profit. In simple words, capital is money which is invested for making more money and to own more holdings.

Corporation is never an individually owned organisation. It is owned by entire team, therefore, it can be understood better as team ownership. Team ownership is not collectivist ownership which has its own totalitarian form of governance. Team ownership allows for experts, and their varied inputs of ideas and resources that are necessary in the running of any corporation. Key difference which is displayed by the concepts of 'ownership' and 'stewardship' is in the mindset. Ownership reminds one of the 'rights' that everyone is interested in having, on the other hand, stewardship reminds one of the 'responsibilities' that everyone is not so keen to accept and to be reminded of.

3. Stewardship Theory

Pure stewardship theory considers the situations in which the management acts in the best interests of shareholders without any conflict between principal and agents. Stewardship can produce and maintain trust. It enables the firm to put the ownership at the common good of all concerned. It provides a solution to the problem of aggressive accumulation of assets and greed. It is the greed or aggressive accumulation of wealth which results in increased inequality, rivalry and conflict. Stewardship can be implemented as a framework for running a business. Stewardship concept can be easily operational. Stewards manage property and resources that are not their own. They are expected to meet the expectations and interests of the shareholders and other stakeholders.

Stewards are the caretakers of an asset or an estate. They oversee the entire property, and run all the business activities. The board has a role and function of overseeing, and management has the function of managing business affairs. Successful leaders are the successful stewards who protect and add value to the assets which are placed under their trust and control. Steward serves the owner. Steward is accountable to the owner for the protection, appreciation and well-being of the assets. Stewardship can be used as a basis for corporate governance where there is a clear separation of management and ownership. It can produce responsible growth of the business. It can guide, direct and enable the people to make their contribution.

The concept of stewardship includes an idea that the rightful owner is someone other than oneself. It is this absence of the self, absence of egòism, absence of corporate ego of CEO and other managers that protects the property of the rightful owner. Stewardship can create spiritual connection of the stewards with the other people and the environment. It creates an organisation which effectively employs the present resources without harming the needs of the future. It creates and maintains trust which enables the organisation to put the ownership at the common good of all the concerned people.

Managers are hired because they are the experts, and directors are chosen because they know how business world functions and corporation operates. Knowledge and expertise of the executives and directors ultimately results in the growth of the firm and maximisation of its financial performance. Stewardship theory works best when the interests of the stewards and all the stakeholders are well aligned. The general assumption of stewardship theory is that the attainment of corporate objectives also satisfies the manager's objectives.

4. Stakeholder Theory

Stakeholders include all the individuals and groups who are affected by the policies, decisions and operations of an organisation. The central claim of the stakeholder theory is that corporations are operated or ought to be operated for the benefits of all those who have a stake in the enterprise. Stakeholders are vital to the survival and success of an organisation. As any group or individual, they can affect or are affected by the achievement of the organisation's objectives. Though the relation of each stakeholder group to the corporation is different, each of the constituencies is integral to the operation of the corporation.

In agency theory, the view of the firm is that of the management serving the shareholders, but in stakeholders theory, managers have a number of stakeholder relationships to serve. There are a number of individuals or groups who are associated with the organisation. Their legitimate interests in participating in the organisational activities is to obtain the benefits.

Stakeholder's theory is justified from three mutually supportive aspects:

- Descriptive Justification
- Instrumental Justification
- Normative Justification

Descriptive Justification

The stakeholder's theory describes the corporation as a collection of cooperative and competitive interests of various stakeholders. It explains the past, present and future affairs of corporation and its stakeholders.

Instrumental Justification

A framework for the analysis and investigation of the links between the practice of stakeholder management and the attainment of organisational goals, is provided by the stakeholder theory. The linkage between managerial action and corporate performance gives instrumental justification for the theory.

Normative Justification

The normative justification of stakeholder theory is acquired from the moral and ethical position of the theory. The normative aspect involves acceptance of stakeholders with legitimate interests in the procedures, processes and substantive aspects of firm's activities. The interests of the stakeholders are considered to be of intrinsic value. Stakeholder theory formulates the stakeholder principles which give moral guidance for the operation and management of the firm.

Management Style and Stakeholders

Immoral, moral and amoral managers react with stakeholders in different management styles. Immoral manager's self-interest supersedes the interests of employees, shareholders, customers and the local community. According to them customers are purely revenue generators. They will communicate only what is legally needed for the stakeholder group. Moral managers treat the stakeholders fairly and justly. They develop the code of ethics and incorporate it in their decision-making.

EXERCISES

1. What is the meaning of 'corporate governance'?
2. "Corporate governance refers to the system, structure and process by which companies are directed and controlled". Elucidate.
3. "Corporate governance represents a framework of values and ethics". Discuss.
4. What are the basic ingredients of corporate governance?
5. Explain the mechanisms and control procedures of corporate governance.
6. Discuss the general principles of corporate governance for the guidance of corporate business.
7. Explain different models of corporate governance.
8. Elucidate on various theories of corporate governance.
9. Write short notes on the following:
   - (i) Anglo American Model of Corporate Governance
   - (ii) Agency Theory of Corporate Governance
   - (iii) Ownership Theory of Corporate Governance
   - (iv) Coordinated Model of Corporate Governance
   - (v) Stewardship Theory
   - (vi) Stakeholder Theory
   - (vii) The Board of Directors
   - (viii) Internal Auditors and Control Procedures
   - (ix) Proxy Voting
   - (x) Takeover or Hostile Takeover
   - (xi) Rights of Shareholders
   - (xii) Transparency and Disclosure
   - (xiii) Code of Ethics
   - (xiv) Interests of Stakeholders

16
Corporate Social Responsibility (CSR)

"There is no higher religion than human service".

—Albert Schwitzer

Learning Objectives

A. Conceptual Framework of CSR
B. Approaches to Corporate Social Responsibility (CSR)
   1. Obstructionist Approach
   2. Defensive Approach
   3. Accommodative Approach
   4. Proactive Approach
C. Benefits of Corporate Social Responsibility (CSR)
D. Monitoring CSR
   1. Stakeholder's Audit
   2. Safety Audit
   3. Environmental Audit.
E. Outcomes of CSR
F. Constituents of Corporate social responsibility (CSR)
   - Legal Responsibilities
   - Ethical Responsibilities
   - Economic Responsibilities
   - Discretionary Responsibilities
G. Assessment of CSR Policies
   1. Internal Aspects
   2. External Aspects.
   3. Accountability
   4. Citizenship

H. Corporate social Responsibility to Stakeholders
   1. Responsibilities to Itself
   2. Responsibilities to Shareholders
   3. Responsibilities to Employees
   4. Responsibilities to Customers
   5. Responsibilities to State
   6. Responsibilities to Community at Large

A. Conceptual Framework of CSR

Business organisations were predominantly concerned with maximising their profits in the early twentieth century. In the 1950s, the social activists began to question this singular objective of profit maximisation. The term "Corporate Social Responsibility (CSR)" came into use in the late 1960s and early 1970s after many multinational corporations formed the term "stakeholder". The term was used to refer to those on whom an organisation's activities had an impact. Later, it was used to describe corporate owners beyond shareholders by Edward Freeman in his book '*Strategic Management: A Stakeholder Approach*' in 1984. The concept of social responsibility became popular after the publication of Howard Bowen's book, '*Social Responsibilities of Business*'.

Corporate Social Responsibility (CSR) refers to the obligations of corporate decision-makers to protect the interests of all the stakeholders, to improve the social economy and to undertake welfare activities for the society as a whole along with their own interests. It is an intelligent and objective concern of a company for the welfare of a broader society. This concern puts a moral control on the business and holds it back from socially unethical and destructive activities. A company with corporate social responsibility holds the view that management is equally responsible to the company itself and to all the interest groups with which it interacts. The interest groups like customers, employees, suppliers, creditors, government and society at large are placed in equal status with the shareholders.

It is expected that management does not mislead the customers by its exaggerated and false advertisements. Business organisation restrains itself from involving in hoarding and profiteering. A socially responsible company keeps the prices fair and ensures quality of products and services. Employees are never exploited. Labour laws are honoured and strictly followed. Health, safety and welfare measures are provided. Workers are paid fair and reasonable wages. Company maintains cooperative and healthy relationships with the creditors and suppliers. Relevant and accurate information is provided to them. Company is expected to play an active and proper role in civic affairs. It has to fulfil its social responsibilities by enhancing the well-being of individuals and groups in the society. Management is expected to pay all the taxes on time. It abides by the rules, laws and agreements. A socially responsible management never bribes the public servants. Management protects the interests of the shareholders and uses the resources effectively and efficiently.

'Corporate Sustainable Development', 'Corporation Philanthropy', 'Corporate Citizenship', 'Corporate Social Performance', and 'Corporate Community Involvement' are other terms used for describing Corporate Social Responsibility.

Andrew Carnegie's (1835-1919) views on social responsibility were based on two principles—'Charity' and 'Stewardship'. The former principle required the more fortunate members of society to provide for the least fortunate and the latter rooted itself in the Bible bestowing businesses and wealthy individuals with the right to protect wealth.

According to European Commission (EU, 2001 a:8) and (EU, 2001, b:5), "Corporate Social Responsibility is a concept whereby companies integrate social and environmental concerns in their business operations and in their interaction with their stakeholders on a voluntary basis".

Dahl, R. (1972) states, "Every large corporation should be thought of as a social enterprise; that is an entity whose existence and decisions can be justified in so far as they serve public or social purposes".

According to Shaw, E. (2004: 196), the principal characteristics of social responsibility are: (i) the orientation—"directly involved in producing goods and providing services to the market, making an operating surplus", and (ii) the aim—"explicit social aims (job creation, training, or provision local services), strong social values and mission (commitment to local capacity building), accountable to their members and wider community for their social, environmental and economic impact. The profits are to their stakeholders or for benefit of the community".

Michael Hopkins (1998) opines, "Corporate social responsibility is concerned with treating the stakeholders of the firm ethically or in a socially responsible manner. Stakeholders exist both within a firm and outside. Consequently, behaving socially responsibly will increase the human development of stakeholders within and outside the corporation".

Kailash Sodani and Renu Jatana (2007) define CSR as "a strategy or visionary plan which targets the bull's eye profit encompassing environmental aspects along with commitment of duty towards the society".

According to Vijay and Harshita Shrimali (2007), "Social responsibility refers to what the business does, over and above the statutory requirement for the benefit of the society. The word responsibility connotes that the business has some moral obligation to the society".

The Prince of Wales Business Leaders Forum defined CSR as "Open and transparent business practices that are based upon ethical values and respect for employees, communities and the environment—(and) designed to deliver sustainable value to society at large as well as to shareholders".

Milton Friedman opined that, "business should use their resources and energies in activities that increase its profits as long as they perform and carry out fair and open practices without deception and fraud".

According to 'World Business Council for Sustainable Development'—"Corporate Social Responsibility is the continuing commitment by business to behave ethically and contribute to economic development while improving the quality of life of the work force and their families as well as of the local community and society at large".

Slaughter (1997) describes corporate social responsibility as "An action that goes beyond the legal or regulatory minimum standard with the end of some perceived social good rather than the maximisation of profits".

Parkinson (1996) distinguishes between relational responsibility and social activism. Relational responsibility refers to assistance to groups such as employees, suppliers, consumers or the community who are affected by the company's business activities. On the other hand, social activism benefits groups who fall outside the scope of company's business activities.

According to K. Koteswara Rao, (2007), "CSR is a concept whereby companies integrate social and environmental concerns in their business operations and in their interactions with their stakeholders on a voluntary basis".

Bowen defines the concept of social responsibility as "the obligation of managers to pursue those policies, to make those decisions or to follow those lines of action which are desirable in terms of the objectives and values of our society".

Koontz and O'Donnell have defined the social responsibility as "the personal obligation of the people as they act in their own interests to assure that the rights and legitimate interests of others are not infringed".

According to Steiner, "Social responsibility is to understand public consensus, to recognise it, and to cooperate in achieving this. Each business has responsibilities in some way commensurate with its power".

According to Balachandran and Solomon Prabakar (2007), "Social responsibility is nothing but commitment and answerability to the needs of society based on sense of subjective judgments involving varied relationships based on change in character and composition of society".

B. Approaches to Corporate Social Responsibility (CSR)

Corporate social responsibility depends on the recognition of the rights of all stakeholders, managerial activities to promote the welfare and well-being of stakeholders and society as a whole, and the accountability of the business in this wider context. The economic view of accountability only to the owners has been subject to debate to a considerable extent. There are variety of other stakeholders who have a concern with the activities of business organisations because they are affected by those activities. Therefore, traditional ownership approach is challenged recently by the critics who uphold a stakeholder approach that recognises the wide stakeholder community.

Corporate activities have an effect not just upon itself but also upon the external environment within which that organisation operates. This environment includes the business environment of the firm, local societal environment and the wider global environment. The effects of the corporate activities on these environment can be in diverse forms. There can be transformation of the landscape due to raw material extraction or waste product storage and dumping. Natural resources are utilised as a part of firm's manufacturing processes. The economic status of the local community can be upgraded by creating employment opportunities for them. Competition of the firm with the other firms, and the judicious distribution of wealth created by the firm, have diverse effects on the owners, workers and society at large. Therefore, corporate activities must be based on its commitment to social responsibilities. Organisational commitment depends on the approaches of management towards the social responsibilities.

1. Obstructionist Approach

In obstructionist approach, managers show negative attitude towards social responsibilities. They do not like to fulfil their social obligations. They make effort to hide information regarding violation of standards, adulteration, etc. A pharmaceutical company which produces unsafe and low quality drugs, falls in the class of such organisations. They take care that the news of their illegal and unethical behaviour does not reach to the other stakeholders.

2. Defensive Approach

Defensive approach shows very little active interest in the corporate social responsibility. Defensive approach signifies minimum required commitment to fulfil social obligations. The organisational behaviour is strictly within the bounds of law, and it does not cross the bounds of ethicality. But such activities are constrained to the minimum required. In defensive approach, managers are not expected to make socially responsible business decisions. They simply abide by rules, laws and other specifications to enhance their profits. They usually do just minimum required so as to ensure that rules and laws are adhered. They give first priority to the interests of the shareholders even at the expense of other stakeholders. If obstructionist approach is the lowest end of the social responsibility continuum, the defensive approach falls just below the average end of the social responsibility continuum.

3. Accommodative Approach

In accommodative approach, management believes that they should behave legally, ethically and in a socially responsible way. Company appreciates the need for supporting the idea of social responsibility. Managers are equally concerned about the interests of the shareholders and those of the other stakeholders. They appear to be just and reasonable in the eyes of all the stakeholders. Though they are not at the highest level of the continuum, they keep themselves at the high level of continuum.

4. Proactive Approach

Some corporate organisations take proactive actions to cause changes for the upliftment and welfare of all the stakeholders. They initiate socially desirable programmes and projects. Managers take initiatives to do the things which promote economic development and social benefits for all the stakeholders. They are eager to learn about the interests of all the stakeholders groups, and take action to behave in a socially responsible manner.

C. Benefits of Corporate Social Responsibility (CSR)

Moral responsibility is one of the most motivating factors behind corporate expenditure on variety of activities like community projects, pollution control, providing safe and pleasant working conditions, ensuring quality of the products and services, sponsoring education, art, etc. However, such expenditure can bring various benefits to the organisation. These benefits include—

1. Customer satisfaction
2. Increased productivity
3. Enhanced quality of products and services
4. Reduction in costs
5. Tax rebates, when a company contributes to social welfare
6. Increased ability to attract and retain loyal and competent workforce
7. Enhanced brand image and reputation
8. Increased customer loyalty
9. Favourable positioning
10. Sponsorship of education and arts
11. Paying competitive wages, providing better working conditions, motivating the workforce and ultimate maximisation of productivity
12. Reduction in regulatory oversight
13. Increased market share

14. Involvement in community projects can raise the morale of the employees and the community at large. This can result in improved local economy. Survival of company depends upon the local economy
15. When company addresses social and environmental problems, it is not necessary for the government to find their own solutions through compulsory regulations, interventions, prohibitive legislations and increased taxation.

D. Monitoring CSR

It is necessary to create the systems or methods to encourage, ensure and monitor the social responsibilities of corporations. For this purpose three audit methods can be recommended:

1. Stakeholder's Audit
2. Safety Audit
3. Environmental Audit

1. Stakeholder's Audit

There should be an effective reporting system to report ongoing performances of the firm in various fields of social responsibility. This system can enable the management to be in a position to appraise its responsiveness to the needs and interests of all the stakeholders. The stakeholder's audit may include the other types of audits as its integral parts.

2. Safety Audit

Some companies rush their products to market before they are properly tested about its use, and the side effects that may result from their use. There are different dimensions of safety and safety measures, for example, keeping the floors and stairs free from obstruction, securely fencing the dangerous parts of machinery, periodic examination of lifts, hoists, chains, cranes, etc. Safety audit is useful to measure the safety measures provided to the employees in the organisation. It can control or eliminate the work related safety hazards.

3. Environmental Audit

Many companies are not adequately responsive about issues related to environmental liabilities. They fail to provide appropriate disclosures about their environmental liabilities. Pressure from stakeholders can encourage more companies to be more forthright about their disclosures of these liabilities. Environmental audit can clearly indicate the potential risks to the natural environment due to the activities of the companies. Environmental audit can be used to assess the company's efforts to ensure that the natural environment is not polluted or depleted.

E. Outcomes of CSR

Corporate managers have to build a good corporate 'image' and corporate 'brand' globally. They have to pursue their founder's values, visions and mission. They have to fulfil the requirements of their business partners and adhere to legal compliance. They have to promote shareholder value and pursue long-term business interests. They have to build and improve relations with internal customers and penetrate the global market. They have to take initiatives to do things which promote benefits and welfare of all stakeholders.

K.B. Boal and N. Peery (1985) suggest that there are sixteen outcomes from corporate decisions concerning social responsibility. These are:

1. Decisions regarding management (organisational) result in—
   (a) promoting economic interests of business
   (b) maintaining high levels of productivity
   (c) promoting long-range survival of business
   (d) promoting interests of stockholders.
2. Decisions regarding organisational participants (Employees) result in—
   (a) safe working conditions
   (b) jobs that allow employees to use valued skills and abilities
   (c) promoting employee rights
   (d) job security for employees
3. Decisions regarding consumers result in—
   (a) producing goods desired by customers

(b) fair prices of the products and services
(c) maintaining high quality of products and services
(d) producing safe merchandise

4. Decisions regarding societal issues result in—
(a) obeying the rules and laws by company
(b) promoting social justice
(c) supporting social and cultural activities
(d) not degrading the natural environment

F. Constituents of Corporate Social Responsibility (CSR)

A.A. Berle (1931), in his "corporate powers as powers in trust", and E. Merrick Dodd (1932), in his "For whom Are Corporate Managers Trustees?" have discussed the components of corporate social responsibility. However, it was Howard Bowen (1953) who made a first comprehensive attempt to develop the concept of corporate social responsibility in his book "*Social Responsibilities of the Business*". Archie Carroll (1979) presented a three-dimensional model of corporate performance to answer the questions like—What components should be included in the definition of corporate social responsibility? What are the overall external social issues that the firm must acknowledge? and, How will the firm address the social issues that impact its operations? Carroll argues that total corporate responsibilities are based on economic, legal, ethical and discretionary responsibilities.

1. Legal Responsibilities

The components of a firm's legal responsibilities include firm's performance which is consistent with legal and government expectations, compliance with local, state, federal and international laws and regulations. The firms have to fulfil their economic responsibilities while following the legal requirements. All the goods and services produced by the firm must meet the minimal legal standards.

2. Ethical Responsibilities

A firm should have ethical responsibilities that are beyond just meeting the legal requirements. These responsibilities include the firm's performance that meets the expectations of social and ethical norms, adapting to new or changing ethical norms, ensuring that ethical norms are not compromised while achieving the objectives of firm.

3. Economic Responsibilities

Economic responsibilities are based on the objective of developing the economic value. The firm has a responsibility to use the resources available to produce the goods and services for society. The economic responsibilities of the firm lay foundation to support the other three responsibilities of the firm. Maximising per share earnings, generating consistent level of profitability, establishing and maintaining a strong competitive position are some of the components of firm's economic responsibility.

4. Discretionary Responsibilities

These responsibilities are left to the managers to decide the firm's courses of action for the welfare of the society. Discretionary responsibilities include firm's programmes for charity, programmes to help the drug addicted people, providing day care centres to help the families, etc. If a firm does not want to participate in such programmes, it cannot be considered as an unethical organisation. Therefore, such responsibilities are called discretionary responsibilities.

G. Assessment of CSR Policies

Richard Welford (2005) identifies twenty elements which can be used to assess the corporate policies for corporate social responsibility. There are four overall areas under which these elements are classified: internal aspects, external aspects, accountability and citizenship. Specific areas are given below:

1. Internal Aspects

These are the five elements which can be used to assess the internal aspects of corporate policies for corporate social responsibility: (i) Written policies on non-discrimination in the workforce; (ii) statements on normal working hours, maximum overtime, and fair wage structure; (iii) staff development, in-house education, and vocational training; equal opportunity statements and implementation plans; (iv) the freedom of association, the right to collective bargaining, and complaints procedures; and, (v) the protection of human rights within the company's operations.

2. External Aspects

These are the nine elements which can be used to assess the external aspects of corporate policies for corporate social responsibility. (i) Policy on labour standards adopted by suppliers in developing countries; (ii) policy on restrictions on the use of child labour; (iii) commitment to the protection of human rights in the company's sphere of influence; (iv) inspection of suppliers' facilities for health, safety, and environmental aspects; (v) commitment to local community protection and engagement; (vi) policy on responding to stakeholders, including procedures for the resolution of complaints; (vii) policies on fair trade, equitable trade, and end-price auditing; (viii) policies on the protection of indigenous populations and their rights; and (ix) code of ethics, including bribery and corruption.

3. Accountability

These are two elements which can be used to assess the accountability: (i) Commitment to reporting on corporate social responsibility and/or sustainable development; (ii) policies and procedures for engaging a wide range of stakeholders in two-way dialogue.

4. Citizenship

These are the three elements which can be used to assess citizenship: (i) Direct support for third-party social and sustainable development-related initiatives; (ii) educational programmes for the promotion of corporate citizenship, and (iii) Corporate social Responsibility the external campaign programmes for raising social and sustainable development issues.

H. Corporate Social Responsibility to Stakeholders

Shareholders, customers, employees, government and community at large have various expectations from the corporate organisations. They have different views about the corporate social responsibility. Let us consider the responsibilities of an organisation to itself, shareholders, employees, customers, the state and the community at large.

1. Responsibilities to Itself

Every business corporation has to work towards it's growth and expansion, and earn enough of profit to stay in business. After attaining stability, it has to grow through innovation and expansion. It has to achieve its own efficiency in order to achieve its social and economic goals. It achieves technical efficiency when it can produce the goods and services at the lowest possible cost. Its economic efficiency is achieved when it can provide the right quantity of goods and services, at the right time, and according to demands of the customers.

2. Responsibilities to Shareholders

A sole proprietor has no responsibilities to other shareholders or owners. However, in a business corporation, the management or the board of directors have to consider the interests of the shareholders who give them their authority and responsibility. The main responsibility of the management is to safeguard the shareholder's investment, and secondly, to provide a reasonable return on their investment.

3. Responsibilities to Employees

The role of employees is of great importance in the ultimate success of any organisation. Management is expected to create such an environment in the organisation that it can satisfy the psychological, physical and social needs of the employees along with the accomplishment of goals of the company. The main function of the management is to manage the work and the workers. The growth and development of a firm depends mainly on the employees and their work potentiality. The employees have the right to be viewed as unique individuals who have the right to be treated with respect, right to be informed, and right to be treated in a fair and honest fashion by the management of a firm. The employee should feel that he is needed in the firm and he is making valuable contribution to the firm through his works and ideas.

4. Responsibilities to Customers

Creating customers and building customer loyalty is the purpose of business. The fate of every business depends on the customers. Therefore, the corporations must fulfil their contractual obligations to their customers. Corporations should provide reliable and adequate information about their products, services, and also about the ethical uses of those products and services. Consumer satisfaction should be the ultimate objective of all the business activities. Company should offer its products and services at lowest possible prices. There should not be any fraudulent use of false weights or measures, adulteration of drugs, supply of substandard quality of goods and services, misleading and dishonest advertising, lack of courtesy to consumers, etc. Business enterprises should not violate their responsibilities towards the customers.

5. Responsibilities to State

The government's role as a stakeholder is essentially based on compliance issues. An ethical organisation fulfils all its legal obligations, and all the goods and services provided by the firm meets at least the minimal legal standards. The business corporations are expected to perform in a way which is consistent with government and legal requirements. If an organisation does not comply with the law, the government has the authority punish it. Today, business is not only a pursuit of economic gains, but it is also a social function. In socialist economies, social obligations are imposed by the State; but, in democratic economies, these obligations should be voluntarily fulfilled by the business corporations. The state grants protection and facilities to the corporations as and when needed. Therefore, the business corporations must pay the taxes and other dues to the state.

6. Responsibilities to Community at Large

Business corporations have definite responsibility towards community. They can contribute generously to the education, cultural, social and charitable causes. They can extend help to the people in times of floods, famine and draughts. They can establish industries in the economically backward regions, help the cause of socio-economic development and generate employment for the rural people. They should play a proper role in civic affairs and help to enhance the well-being of the members of the society.

Business organisations are a part of the society, therefore, they must respond to the demands of the society. As a social sub-system, corporation has a responsibility to contribute to the system as a whole. Long-run self-interests of the business corporations can be served by creating better public image among the various sections of society. From the philanthropic point of view, corporations should freely give the financial support or other help to the people who need it. They can support the causes such as the fine arts and the performing arts to enrich the society culturally. They have to support voluntarily the community projects to improve the overall quaiity of community life. They should provide financial and non-financial assistance to various charitable organisations and educational institutions.

Beside the corporate social responsibility of making possible contributions to furthering social causes, business organisations have another major responsibility of preventing environmental pollution and preserving the ecological balance.

EXERCISES

1. Explain the conceptual framework of corporate social responsibility.
2. "Corporate social responsibility refers to the obligations of corporate decision-makers to protect the interests of all the stakeholders". Discuss.
3. "Corporate social responsibility is the continuing commitment by business to behave ethically". Elucidate.
4. Discuss different approaches of corporate managements towards their social responsibilities.
5. What are the benefits of corporate social responsibility?
6. What are the methods of auditing and monitoring corporate social responsibility?
7. Explain various outcomes of corporate social responsibility.
8. What are the constituents of corporate social responsibility?
9. How would you asses the corporate policies for corporate social responsibility?
10. What are corporate social responsibilities to stakeholders?
11. Write short notes on the following:
    (i) Approaches to CSR
    (ii) Stakeholders' Audit
    (iii) Ethical Responsibilities
    (iv) Legal Responsibilities

(v) Economic Responsibilities
(vi) Discretionary Responsibilities
(vii) Corporate Citizenship
(viii) Corporate Accountability
(ix) Corporate Social Responsibility to Stakeholders
(x) Safety and Environmental Audit

17

CSR: Law, Policy and Guidelines

3. Accountability's AA1000 Series of Standards
4. SA 8000 Standard: Social Accountability
5. UN Millennium Development Goals
6. The LBG Model
7. OECD Guidelines for Multinational Enterprises
8. ILO's Tripatriate Declaration of Principles on Multinational Enterprises and Social Policy
9. UN Global Compact Principles

A. Introduction

Indian Corporate sector has generated wealth and value for the shareholders since independence. However, the nation faces the problems of illiteracy, malnutrition, poverty, unemployment, etc. The corporate growth and emergence of strong India is sometimes seen as widening the gap between India and Bharat. There is a need to bridge this gap. The business sector needs to undertake socially responsible business practices in order to ensure distribution of wealth and well-being of the communities. It has to integrate the interests of the business with that of the communities in which it operates. It has to exhibit the ethically, socially and environmentally responsible behaviour in its corporate governance. It has to generate value and long-term sustainability for itself while making positive efforts for the betterment of the communities.

Businesses are an integral part of society. Therefore, they are expected to uphold the ethical practices and good governance. They have an important role to play in fostering social inclusiveness and equity. They have to make positive efforts for the sustenance and improvement of healthy environment. Corporate Social Responsibility is viewed as "a way of conducting business which enables the creation and distribution of wealth for the betterment of its stakeholders through the implementation and integration of ethical systems and sustainable management practices.

India became the first country in the world to mandate spend on Corporate Social Responsibility activities when the President of India gave assent to the Companies Bill, 2013. Many corporate houses in India have been traditionally engaged in CSR activities voluntarily, but the CRS provisions in New Companies Act, 2013 has put the formal and greater responsibility on corporate sector to set out the clear framework and process to ensure strict compliance. The draft

CSR rules suggest that CSR provisions will be made effective from financial year 2014-15.

B. Development of CSR in India

The history of CSR in India indicate four phases of development. Philanthropy and charity were the main drivers of CSR in the first phase. During the pre-industrialization period wealthy merchants shared a part of their wealth by building temples, and by helping the society during the phases of famine and epidemics by providing food and money. After 1850s, the industrial families like Tata, Birla, Godrej, Singhania, Modi, etc. made efforts towards social and industrial development.

The second phase covers the period of independence movement when Indian industrialists demonstrated their dedication to social cause. When Mahatma Gandhi introduced the notion of "trusteeship", the industrial leaders were motivated to manage their wealth for the benefit of common man. Industrialists were urged to act towards building the nation and socio-economic development. Mahatma Gandhi called Indian companies as the "temples of modern India". Under Mahatmaji's influence business houses established trusts for schools, colleges and other social institutions.

The third phase of CSR in India (1950-1980), was characterized by the emergence of PSUs, 'mixed economy', labour laws and environmental standards. This period is also described as an "era of command and control" because of the stringent rules and regulations on the activities of the private sector companies. Governments' policy of licensing, high taxes and restrictions on private sector led to corruption and other malpractices. PSUs were established by the state but they were effective only to a limited extent. It resulted in the shift of expectations from PSUs to private sector industries for the socio-economic development of the country.

The fourth phase (1980 onwards) is characterized by 'globalization', 'economic liberalization' and sustainable business strategy. Licensing system and controls were partly done away which resulted in the rapid growth of industries and economy of the country. Globalization has transformed India into an attractive destination of MNCs for production, manufacturing and marketing. Indian companies who produce goods and export them to the developed world, are paying close attention to the labour and environmental standard.

C. CSR Provisions in Companies Act 2013

1. Clause 135 of the Companies Act, 2013

The Companies Act, 2013, was passed by both houses of Parliament and enacted on 29th August 2013, on accord of the assent of Hon'ble President of India. It aims to improve the corporate governance, enhance the interests of minority investors and simplify the regulations. The new law replaces the nearly sixty year old Companies Act, 1956. The Act has introduced several provisions that will change the way Indian corporates do the business.

The concept of Corporate Social Responsibility (CSR) is governed by Clause 135 of the Companies Act, 2013. The CSR provisions within the Act is applicable to companies with an annual turnover of 1000 crore INR and more, or a net worth of 500 crore INR and more, or a net profit of five crore INR and more. These rules which are applicable from the fiscal year 2014-15 onwards, require companies to set up a CSR committee. It will consist of their board members.

2. CSR Committee

- The CSR committee would consist of three or more directors out of which at least one director should be independent;

The mandate of the CSR committee should be:

- To formulate and recommend to the Board, a Corporate Social Responsibility Policy, which shall indicate the activities to be undertaken by the company as specified in Schedule VII;
- To recommend the amount of expenditure to be incurred on the activities referred to above;
- To monitor the CSR Policy of the company from time to time.

The role of the Board is to:

- Form a CSR Committee
- Approve the CSR policy

- Ensure implementation of the activities under CSR
- Ensure 2 per cent spend
- Disclose reasons for not spending the amount (if applicable).

3. CSR Policy

(i) Creating CSR Policy

The Companies Act, 2013 mandates the companies to spend at least 2 per cent of their average net profit in the previous three years on CSR activities. The rules of the new Act have some guidance on what the CSR policy should and should not include. In creating CSR policy the following guidelines are given:

- The policy should specify the projects and programmes that are to be undertaken.
- The policy should include a list of CSR projects/programmes which the company plans to undertake during the year of implementation.
- It should specify modalities of execution and an implementation schedule for each programme/project.
- In specifying the CSR projects/programmes the policy should give preference to the local areas around it and where it operates.
- The CSR projects/programmes may focus on integrating business models with social and environmental priorities and processes in order to create shared value.
- Any financial surplus arising out of CSR activity will not be part of business profits of a company.
- The Committee should prepare a transparent monitoring mechanism. It should ensure implementation of the projects/ programmes proposed in the policy.
- The policy should give all the details of the CSR activities and what budget will be spent on them. This should be published on the company's website.
- At the end of each year the details of the CSR initiatives undertaken by the company must be reported in the Director's Report and on company's website.
- The two per cent CSR spending needs to be computed as two per cent of the average net profits made by the company during every block of three years.

(ii) Core Elements in CSR Policy

(a) *Care for All Stakeholders*: The companies should respect the interests of, and be responsive towards all stakeholders, including shareholders, employees, customers, suppliers, project affected people, society at large, etc. and create value for all of them. They should develop mechanism to actively engage with all stakeholders, inform them of inherent risks and mitigate them where they occur.

(b) *Ethical Functioning*: Governance systems of the companies should be underpinned by Ethics, Transparency and Accountability. They should not engage in business practices that are abusive, unfair, corrupt or anti-competitive.

(c) *Respect for Worker's Rights and Welfare*: A workplace environment of the companies should be safe, hygienic and humane and it should uphold the dignity of employees. Companies should provide all employees with access to training and development of necessary skills for career advancement, on an equal and non-disseminatory basis. They should uphold the freedom of association and the effective recognition of the right to collective bargaining of labour, and have an effective grievance redressal system. They should not employ child or forced labour and provide and maintain equality of opportunity without any discrimination on any grounds in recruitment and during employment.

(d) *Respect for Human Rights*: Companies should respect human rights for all and avoid complicity with human rights abuses by them or by third party.

(e) *Respect for Environment*: Companies should take measures to check and prevent pollution; recycle, manage and reduce waste, should manage natural resources in a sustainable manner and ensure optimal use of resources like land and water. They should proactively respond to the challenges of climate change by adopting cleaner production methods, promoting efficient use of energy and environment friendly technology.

(f) *Activities for Social and Inclusive Development*: Depending upon their core competency and business interest, companies should undertake activities for economic and social development of communities and geographical areas, particularly in the vicinity of their operations. These could include—education, skills building for livelihood of people, health, cultural and social welfare etc., particularly targeting at disadvantaged sections of society.

(iii) Guidance for Implementation of CSR Policy

(a) The CSR policy of the business entity should provide for an implementation strategy which should include identification of projects/activities, setting measurable physical targets with timeframe, organizational mechanism and responsibilities, time schedules and monitoring.
Companies may partner with local authorities, business associations and civil society/non-governmental organizations. They may influence the supply chain for CSR initiative and motivate employees for voluntary effort for social development. They may evolve a system of need assessment and impact assessment while undertaking CSR activities in a particular area. Independent evaluation may also be undertaken for selected projects/activities from time to time.

(b) Companies should allocate specific amount in their budgets for CSR activities. This amount may be related to profits after tax, cost of planned CSR activities or any other suitable parameter.

(c) To share experiences and network with other organizations the company should engage with well established and recognised programmes/platforms which encourage responsible business practices and CSR activities. This would help companies to improve on their CSR strategies and effectively project the image of being socially responsible.

(d) The companies should disseminate information on CSR policy, activities and progress in a structured manner to all their stakeholders and the public at large through their website, annual reports, and other communication media (CSR Voluntary Guidelines, India Corporate Week Dec. 14-21, 2009, MCA, Government of India.)

4. Eligible CSR Spend

(i) CSR Activities

Activities which may be considered as eligible for CSR spend are given in Schedule VII of the Act. The specified activities are given below:

- Eradicating hunger and poverty
- Promotion of education
- Promoting gender equality and empowering women
- Reducing child mortality and improving maternal health
- Combating HIV, AIDS, malaria and other diseases.
- Ensuring environmental sustainability.
- Improvement of Health.
- Enhancing employment generation and imparting vocational skills.
- Social Business Projects.
- Contribution towards central and state government funds for socio-economic development and relief.
- Such other matters as may be prescribed.

The companies should give preference to the local area and the area around it where it operates for spending the amounts earmarked for CSR activities.

(ii) Setting up Trusts, Foundations and Collaborations

The companies can set up a not-for-profit organization in the form of trust, society or non-profit company to facilitate implementation of its CSR activities. However, the contributing company shall specify projects/programmes to be undertaken by such an organization. The company shall establish monitoring mechanism to ensure that the allocation to such organization is spent for the intended purpose only. A company may also implement its CSR programmes through not-for-profit organizations that are not set up by the company itself. Such spends may be included as part of company's prescribed CSR spend only if such organizations have an established track record of at least three years in carrying on activities in related areas.

Companies may also collaborate or pool resources with other companies to undertake CSR activities. Only CSR activities undertaken in India would be considered as eligible CSR activities. CSR activities may generally be conducted as projects or programmes which are either new or ongoing. However, these activities exclude the activities which are undertaken in pursuance of the normal course of business of a company. CSR projects/programmes may also focus on integrating business models with social and environmental priorities and processes in order to create shared value. CSR activities shall not include activities exclusively for the benefit of employees and their family members.

(iii) Tax Treatment of CSR Spend

"Net profit" for the Section 135 and these rules shall mean net profit before tax as per books of accounts and shall not include profits arising from branches outside India. Reporting will be done on an annual basis commencing from FY 2014-15. Tax treatment of CSR spend will be in accordance with the IT Act as may be notified by the Central Board of Direct Taxes (CBDT). Surplus arising of the CSR activities will not be part of business profits of a company. The CSR Committee should specify that the corpus would include two per cent of the average net profits, any income arising therefrom, and surplus arising out of CSR activities.

(iv) Queries and Clarifications

There is a debate as to whether any penal consequences will emanate on failure to spend. There may be reluctance in compliance, especially in case of companies which are not profitable, but fall under the designated category due to triggering net worth or turnover criteria. It is not clear what all constitutes CSR activities as the list specified under Schedule VII of the Act seems like an inclusive list and not an exhaustive list.

The concepts of 'business process integration' and 'shared value' are not defined in the Act/draft CSR rules. While the draft CSR rules specify that CSR activities shall not be exclusively for the benefit of employees/their families, it does not provide any objective criteria of certain benefits given to employees/their families that could be regarded as CSR activities. While the draft CSR rules suggest that tax treatment of CSR spend will be in accordance with the Income-Tax Act, 1961 as may be notified by Central Board of Direct Taxes, one will have to wait and watch for the notification from CBDT and whether the same provides adequate certainty on tax treatment of CSR spend.

5. CSR and Sustainability

(i) Impact of UN Global Compact

The UN Global Compact was the first major initiative to lay down a charter of ten principles for all companies globally to be respected and followed in their business operations. It sets the agenda for CSR for all the corporate enterprises. It provides a framework for initiation and practice of sustainability policies. CSR is the responsibility which the corporate houses accept for social, economic and environmental impact their activities have on the stakeholders. The stakeholders include employees, consumers, investors, shareholders, civil society groups, government, non-governmental organizations, communities and the society at large.

(ii) What is Sustainability?

Sustainability practiced through CSR involves the conduct of business in such a way that it minimizes harm to the environment and local communities, and benefits consumers and employees. Sustainability includes development of new range of goods and services, and innovative production methods that are environmental and consumer friendly and cost effective. It enhances consumer satisfaction and boosts profitability and business growth.

CSR and sustainability is a commitment of corporate enterprise to its stakeholders to conduct business in an economically, socially and environmentally sustainable manner. CSR and sustainability is not limited to its own operations and activities, but extends to its supply chain also. The supply chain includes service providers, vendors, contractors and other outsourced agencies. Multinational companies are nowadays careful in their selection of partners, agents, vendors and contractors abroad. They prefer to do a thorough check of the credentials of theirs partners agents, vendors and contractors abroad in CSR and sustainability.

(iii) Sustainability Reporting

Sustainability reporting is on the increase and a large number of organizations and companies worldwide have voluntarily adopted internationally accepted standards and frameworks like GRI for disclosure and reporting. Attempts are made to devise some common matrices for measuring the performance of the companies in CSR and sustainability. Some notable of these initiatives are 'Global Reporting Initiatives' (GRI); Sustainability Reporting Guidelines; Accountability's AA1000 Standard based on John Elkington's Tripple

Bottom Line (3 BL) Reporting; Social Accountability International's SA 8000 standard; and, the ISO 14001 Environmental Management Standard. Growing investor pressure, competitive labour markets, increased customer interests, greater oversight over suppliers in the supply chain network, and increasing globalization of business has led to growing demand for greater disclosure and audit of CSR and sustainability reporting.

(iv) Benefits of CSR and Sustainability

If CSR and sustainability is discharged sincerely, it brings several benefits for the companies. CSR and sustainability results in improving the brand image, preparing it for risk management through public goodwill in the event of a crisis, winning the confidence of the investors and shareholders, attracting and retaining talent for the organization, winning the confidence of the investors and shareholders, positioning the company for competitive business advantage, and improving its relations with the important stakeholders.

CSR and sustainability activities which are prompted by 'Genuine Concern' for social and environmental issues produce the implementation models that differ from those which are motivated by the 'Enlightened Self-interest' of a company. CSR and sustainability activities which are undertaken as a part of 'public relations' campaign for earning public goodwill are different from CSR and sustainability activities which are taken up by a company to obtain 'License to operate' in certain areas. Good CSR practices can bring in certain benefits, some of which are as follow:

- Robust CSR programmes meet the aspirations of the communities. In India many companies have realised that the 'Licence to operate' is no longer given by governments alone but also by the communities that are impacted by a company's operations. If CSR programmes meets the aspirations of local communities, they provide the licence to operate, and help the company to maintain that licence.
- Company's ability to attract, retain and motivate employees is linked with its CSR commitments. CSR activities increase employee morale and a sense of belonging to the company.
- In certain innovative CSR initiatives, companies have invested in enhancing community livelihood by incorporating

them into their supply chain. It has increased the income levels of the communities. It has also provided an additional and secure supply chain to the companies.

- Companies that operate effective CSR programmes, get the benefit of generating goodwill and creating positive image. This enables companies to position themselves as responsible corporate citizens.

(v) Doctrine of Shared Value

Strategic CSR and sustainability activities based on 'Enlightened Self-interests' of the company have found favour with the private multinational companies of the developed economies. This strategic approach is supported by the doctrine of 'Shared Value.' This doctrine was propounded by eminent Harvard economists Michael Porter and Mark Kramer. Creating 'Shared Value' means creating new business opportunities and developing new products that are profitable for companies while simultaneously contributing to social development. According to Porter and Kramer, through 'Strategic CSR' companies seek to exploit opportunities to achieve social and economic benefits simultaneously. In other words, companies seek business opportunities in socio-economic problems of the communities. According to Porter and Kramer, 'the essential test that should guide CSR is not whether a cause is worthy, but whether it presents an opportunity to create Shared Value, that is, a meaningful benefit for society that is also valuable to the business.'

6. CSR and Sustainability Guidelines for CPSEs

(i) Major Guidelines

Public Sector Enterprises are required to have a CSR and sustainability policy approved by their respective Board of Directors. However, the Central Public Sector Enterprises (CPSEs) should frame their CSR and sustainability policies and plan their activities in this regard within the framework of DPE's guidelines on the subject. CPSEs are expected to adhere to the global standards in this regard and keep in mind the UN Global Compact and the UN Millennium Development Goals.

Each CPSE shall have a Board level committee headed by either the Chairman and/Managing Director, or an Independent Director to oversee the implementation of the CSR and sustainability policies of the company. To facilitate co-ordination of CSR and sustainability initiatives of different department within the organization, to report on their separate endeavours. to issue policy directives on the subject, and to devise an appropriate corporate communication strategy in this regard, it is expected that the public sector enterprises will appoint a fairly senior officer not less than one rank lower to the Board level to function as the Nodal Officer. The Board level committee and the designated nodal officer's team of officers together will constitute the two-tier organizational structure to steer the CSR and Sustainability agenda of the company.

Public sector enterprises are expected to have knowledge about their important stakeholders and be aware of their expectations of how business should be conducted. Their CSR and sustainability policies should address social, economic and environmental concerns.

CPSEs should refrain from taking up activities which are clearly mandated to be performed by the Government and/or for which Central/State Government's schemes have been sanctioned, as it could result in unnecessary duplication. The companies should disclose their CSR and Sustainability initiatives on their official websites. A brief summary of these activities should also be included in their Annual Report.

Public sector enterprises, especially those having global operations and dealings are encouraged to adopt global standards. Such companies are also advised to practice CSR and Sustainability Policies as applicable to the conditions prevailing in the host countries where they carry out their business operations.

Corporate enterprises are expected to produce goods and services that are safe and healthy for the consumers and the environment, with reduced cost to the company in the long run. They are expected to effectively use the services of their R&D Departments in leveraging technology for production of goods and services which are resource efficient, consumer friendly and environmentally sustainable throughout their life cycles.

In brief, it is generally expected that socially responsible public sector enterprises would take initiatives to:

(a) Promote organizational integrity and ethical business practices through transparency in disclosure and reporting procedures.

(b) Leverage green technologies, processes and standards to produce goods and services that contribute to social and environmental sustainability.

(c) Contribute to inclusive growth and equitable development in society through capacity building measures. empowerment of the marginalised and underprivileged sections/ communities.

(d) Promote welfare of employees and labour (casual or contractual), by addressing their concerns of safety, security, professional enrichment and healthy working conditions, whether mandated or otherwise. However, expenditure on mandated activities cannot qualify for CSR's financial components.

(ii) Financial Component

Every year, each CPSE shall with the approval of its Board of Directors make a budgetary allocation for CSR and sustainability activities/projects for the year. Budgetary allocation will be determined by the Profit After Tax (PAT) of the company in the previous year as shown hereunder:

PAT of CPSE in the previous year	*Range of Budgetary Allocation for CSR and Sustainability Activities (PAT in Previous Year)*
1. Less than Rs. 100 crore	3% – 5%
2. Rs. 100 crore to 500 crore	2% – 3%
3. Rs. 500 crore and Above	1% – 2%

For all CPSEs having PAT above Rs. 500 crores in the previous year, the range of budgetary allocation for CSR and sustainability activities has been raised to 1% – 2%.

(iii) Implementation

Implementation of CSR and sustainability projects requires specialised knowledge and skills. Public sector companies normally do not have such in-house expertise and dedicated staff to carry out this task. Therefore, in such cases CPSEs should seek the services of external specialised agencies for the implementation of such CSR and sustainability projects. A public sector company may take up the implementation of CSR activity with its manpower and resources, if it feels confidents of its organisational capability to execute such project. In such a case it is advisable that monitoring is done by an external agency even though the staff of the CPSE may be associated with it. While engaging or partnering with external agencies, care should be taken in selecting only such specialised agencies which have the necessary capabilities and expertise to implement the CSR projects. Specialised agencies may include government department, semi-government, or non-governmental organizations (NGOs), autonomous organizations, professional consultancy organizations, registered Trusts/Missions, community based organizations, local bodies such as Panchayati Raj Institutions, academic institutions, etc.

(iv) Monitoring, Reporting and Disclosure

Monitoring is essential to assess if the progress is on expected lines in terms of timeliness, budgetary expenditure and achievement of physical targets. Monitoring should be done periodically with the help of identified key performance indicators; the periodicity being determined largely by the nature of performance indicators. Monitoring should be done in project mode with continuous feedback mechanism. The final evaluation must always be entrusted to an external agency. Implementation and monitoring of the CSR and sustainability activities will be overseen by a Board level committee headed by either the Chairman and/or Managing Director, or an Independent Director. The composition of the committee is to be decided by the Board of Directors of the company, but it is mandatory to have at least one Independent Director as a member of this committee.

Sustainability Reporting and Disclosure to the stakeholders is a practice of disclosing the economic, social and environmental initiatives taken by a company. Disclosure of a company's financial performance is a traditional practice, but disclosures in non-financial parameters is a relatively recent phenomenon which is rapidly gaining acceptance and recognition as a good corporate practice that enhances the reputation, improves the financial performance and increases the competitive advantage of the company in the long run.

A large number of corporates, including Indian companies are resorting to sustainability reporting on the internationally accepted reporting frameworks like the Global Reporting Initiatives (GRI). According to the policy directives of Securities and Exchange Board of India (SEBI), all listed companies have to report on their environmental, social and governance initiatives in their Annual Reports. Reporting and disclosure of all CSR and sustainability activities undertaken by CPSEs is mandatory. By reporting transparently and with accountability, public sector companies can gain and reinforce the trust of the stakeholders.

7. CSR of Small and Medium Enterprises

Small and Medium Enterprises (SMEs) employ nearly 40 per cent of India's workforce. They contribute around 45 per cent to India's manufacturing output. They generate employment and industrialise the rural and backward regions of India. Their business activities in proximity to the locals enable them to be aware of the needs of community and to develop CSR programmes appropriately.

CSR clause in the Companies Act, 2013 covers companies that have a net profit of five crore and above. Therefore, it is expected that many small and medium enterprises will quality for it. The quantum of revenue available for CSR with individual small and medium enterprise is can be small, but if all eligible enterprises in a specific geographical cluster pool their resources together, a sizable CSR fund can be created. Such collaboration can be formed in a cluster of SMEs because they interest with the same communities and have established associations that cater to the needs of business units.

A common organization or collaboration of SMEs can carry out CSR activities collectively and reduce the operational cost of CSR management. They can undertake long-term CSR programmes which lead to better community relations. It helps to ensure avoiding situations at community unrest that hamper the business activities. A common entity with multiple SMEs from the cluster can help to assess the needs of the community and to undertake the relevant programmes based on past experiences.

The process can begin with creating an alliance of interested SMEs. Then the alliance should form a committee with their representatives. The Steering Committee should decide thematic areas from Schedule VII of the Companies Act, 2013, the beneficiary groups, the geographical area, individual contribution by member

SMEs and their utilization, planning and development of projects, implementation and operationalising institutional mechanism, contracting, budgeting and payments monitoring, reporting and impact measurement. If the total funds are insufficient to cover the cost of CSR programmes, the SMEs can have the option of contributing to the Prime Minister's National Relief Fund or any other fund set up by Central/State Governments as activity IX of the Schedule VII of the Companies Act, 2013.

D. Global Guidelines for CSR and Sustainability

Some of the globally recognised guidelines, principles and frameworks that relate to the larger concept of CSR and sustainability are given below. They are useful to mainstream the adoption of sustainable and socially responsible policies by business around the world.

1. The UN Guiding Principles on Business and Human Rights

These principles provide guidelines to governments and business enterprises to fulfil their obligations towards human rights, fundamental freedoms and the existing laws. These principles act as global standards for addressing the problems of human rights violation related to business activity. They focus on the protection of human rights by both, the state and the business enterprises.

(www.ohchr.org/Documents/Publications/GuidingPrinciplesBusinessHR_En.pdf)

2. The OECD CSR Policy Tools

The OECD CSR policy tool helps the companies to gain insight into their CSR activities. It assists them to assess and evaluate the CSR projects. It guides the companies to determine other CSR activities that can be undertaken. It is based on the OECD Guidelines and the ISO 26000 implementation guidelines. The policy tool provides guidelines regarding action plan, tasks, responsibilities, monitoring, communication strategy, etc.

(www.oecdguidelines.nl/get_started/creating_a_csr_policy/)

3. Accountability's AA1000 Series of Standards

Account Ability's AA1000 Series of Standards consists of the (1) AA1000 accountability principles (AP) standard, (2) AA 1000 assurance standard (AS) and (3) AA1000 Stakeholder Engagement Standards (SE). This series of standards enable business enterprises to become accountable, responsible and also sustainable. These standards have been formulated through a multi-stakeholder consultation process. Therefore, they ensure that those impacted (enterprises, governments and civil societies) stand to gain.

(www.accountability.org/standards/)

4. SA 8000 Standard: Social Accountability

International (SAI) SA 8000 standard is one of the worlds first auditable social certification standard. This standard protects the basic human rights of workers. It is based on ILO, UN and national law conventions. The nine basic elements of this standard include: (i), Child labour, (ii) Forced and Compulsory Labour, (iii) Health and Safety, (iv) Disciplinary practices, (v) Discrimination, (vi) Freedom of association and the right to collective bargaining, (vii) Working hours, (viii) Remuneration, and (ix) Management systems.

(www.sa-intl.org/index.cfm?fuseaction=pago.viewPage&PageID=937)

5. UN Millennium Development Goals

The largest gathering of world leaders in history adopted the 'UN Millenium Declaration' at the Millenium Summit in September 2000. They committed their nations to a new global partnership to reduce extreme poverty and set out a series of time bound targets, with a deadline of 2015. These have become known as the Millennium Development Goals (MDGs).

"The Millennium Development Goals set time bound targets, by which progress in reducing income poverty, hunger, disease, lack of adequate shelter and exclusion—while promoting gender equality, health, education and environmental sustainability—can be measured. They also embody basic human rights—the rights of each person on the planet to health, education, shelter and security. The Goals are ambitious but feasible and, together with the Comprehensive United Nations development agenda, set the course for the world's efforts to alleviate extreme poverty by 2015."

UN Secretary General, Ban–ki–Moon

(http://www.un.org/millenniumgoals/bkgd/shtml)

6. The LBG Model

LBG's measurement model is adopted by the companies across the world to assess the real value and impact of their community investment to both, the business and society. This model helps the companies to track the manner in which their community programme supports business goals like building employee morale or creating reputational advantages. It helps to measure the impact made by the programmes on the community at large. Under this model the member companies share data and best practices that helps them in benchmarking process.

(www.lbg.online.net/about-lbg.aspx)

7. OECD Guidelines for Multinational Enterprises

OECD Guidelines for Multinational Enterprises were adopted on 21st June 1976 by the member states. These guidelines are non-binding recommendations covering all major areas of business ethics addressed by the governments to multinational enterprises operating in or from adhering countries. The last update of the OECD Guidelines was adopted in May 2011. It establishes that enterprises should avoid causing or contributing to adverse impacts through their own activities or through business relationships.

The OECD Guidelines provide voluntary principles and standards for responsible business conduct in the areas of Information disclosure, Human Rights, Employment, Combating bribery, bribe solicitation, and extortion, consumer interests, science and technology, competition, Taxation, Respect for labour standards, contribution to sustainable development, supply chain responsibility, and whistle blower protection. (http://oecdwatch.org/about-oecd/guidelines)

8. ILO's Tripatriate Declaration of Principles on Multinational Enterprises and Social Policy

Adoption of this declaration by governments, multinational organizations and employers ensures labour and social standards. This declaration is particularly for organizations that operate across multiple countries. It focuses on labour standards like right to collective bargaining, freedom of association, prohibition of discrimination, bonded and forced labour, no trade union restrictions, provision of a forum to lodge complaints in case of labour standard violation, regular discussions between management and labour, job security, improved working and living conditions, ensuring wages on par with those of other enterprises in the same country, etc.

(www.ilo.org/empent/publications/wcms_094386/lang_en/index.htm)

9. UN Global Compact Principles

The UN Global Compact's ten principles are derived from: (1) The Universal Declaration of Human Rights (2) The International Labour Organization's Declaration on Fundamental Principles and Rights at Work. (3) The Rio Declaration on Environment and Development. (4) The United Nations Convention Against Corruption:

The UN Global compact asks companies to embrace, support and enact, within their sphere of influence, a set of core values in the areas of human rights, labour standards and anti-corruption:

Principle 1: Business should support and respect the protection of internationally proclaimed human rights.

Principle 2: Make sure that they are not complicit in human rights abuses.

Principle 3: Businesses should uphold the freedom of association and the effective recognition of right to collective bargaining.

Principle 4: The elimination of all forms of forced and compulsory labour.

Principle 5: The effective abolition of child labour.

Principle 6: The elimination of discrimination in respect of employment and occupation.

Principle 7: Businesses should support a precautionary approach to environmental challenges.

Principle 8: Undertake initiatives to promote greater environmental responsibility.

Principle 9: Encourage the development and diffusion of environmentally friendly technology.

Principle 10: Businesses should work against corruption in all its forms including extortion and bribery.

(www.unglobalcompact.org/aboutthegc/thetenprinciples/index.html)

EXERCISES

1. 'Corporate sector has to integrate the interests of the business with that of the communities in which it operates'. Discuss.
2. Write a note on the phases of CSR history in India.
3. What are the CSR provisions in the Companies Act, 2013?
4. What are the responsibilities of CSR Committee?
5. Which guidelines should be followed in creating CSR policy?
6. Explain the core elements in CSR policy.
7. Write a note on implementation of CSR policy.
8. Which activities are eligible for CSR spend?
9. Why should companies set up foundations, trusts and collaborations for CSR activities?
10. Explain the tax-treatment of CSR spend.
11. 'CSR is the responsibility which the corporate houses accept for social, economic and environmental impact their activities have on the stakeholders'. Elucidate.
12. How can sustainability be practiced through CSR activities.
13. What is 'Sustainability'?
14. What are the benefits of CSR and sustainability?
15. Write an essay on the CSR and sustainability guidelines for CPSE.
16. 'A common organization or collaboration of small and medium enterprises can carry out CSR activities collectively.' Comment.
17. Discuss some globally recognised guidelines, principles and frameworks that relate to CSR and sustainability.
18. Write short-notes on the following:
    (i) Clause 135 of the Companies Act 2013.
    (ii) CSR Committee
    (iii) Core Elements in CSR Policy
    (iv) Eligible CSR Spend

(v) CSR Activities
(vi) Sustainability
(vii) Impact of UN Global Compact
(viii) Sustainability Reporting
(ix) Doctrine of 'Shared Value'
(x) Financial Component of CSR
(xi) Implementation of CSR
(xii) CSR Monitoring and Reporting
(xiii) CSR of SMEs
(xiv) The LBG Model
(xv) SA 8000 Standard
(xvi) UN Guiding Principles on Business and Human Rights
(xvii) OECD CSR Policy Tool
(xviii) AccountAbility's AA1000 Standards
(xix) UN Global Compact Principles
(xx) OECD Guidelines for Multinational Enterprises

Bibliography

Ackerman, R. and Baner, R., (1976), "*Corporate Social Responsiveness*", VA: Reston, Reston.

Ansolf, H.L., (1988), "*The New Corporate Strategy*", John Wiley, New York.

Armstrong, S. and Botzler (Eds.), (1993), "*Environmental Ethics*", McGraw-Hill, New York.

Armstrong, M.B., (1993). "*Ethics and Professionalism*", South-Western, Cincinnati.

Agarwal, Sanjiv, "*Corporate Excellence*", Vistar, New Delhi.

Arrow, K., (1951), "*Social Choice and Individual Values*", Yale University, Press, New Haven.

Arthur, John and Shaw, W.H. (Eds.), "*Justice and Economic Distribution*", Prentice Hall, Englewood Cliffs, N.J.

Attfield, Robin (1991), "*The Ethics of Environmental Concern*", University of Georgia Press, Athens.

Arya, P.P., Tandon, B.B. and Vashist, A.K. (Eds.) (2003), "*Corporate Governance*", Deep & Deep Publications, New Delhi.

Broad, C.D. (1930), "*Five Types of Ethical Theory*", Marcourt Brace & Co., New York.

Bayles, M.D. (1989), "*Professional Ethics*", Wadsworth, Belmont, CA.

Bennett, W.J. (1993), "*The Book of Virtues*", Simon & Schuster, New York.

Boatright, J.R. (1997), "*Ethics and the Conduct of Business*", Prentice Hall, NJ.

Bowie, N. (1982), "*Business Ethics*", Prentice Hall, NJ.

Brown, M.T. (1990), "*Working Ethics*", Jossey-Bass, San Francisco.

Barry, Vincent (1986), "*Moral Issues in Business*", Wadsworth, Belmont, CA.

Blum, L.A. (1994), "*Moral Perception and Particularity*", Cambridge University Press.

Brandt, Richard B. (1979), "*A Theory of the Good and the Right*", OUP, New York.

Beauchamp, T.L. and Bowie, N. (eds.) (1979), "*Ethical Theory and Business*", Prentice Hall, Englewood Cliffs, NJ.

Burns, J.M. (1985), "*Leadership*", Harper & Row, New York.

Berle, A.A. (1931), "Corporate Powers as Powers in Trust", *Harvard Law Review*, 44 (1931).

Boal, K.B. and Peery, N. (1985), "The Cognitive Structure of Corporate Social Responsibility", *Journal of Management*, 11 (1985), 71-82.

Barucha, Erach (2005), "*Textbook of Environmental Studies*", Universities Press (India) Ltd., Hyderabad.

Bhatia, S.K. (2008), "*Business Ethics and Global Values*", Deep & Deep Publications, New Delhi.

Boatright, J.R. and Patra, B.P. (2011), "*Ethics and the Conduct of Business*", Dorling Kindersley (India) Pvt. Ltd.

Bajaj, P.S. and Agrawal, R. (2004), "*Business Ethics*", Biztantra, New Delhi.

Callahan, D. and Bok, S. (Eds.) (1980), "*The Teaching of Ethics in Higher Education*", Hastings-Hudson, Hastings Centre, NY.

Carroll, A.B. (1996), "*Business and Society*", South-Western, Cincinnati, OH.

Cederblom, J. and Dougherty, C.T. (1990), "*Ethics at Work*", Wadsworth, Belmont, CA.

Carroll, Archie (1979), "A Three Dimensional Conceptual Model of Corporate Performance", *Academy of Management Review*, 4 (1979).

Clapham, W.B. Jr. (1983), "*Natural Ecosystems*", Macmillan, New York.

Chhokor, K.B., Pandya, M. and Raghunath, M. (2005), "*Understanding Environment*", Sage, New Delhi.

Dean Rashdal, (1924), "*The Theory of Good and Evil*", Oxford University Press, London.

Dewey and Fufs, (1932), "*Ethics*", Henry Holt & Co., New York.

DeGeorge, R.T. (1997), "*Business Ethics*", Prentice Hall, NJ.

Doming, W.E. (1982), "*Quality, Productivity and Competitive Position*", MIT, Cambridge.

Diladova, L. (1990), "*Instructor's Manual to Becoming a Master Manager*", John Wiley, New York.

Donabue, W. and Kolt, R. (1992), "*Managing Interpersonal Conflict*", CA: Sage, Newbury Park.

Donaldson, T. (1989), "*The Ethics of International Business*", *OUP*, New York.

Downie, U.S. (1971), "*Roles and Values: An Introduction to Social Ethics*", Methuen, New York.

Driscoll, D.M., Hoffman, M.W. and Petry, E.S. (1995), "*The Ethical Edge*", Master Media, New York.

Dworkin, R. (1978), "*Taking Rights Seriously*", Harvard University Press, Cambridge, MA.

Dworkin, R. (1985), "*A Matter of Principle*", Belknap Cambridge, MA.

Donagan, A. (1977), "*The Theory of Morality*", The University of Chicago Press, Chicago.

Davis, K. and Blomstrom, R.L. (1975), "*Business and Society*", McGraw Hill, New York.

Donaldson, Thomas (1982), "*Corporations and Morality*", Prentice Hall, Englewood Cliffs, NJ.

DesJardins, J.R. and McCall, J.J. (Eds.) (2000), "*Contemporary Issues in Business Ethics*", Wadsworth, Belmont, Califf.

Duska, R.P. and Duska, B. (2003), "*Accounting Ethics*", Blackwell Publishing, Oxford.

Everett, W.G. (1918), "*Moral Values*", Henry Holt & Co., New York.

Emmet, D. (1966), "*Rules, Roles and Relations*", Beacon, Boston.

Etzioni, A. (1988), "*The Moral Dimension*", Free Press, New York.

Ethics Teaching Group (1992), "*Integrity and Management*", Harvard Business School, Boston.

Ewing, D.W. (1977), "*Freedom Inside the Organisation*", McGraw Hill, New York.

Feinberg, J. (1970), "*Essays on the Theory of Responsibility*", Princeton University Press, Princeton, NJ.

Fernandez, J. (1991), "*Managing a Diverse Workplace*", Free Press, New York.

Fiedler, F. and Chemers, M. (1982), "*Improving Leadership Effectiveness*", John Wiley, New York.

Finnis, J. (1980), "Natural Law and Natural Rights", *OUP*, New York.

Flores, A. (1988), "*Professional Ideals*", Wadsworth, Belmont CA.

Freeman, R.E. and Gilbert, D., Jr. (1988), "*Corporate Strategy and the Search for Ethics*", Prentice Hall, NJ.

Fukuyama, F. (1995), "*Trust: The Social Virtues and Creation of Prosperity*", Free Press, NY.

Fuller, L.L. (1964), "*The Morality of the Law*", Macmillan, New York.

Fried, Charles (1970), "*An Anatomy of Values*", Harvard University Press, Cambridge.

Feldman, Fred (1978), "*Introductory Ethics*", Prentice Hall, NJ.

Freeman, R. and Gilbert, D. (1988), "*Corporate Strategy and the Search for Ethics*", Prentice Hall, Englewood Cliffs, NJ.

Ferell, O.C. and Fraedrich, J. (1991), "*Business Ethics: Ethical Decision-Making and Cases*", Houghon Mifflin Co., Boston.

Ewing, A.C. (1965), "*Ethics*", Free Press, New York.

Garvin, L.A. (1953), "*A Modern Introduction to Ethics*", Houghton Mifflin Co., Cambridge.

Gauthier, D. (1986), "Morals by Agreement", *OUP*, Oxford, UK.

Gilligan, C., Ward, J.V. and Taylor, J.M. (Eds.) (1989), "*Mapping the Moral Domain*", Harvard University Press, Cambridge, MA.

Gordner, H.F. (1991), "*Ethics for Public Managers*", Praeger, New York.

Green, D.M. (1994), "*The Ethical Manager*", Macmillan, New York.

Holmes, R.L. (1993), "*Basic Moral Philosophy*", Wadsworth, Belmont, CA.

Hosmer, L.T. (1994), "*Moral Leadership in Business*", Irwin, Burr Ridge. IL.

Hosmer, L.T. (1996), "*The Ethics of Management*", Irwin, Burr Ridge, IL.

Garrett, T.M and Klonoski, R.J. (1986), "*Business Ethics*", Prentice Hall, NJ.

Harris, C.E., Jr. (1986), "*Applying Moral Theories*", Wadsworth, Belmont, CA.

Goodpaster, K.E. (1983), "*Ethical Frameworks for Management*", Harvard Business School, Boston.

Hiff, W. (1990), "*Ethics and Leadership*", Batlelle Press, Columbus.

Gibson, Mary (1983), "*Worker's Rights*", Rowman & Allanheld, Totowa, NJ.

Heywood, V.H. and Watson, R.T. (1995), "*Global Biodiversity*", Cambridge University Press.

Klein, T.A. (1977), "*Social Costs and Benefits of Business*", Prentice Hall, NJ.

Kant, Immanuel (1964), "*Groundwork of the Metaphysics of Morals*", Harper & Row, New York.

Jackall, R. (1988), "Moral Mazes", *OUP*, New York.

Janis, I.L. (1983), "*Groupthink*", Houghton Mifflin, Boston.

Johannsen, R.L. (1990), "*Ethics in Human Communication*", Waveland.

Koehn, D. (1995), "*The Ground of Professional Ethics*", Routledge & Kegan Paul, Boston.

Kohlberg, L. (1984), "*The Psychology of Moral Development*", Harper & Row, New York.

Kramer, R.M. and Tyler, T.R. (Eds.) (1995), "*Trust in Organisations*", Sage, Newbury Park, CA.

Kennedy, R.E. and Rafael Di Tella (2001), "*Corruption in International Business*", Harvard Business School, Boston.

Mill, John Stuart, (1957), "*Utilitarianism*", The Bobs-Merrill Co., Indianapolis.

Michales, A.C. (1995), "*A Pragmatic Approach to Business Ethics*", Sage Publications, Thousand Oaks, CA.

LaCroix, W.L. (1976), "*Principles for Ethics in Business*", University Press of America, Washington.

Larrabee, M.J. (Ed.) (1993), "*An Ethic of Care*", Routledge & Kegan Paul, Boston.

Macedo, S. (1990), "Liberal Virtues", *OUP*, New York.

Manley, W. (1991), "*Executive Handbook of Model Business Conduct Codes*", Prentice Hall, NJ.

Martin, M.W. (1995), "*Everyday Morality*", Wadsworth, Belmont, CA.

Mason, R., Mason, F. and Culnan, M.J. (1995), "*Ethics of Information Management*", Sage, Newbury Park, CA.

Miles, H.H. (1987), "*Managing the Corporate Environment*", Prentice Hall, U.S. River, NJ.

Milo, R.D. (1984), "*Immorality*", Princeton University Press, Princeton, NJ.

Mintzberg, H. (1994), "*The Rise and Fall of Strategic Planning*", Free Press, New York.

Moore, M.H. (1995), "*Creating Public Value*", Harvard University Press, Cambridge, MA.

Moore, M.H. and Sparrow, M.K. (1990), "*Ethics in Government*", Prentice Hall, Upper Saddle River, NJ.

Mortimer, G.W. (1971), "*Weakness of Will*", St. Martin's, New York.

Murphy, K.R. (1993), "*Honesty in the Workplace*", Brooks/Cole, Pacific Grove, CA.

Luecke, Richard (2006), "*The Ethics of Power, Influence and Persuasion*", Harvard Business School Press, Boston.

Lippke, R.L. (1995), "*Radical Business Ethics*", Rowman & Littlefield, Lanham, Md.

LeMoncheck, Linda and Hajdin, M. (1997), "*Sexual Harassment*", Rowman & Littlefield, Totowa, NJ.

Navran, F.J. (1991), "*Desktop Guide to Total Ethics Management*", Navran Associates, Allanta, GA.

Navran, F.J. (1995), "*Trust and Truth*", Athabasca University Press, Alberta, Canada.

Newton, K.H. and Schmidt, D.P. (1996), "*Wake-up Calls: Classic Cases in Business Ethics*", Wadsworth, Belmont, CA.

Naddings, N. (1984), "*Caring: A Feminine Approach to Ethics*", University of California Press, Berkeley.

Nussbaum, M.C. (1986), "*The Fragility of Goodness*", Cambridge University Press, Cambridge, UK.

Nozick, Robert (1971), "*Anarchy, State and Utopia*", Basic Books, New York.

Paine, L.S. (1994), "Managing for Organisational Integrity" *Harvard Business Review*, 2, 106-117.

Paine, L.S. (2006), "*Ethics: A Basic Framework*", Harvard Business School, Boston.

Panda, Sunakar (2005), "*Environment and Ecology*", Vrinda Publications, Delhi.

Peery, N.S. Jr. (1995), "*Business Government and Society*", Prentice-Hall, Upper Saddle River, NJ.

Pegis, A.C. (Ed.), "*Basic Writings of Saint Thomas Aquinas*", Random House, New York.

Pepper, G.L. (1995), "*Communicating in Organisations*", McGraw Hill, New York.

Petric, J.A. and Furr, D.S. (1995), "*Total Quality in Managing Human Resources*", St. Lucie, Delray Beach, FL.

Petrick, J.A. and Quinn, J.F. (1997), "*Management Ethics*", Response Books, New Delhi.

Pojman, Louis P. (Ed.), "*Ethical Theory*", Wadsworth, Belmont, Calif.

Post, James (1978), "*Corporate Behaviour and Social Change*", Reston Publishing Co., Reston, VA.

Poter, M. (1980), "*Competitive Strategy*", Free Press, New York.

Powell, G. (1993), "*Men and Women in the Workplace*", Sage, Newbury Park, CA.

Reskin, Barbara and Padavic, Irene (1994), "*Women and Men at Work*", Pine Forge Peers, Thousand Oaks CA.

Rawls, John (1971), "*A Theory of Justice*", Harvard University Press, Cambridge.

Rothfeder, J. (1992), "*Privacy for Sale*", Simon & Schuster, New York.

Rachels, James (1986), "*The Elements of Moral Philosophy*", Random House, New York.

Reidenbach, R.E. and Robin, D.P. (1989), "*Ethics and Profits*", Prentice-Hall, NJ.

Rahim, M.A. (1986), "*Managing Conflict in Organisations*", Praeger, New York.

Rest, J.R. (1979), "*Development in Judging Moral Issues*", University of Minnesota Press, Minneapolis.

Rest, J.R. and Narvaez, D. (Eds.) (1994), "*Moral Development in the Professions*", Lawrence Erlbaum, Hillsdale, NJ.

Rion, M. (1990), "*The Responsible Manager: Practical Strategies for Ethical Decision-Making*", Harper Collins, New York.

Rost, J. (1991), "*Leadership for the 21st Century*", Praeger, New York.

Sherlekar, S.A., "*Ethics in Management*", Himalaya Publishing Co., Mumbai.

Sidgwick, Henry (1962), "*Methods of Ethics*", University of Chicago Press, Chicago.

Searle, John R. (1995), "*The Construction of Social Reality*", Oxford Press, New York.

Stevens, Edward J. (1969), "*Making Moral Decisions*", Paulist Press, New York.

Singer, Marcus, G. (1961), "*Generalisation in Ethics*", Alfred Knopf, Inc., New York.

Smart, J.J.C. and B. Williams (1973), "*Utilitarianism: For and Against*", Cambridge University Press, Cambridge.

Samant, J.S. (2008), "*Environmental Studies*", Shivaji University Press, Kolhapur.

Santra, S.C. (2008), "*Environmental Science*", New Central Book Agency, Kolkata.

Schutz, W. (1994), "*The Human Element*", Jossey-Bass, San Francisco.

Shaw, W.H. and Barry, V. (1995), "*Moral Issues in Business*", Wadsworth, Belmont, CA.

Sheppard, B.H., Lewicki, R.J. and Minton, J.W. (1992), "*Organisational Justice*", Lexington Books, Lexington, MA.

Shinner, R. (1992), "*Norm and Nature*", Clarendon, Oxford, UK.

Shrivastava, P. (1996), "*Greening Business*", Thomson Executive Press, Cincinnti.

Slote, M. (1992), "*From Morality to Virtue*", OUP, New York.

Smith, H.H. (1994), "*Managing Privacy*", University of North Carolina Press, Chapel Hill.

Synder, C., Higgins, R. and Stucky, R. (1983), "*Excuses*", John Wiley, New York.

Soloman, R.C. (1990), "*A Passion for Justice*", Addison – Wesley, Reeding, MA.

Solomon, R.C. (1992), "Ethics and Excellence", *OUP*, New York.

Solomon, R.C. and Higgins, K.M. (1996), "A Short History of Philosophy", *OUP*, New York.

Sullivan, W.M. (1995), "*Work and Integrity*", Harper Business, New York.

Sher, George (Ed.) (1998), "*Moral Philosophy*", Harcourt Brace Jovanorich, San Diego.

Shaw, William H. (1999), "*Contemporary Ethics*", Oxford: Blackwell.

Shaw, William H. (2002), "*Business Ethics*", Wadsworth, Singapore.

Singer, Peter (Ed.) (1991), "*A Companion to Ethics*", Blackwell, Cambridge, Mass.

Smith, N.C. and Quech, J.A. (1993), "*Ethics in Marketing*", Irwin, Homewood, Ill.

Stanwick, P.A. and Stanwick, S.D. (2009), "*Understanding Business Ethics*", Dorling Kindersley (India) Pvt. Ltd., New Delhi.

Sarangi, S.K. (2004), "*Values and Ethics of Profession and Business*", VMP Publishers, Mumbai.

Trorne, D., Ferrell, O.C. and Ferrell L. (2003), "*Business and Society*", Houghton Mifflin, Boston.

Thompson, D.F. (1987), "*Political Ethics and Public Office*", Harvard University Press, Cambridge, MA.

Thompson, D.F. (1995), "*Ethics in Congress*", Brookings Institution, Washington, D.C.

Toffler, B.L. (1991), "*Managers Talk Ethics*", John Wiley, New York.

Tomasko, R.M. (1990), "*Downsizing*", MACOM, New York.

Transparency International (1996), "*International Corruption Perception Index*", Gottingen University, Gottingen, Germany.

Trevino, L.K. and Nelson, K. (1995), "*Managing Business Ethics*", John Wiley, New York.

Tronto, J. (1993), "*Moral Boundaries*", Routledge, New York.

Taylor, Paul (1986), "*The Ethics of Respect for Nature*", Princeton University Press, Princeton.

Timmons, Mark (Ed.) (1999), "*Conduct and Character*", Wadsworth, Belmont, Calif.

Velasquez, M.G. (2006), "*Business Ethics*", Prentice Hall of India, New Delhi.

Weir, Walter (1963), "*Truth in Advertising*", McGraw Hill Co., New York.

Wirtenberger, H.J. (1962), "*Morality and Business*", Loyola University Press, Chicago.

Weiss, Joseph W. (1994), "*Ethics: A Managerial Stakeholder Approach*", Wadsworth, Belmont, CA.

Vogel, D. (1992), "Globalisation of Business Ethics", *California Management Review*, 35 (1), 30-49.

Vroom, V.H. (1964), "*Work and Motivation*", John Wiley, New York.

Wallace, J.D. (1978), "*Virtues and Vices*", Cornell University Press, Ithaca, NY.

Walton, C.C. (1988), "*The Moral Manager*", Harper Business, New York.

Walzer, M. (1983), "*Spheres of Justice*", Basic Books, New York.

Wellman, C. (1975), "*Morals and Ethics*", Scot, Foresman, Glenview, IL.

Wever, G.H. (1996), "*Strategic Environmental Management*", John Wiley, New York.

Wilkins, A.L. (1989), "*Developing Corporate Character*", Jossey-Bass, San Francisco.

Willig, J.T. (1994), "*Environmental TQM*" McGraw Hill, New York.

Wilson, J.Q. (1993), "*The Moral Sense*", Free Press, New York.

Wilson, R. (Ed.) (1996), "*Character Above All*", Simon & Schuster, New York.

Wood, D.T. (1994), "*Business and Society*", Harper Collins, New York.

Williams, Bernard (1985), "*Ethics and the Limits of Philosophy*", Harvard University Press, Cambridge, Mass.

Wagner, K.D. (1998), "*Environmental Management*", W.B. Saunders Co., Philadelphia.

Index